GIVING USA™ 2007

An index, information about revisions to prior years, and other additions to *Giving USA 2007* are online at www.givingusa.org/downloads2007.

User id: givingusa

Password: givingusa2007

GIVING USA™
2007

The Annual Report on Philanthropy for the Year 2006

52nd Annual Issue

Researched and Written at

The Center on Philanthropy
AT INDIANA UNIVERSITY

INDIANA UNIVERSITY—PURDUE UNIVERSITY INDIANAPOLIS

Publisher

FOUNDATION

Photo credits and information

Front cover:

A young philanthropist sorting coins at the Penny Power tables at the Harrisburg Relief Sale, Harrisburg, Pennsylvania. Penny Power is a program that encourages children and adults to collect coins for MCC's food, water and health projects throughout the world. Each year Mennonite and Brethren in Christ churches collect pocket change and take it to local auction events to be counted. In 2006, Penny Power raised more than $500,000.
Organization: Mennonite Central Committee, Akron, PA
Photographer: Melissa Engle

Back cover:

"We learn that life doesn't have to be complicated." Mr. R.V. loves his wife, BB King music, and fried chicken. This true Southern gentleman shows us that physical and mental challenges don't have to impede the things that really matter. (Mr. R.V. is a Joy's House guest.).
Organization: Joy's House—Care and Community for Adults, Indianapolis, IN
Photographer: Angie Cinnamon

Giving USA Foundation™ welcomes the use and citation of information from *Giving USA*. The preferred citation for *Giving USA* is: *Giving USA*, a publication of the Giving USA Foundation™, researched and written by the Center on Philanthropy at Indiana University. For scholarly citations, the preferred form is the American Psychological Association style for a periodical published annually, as follows: Title of chapter, *Giving USA 2007*, page number. Speakers are encouraged to cite *Giving USA* and should credit the publication or Giving USA Foundation when using data or charts from this work.

Giving USA is a public outreach initiative of the Giving USA Foundation. The Foundation, established by the Giving Institute: Leading Consultants to Non-Profits, endeavors to advance research and education in philanthropy.

ISSN: 0436-0257
ISBN: 978-0-9786199-2-3

Contributors

We are grateful for the generous gifts to Giving USA Foundation™ for *Giving USA* and wish to recognize in particular the substantial support from the following contributors.

Philanthropy Circle
$15,000

Center on Philanthropy at Indiana University
Marts & Lundy, Inc.

Patron
$5,000–$7,999

Changing Our World, Inc.
Grenzebach Glier & Associates, Inc.
IDC
The Sharpe Group
Viscern/Ketchum/RSI

Partner
$2,500–$4,999

Alexander Haas Martin & Partners, Inc.
The Alford Group Inc.
Jimmie R. Alford & Maree G. Bullock
Benevon (formerly Raising More Money, Inc.)
CCS Fund Raising
Campbell & Company
Claude Grizzard, Sr.
Hodge, Cramer & Associates, Inc.
The Kellogg Organization, Inc.
Raybin Associates, Inc.
Ruotolo Associates Inc.

Developer
$2,000–$2499

Arnoult & Associates, Inc.

Builder
$1,000–$1,999

A.L. Brourman Associates, Inc.
Alexander Macnab & Company
Diane M. Carlson
L. Gregg Carlson
The Collins Group

Builder (continued)
$1,000–$1,999

The Dini Partners, Inc.
The EHL Consulting Group
Jaques & Company, Inc.
Jeffrey Byrne & Associates
Joyaux Associates
Thomas W. Mesaros, CFRE
Miller Group Worldwide, LLC
National Community Development Services, Inc.
Payne, Forrester & Associates, LLC
The Robert B. Sharp Company of Colorado, Inc.
Semple Bixel Associates, Inc.
Smith Beers Yunker & Company, Inc.
StaleyRobeson®

Sponsorship
$500–$900

Blackburn Associates, Inc.
Cardaronella Stirling Associates
Carlton & Company
Edith H. Falk, CFRE
Peter J. Fissinger, CFRE
Fund Inc®
The J.F. Smith Group, Inc.
Richard T. Jolly
Sandy Macnab, FAHP, CFRE
Del Martin, CFRE
The Oram Group
Woodburn, Kyle & Company

Friends
$1–$499

Rita Fuerst Adams
David Bergeson, Ph.D., CAE
Melissa S. Brown
Randee Dalzell
eTapestry
Clark and Marilynn Gafke
Thomas Kovach
Ter Molen Watkins & Brandt, LLC
Bruce Wenger

Contents

Foreword

The estimates of Americans' generosity last year, as reported in *Giving USA 2007*, prove again that we are a generous country. To go along with the largesse of such luminaries as Warren Buffett, Bill and Melinda Gates, T. Boone Pickens and others, millions upon millions of average Americans looked at their household budgets and decided philanthropy was worthy of their hard-earned dollars, to the tune of $295.02 billion, a new record.

In constant dollars, the increase was 4.2 percent over 2005; in inflation-adjusted numbers, the increase was 1.0 percent. This change is measured against the extraordinary results for 2005. Charitable giving for that year will always have an asterisk associated with it, because of the overwhelming response to disasters, with $7.37 billion reported. Giving for recovery efforts continued in 2006, with at least $1.17 billion documented in contributions. And the contributions for disaster recovery continue in 2007.

Giving in 2006 broke new ground, setting a record high, partly because two-thirds of U.S. households annually give something to charity. Individuals still comprise the largest slice of the giving "pie," being responsible for approximately 75 percent of all the dollars given, year in and year out. When you add in bequest giving, individuals and families comprise about 80 percent of all giving in the United States.

The individual donors who are so important to charity in the U.S. respond to community needs—and most increase their contributions as their income rises. While giving follows the economy, the economy affects different households in different ways. At the upper echelons of our society, the very strong stock market meant gains in wealth, leading to some of the big gifts announced during 2006. Yet the average American saw rising prices in nearly all categories, leading many to face difficult decisions of where to put their discretionary income. That the vast majority of Americans continued to give to charity is a sign of their trust in the work done by nonprofit organizations.

People working in nonprofits often wish Americans would dig deeper still to help the 1.4 million-plus non-profits whose very purposes shape our society. For 50 years, the trend has been con-tributions at 2 percent or so of Gross Domestic Product. Individuals give about 2 percent of personal income; corporate donors give about 1 percent of pretax income. Foundations are required to expend at least 5 percent of assets in grantmaking activity. On average, charitable bequests are 5 percent to 10 percent of estate value when a charity is named in the will.

To raise more funds, charities have to make the case for philanthropic support as strong as possible—Americans need to feel assured that their charitable dollar will be put to good use and achieve an impact or result that matters in people's lives.

Charities will benefit if they are able to take a long, hard look at how they spend the precious dollars they receive and ensure they are spending that treasure wisely. They will find donors respond positively when they know that there is no question about what is done with the money raised. And how each gift matters in improving lives.

When Americans give to charity, they are saying that they support a given cause and purpose. Year in and year out, in good economic times and bad, they continue to donate. They continue to hear the need, and they continue to respond within their capacities.

The *Giving USA 2007* estimates are reason for optimism about the health of the nonprofit sector in the United States. Our charitable world is getting its messages out, and Americans are hearing them. It is the nonprofit sector that has the capacity and will to respond to needs—in times of disaster and every day. That it can do so is possible only because of the donations made by so many of us.

Richard T. Jolly
Chair
Giving USA Foundation™

George C. Ruotolo, Jr., CFRE
Chair
Giving Institute: Leading
Consultants to Non-Profits

Eugene R. Tempel, Ed.D., CFRE
Executive Director
The Center on Philanthropy
at Indiana University

Acknowledgments

Thanks first and foremost to the Giving USA Foundation and Giving Institute and the chairs of those groups, Richard T. Jolly and George C. Ruotolo, Jr., respectively. The members of these two organizations support *Giving USA* with their wisdom and knowledge of fundraising and charitable giving. They also provide significant financial support, along with other donors, to assure high-quality research within a few months. Data for the various estimates become available in spring and publication is in June.

Among Giving Institute members who give many hours of time are 11 on the Editorial Review Board (ERB), which is chaired by Jim Yunker. Each chapter is reviewed by ERB members, and their comments and suggestions help shape the narrative about giving in the year. The ERB members are named on page 242.

Thanks especially to the cover contest committee, chaired by Del Martin and named on page 242. These "visual experts"—photographers, graphic designers, marketing and communication professionals—who select and produce the cover art, help "put a face" on *Giving USA*.

The members of Advisory Council on Methodology are named on page 243. This group includes 22 researchers from 18 research centers and 6 Giving Institute members, plus staff. Jim Yunker also chairs this council, providing a vital link between the volunteer groups. The Advisory Council reviews the methods each fall, proposes changes that are tested at the Center on Philanthropy, and approves the estimates each spring.

At the Center on Philanthropy at Indiana University, executive director Gene Tempel makes all things possible. Research department director Patrick Rooney has kept the *Giving USA* research team together through regular delivery of pizza and thoughtful critiques of work in progress. Colleagues too numerous to mention here have contributed to this volume. Many are listed on page 244.

Research for *Giving USA* relies extensively on the work of many others. Thanks especially this year to Tom Pollak and the staff of the National Center for Charitable Statistics for sharing data; Woods Bowman, editor of *ARNOVA Abstracts,* for compiling that publication; Joseph Claude Harris of Seattle for work on Catholic giving and the religion chapter generally; and Bill Huddleston in Washington, D.C., for his insights about the Combined Federal Campaign.

Production is possible only because of the professionalism and long hours of Rich Metter at Rich Metter Graphics (New York), Nancy Sixsmith of ConText Editing (Bloomington, Indiana) and J. Heidi Newman of Mark My Word! (Indianapolis, Indiana). Thanks, all.

Families of people involved in this work deserve thanks, too. The entire *Giving USA* team puts in long hours each spring, paid or volunteer. To my own family, for their forbearance, my gratitude.

Melissa S. Brown
Managing Editor, *Giving USA 2007*

1 How you can use this book

Giving USA provides critical information at a critical time

Giving USA is the only resource in the United States that simultaneously estimates the giving of the principal sources of philanthropy and the charitable receipts of the main types of recipients in a given year. It is also the single annual compilation that references major studies conducted about giving and released within a year. These two aspects of *Giving USA* permit fundraisers, nonprofit managers, scholars, and others to see trends, discern patterns, and identify new questions for practice and research.

Giving USA will help your organization:

■ Understand factors that impact philanthropy in general and by subsector;

■ Benchmark fundraising performance against national data;

■ Plan for the future, based on long-term trends in giving;

■ Educate new staff members and board members about the broad context of philanthropic giving, so that they may have a better understanding of the organization's funding patterns and potential;

■ Include up-to-date information about philanthropy overall and by subsector in speeches, publications, press releases, and internal communications; and

■ Learn about and access recent studies and other resources that can help strengthen your fundraising,

grantmaking, or other philanthropic activity.

Giving USA is the only work that provides a long series of data, going back more than 50 years, about charitable giving in the United States. (This volume only contains data tables that cover 1966-2006.)

An overview of the organization of the book

Giving USA presents four different types of information. Each type has its own uses and applications for a nonprofit organization. They are:

■ Estimates of charitable giving by donor type and by type of recipient;

■ Trend line and data covering 40 years by donor type and type of recipient;

■ Reports of major events during the year that inform the estimates; and

■ Key findings from studies done by researchers examining some aspect of charitable giving.

The book is divided into two principal components:

■ Findings for 2006 and the 40-year trend lines, in the section called "The Numbers."

■ Chapters about
  — Each principal source of giving: individuals, charitable bequests, foundations, and corporations; and
  — Each of the main types of recipient organizations tracked by *Giving USA*: religion, education, foundations, human services, health, public-society benefit,

arts, environment/animals, and international affairs.

In addition to these main components, *Giving USA* has some additional material that can be helpful.

- Introductory material that includes a synthesis of critical information about the year, including a foreword and an overview of charitable giving in the year.

- Data tables and a list of gifts of $5 million or more from individuals (not foundations or corporations) that were announced in the year. This section is toward the end of the volume.

- A brief summary of the estimating procedures used, which is on pages 221 to 238. This section includes a glossary and a chart of the National Taxonomy of Exempt Entities (NTEE) in which charitable organizations are coded by the National Center for Charitable Statistics. The subsector definitions tie back to the NTEE codes.

Ideas for ways to use the section called "The Numbers"

The approximately 30 pages headed "The Numbers" contain the new estimates for 2006 giving plus the 40-year trend lines for giving in current dollars and inflation-adjusted dollars. This year's estimates are presented as a percentage of the total, in pie charts.

One of the most frequent uses of *Giving USA* is to educate new board members and new staff about the importance of individual giving. Many people do not realize that individuals

contribute three-quarters or more of the total.

Another frequent use of *Giving USA* is to watch trends that can affect your organization. One of the ways to do this is to monitor the stacked-bar graphs with five-year periods. For example, in the 2001–2006 period, the share of giving coming from foundations is markedly larger than the share from foundations was even ten or fifteen years ago. Knowing this can help your charity implement a strategy to cultivate relationships with foundations, especially any new foundations formed in your area or focused on your work.

The 40-year trend lines show growth over time and can be used to estimate how giving to your type of organization, or from a particular type of donor, might change in the coming five or ten years. For example, international affairs is a rapidly growing subsector. This has implications for charities in that group, as well as some potential impact on other types of charities that appeal to similar donors.

Organization of chapters by type of donor and type of recipient

Each chapter has four segments:

- *Giving USA* findings and in some cases, data tables

- News stories from the year that can help explain giving

- Reports of key findings from other studies, including a table with the three most recent years' data from annual studies when available

- Notes, including references and where available, Web sites where the material can be found.

Ideas for ways to use each segment are below. In all cases, the citations provided can be leads to other studies, whether you are a scholar or a non-profit organization staff member who wants to know more about a specific topic. The news stories serve as a historical record, which can also be useful if your organization is reviewing its performance and wants a refresher about key events in a prior year. Earlier editions of *Giving USA* are available for purchase (back to 2002) from the publisher. Editions from 1955 through 2001 are available free online.[1]

Ideas for how to use the chapters about the sources of giving

The chapters about the sources of giving start with the bullet points that also appear in "The Numbers" section. These are followed by a longer discussion of the *Giving USA* findings. The discussion section typically contains explanatory information about the factors influencing giving by that type of donor. This information can be very useful in understanding overall economic trends as well as explaining to board members and others the economic climate in which your charitable organization operates.

Some readers of *Giving USA* use the chapter information to inform prospective donors about benchmarks. All chapters identify the largest gifts in the prior year, which can help a donor recognize the leadership level giving

by the wealthiest in our country. The corporate chapter reports the trends in giving as a percentage of corporate profits for the largest firms. This can help a corporate donor as it considers its role in the community. The chapter about charitable bequests can be used to help design a planned giving program, as it shows survey results for the average amount received per bequest by different types of charities (by size, which is defined in the glossary, and by subsector).

Ideas for how to use the chapters about the types of recipients

Chapters about the types of recipients of giving start with the bullet points that also appear in "The Numbers" section. These are followed by *Giving USA* findings, including tables summarizing survey results for the subsectors that are surveyed. Religious organizations and foundations are not surveyed. The other subsectors have tables showing the average amount raised, the distribution of responding organizations based on whether their charitable receipts rose, fell, or stayed flat during the year, and average amounts received from bequests among the responding organizations that had bequest revenue. Ideas for using these tables follow.

Table 1: Charitable revenue received, median and average, for two years. This table is provided so that you can determine where your organization fits. If you are at or above the averages, celebrate success. If not, consider whether your program may need strengthening. Recognize that an average is an arithmetic result combining the results from several organizations. It does not represent the reality of any one particular organization.

It is also possible that your organization faces distinctive fundraising circumstances. This can occur if your group is new, in a very small community, or representing an activity that has a limited natural constituency. If this is the case, express that clearly for fundraising staff, board members, and other volunteers.

The median value is the one in the middle if you organize the answers from smallest to largest. It is an actual value reported by one of the survey respondents. Medians are helpful in judging how skewed the average is by a few cases. If the median and the average are fairly close together, you know that outliers in the data—unusual cases to one extreme or the other—are not greatly affecting the average. If the median and average are far apart, you know that outliers are having a relatively large effect on some of the trends in the data. A small number of organizations experienced something dramatically different from the rest of the group. In this case, you might want to measure your organization against the midpoint (median), instead of against the average (mean).

Table 2: Increases or decreases in charitable revenue. This table provides the information you can use to gauge your organization's results when compared with other institutions of similar size and direction of change. In all subsectors and all size groups, some organizations experienced growth and

some saw a decline. These are reported as an average and median change in dollars raised and an average and median percentage change. This gives you information you can use to determine "the company you keep."

You may find it helpful to use the tables over time (they started in *Giving USA 2002*) to see if you are consistently above or below the trends for your size and subsector. The averages and medians can also be useful for planning ahead and setting targets for your own charity. The target amounts should reflect more than a national average; they should incorporate knowledge of your organization's fundraising experience, staffing and volunteer force, and community.

The results from tables 1 and 2 can serve as benchmarks for your board and other volunteers. If you find that your organization is consistently below the national averages or medians, consider recommending a more aggressive investment into your fundraising program in the form of volunteer action and financial resources to pay for additional fundraising initiatives' costs.

Table 3: Bequest dollars received. This table is perhaps most useful in providing benchmarks for planning or goal setting for a planned giving program. There are other tables in the Giving by bequest chapter that show the average number and size of bequest received by type of recipient charity. Combined with Table 3 from the subsector chapters, you can get a good "read" on what organizations are experiencing by size and type.

A new feature:
What this means to you
Within each chapter appear boxed sections "What this means for you" that provide some key information. These boxes include "take-aways" from the chapter and suggestions for fundraising practice from the experts who work at firms that are members of the Giving Institute™: Leading Consultants to Non-Profits.

Why we report important events that may influence giving
We have used newspaper and magazine reports to help identify and summarize key events that may have affected giving for each of the donor types and each subsector studied. *Giving USA* is a "yearbook of philanthropy" and will help readers understand the current context for fundraising and may be consulted in the future to help non-profit managers find events that inspired giving or impelled reductions in contributions. This section in each chapter also includes the largest gifts made in the year by type of donor or type of recipient, information (where available) from other organizations that analyzed giving in the year, and stories that may indicate the beginning of trends.

Ideas about how to use other research about giving
Giving USA summarizes key findings, often with tables and graphs, of other studies appearing about charitable giving. This research typically covers gifts made more than a year ago, but the study was released in 2006. *Giving USA* can be a quick reference guide for data that you might use in a report, when speaking with a news reporter, or when preparing for a meeting.

Ideas about how to use the table presenting three years of information from other studies
Many studies about giving or about nonprofit organization funding appear annually. Some of the findings demonstrate trends. These can include, for example, amount contributed per pupil at independent schools; average amount foundations grant to charities in a subsector; or number of charities registered by subsector.

Giving USA reports three years of data for selected data points and provides citations and references to the original work, including (where available) Web site addresses and contact information. These tables provide a quick reference guide to key studies, a resource of web addresses leading to the primary organizations studying giving for a specific donor type or recipient type, and easy access to information about another subsector.

You may wish to use the national averages from another subsector, for example, as a way to start conversations in your organization about a related subject. Track board giving at independent schools (amount and participation rates) as one way to motivate your board. Check the amount raised per dollar spent, for example, in health, which might be useful for education or arts, among other types of organizations.

Ideas for how to use the data tables

The tables of data toward the end of the book contain 40 years' worth of data. They can be used, for example, to track your organization's rates of change in amount received in charitable gifts against the national findings over time. This may be particularly useful for the past five or ten years.

To calculate a rate of change, start with a time series of data. The example below contains six years of data about the amount raised at an imaginary organization. The rate of change for each year is based on the new value and the prior year's value. The formula is:

$$\frac{New - old}{old} \times 100 = percentage\ change$$

Example for calculating percentage change:

Year	Organization Amount ($ millions)	Change	National Trend (human services)
2001	1,005		
2002	999	-0.6%	10.4%
2003	1,020	2.1%	-6.0%
2004	1,050	2.9%	1.4%
2005	1,200	14.3%	28.9%
2006	1,350	12.5%	-11.3%

Using the percentage change from 2001–2002 as an example:

Subtract the old value from the new value:
999 – 1,005 = (-6)

Divide that difference by the old value:
-6/1,005 = -0.00597

Multiply the result by 100 to get percentage change:
-0.00597 x 100 = -0.6%

If this organization is comparing its results against human services in the same time period, in most years, this organization's rate of change exceeds that of the national trend. The exceptions are 2002 and 2005. In human services organizations nationally, those two years saw high rates of giving related to disasters. If this were a real organization, people working there would be able to explain the results and provide a context for understanding the organization's performance over time.

Conclusion

Giving USA is a unique publication that compiles in one reference work the critically important information your organization needs about fundraising and giving in the United States. Keep this book on your shelf. You will consult it frequently. The information will be in your presentations, plans, and reports. It might help you shape your fundraising strategies. It might even be part of the reason your organization raises more money. The founders of *Giving USA* created it to be a guide for charities in their work and a report about their progress. The Giving USA Foundation™ is proud to continue offering this year's edition as a public service.

---

1   The free online resource, arranged with permission of the Giving USA Foundation™, is in the monograph collection at Philanthropic Resources Online (PRO). PRO is housed at the Joseph and Matthew Payton Philanthropic Studies Library at University Library, Indiana University-Purdue University Indianapolis. The Payton Library's welcome page is www.ulib.iupui.edu/special/psl/. From there, users can find PRO.

2 Overview of giving in 2006

Giving USA combines data from a number of sources to present a series of simultaneous estimates about charitable giving for one year. It is an invaluable resource for understanding current and past charitable giving, which helps organizations anticipate their options for the future. The results included in this issue show that 2006, while setting new records, may not have been "golden" for every charity.

2006 tops the charts

In 2006, headlines announced a new "golden age of philanthropy" when Warren Buffett and Bill and Melinda Gates released news of Mr. Buffett's multiyear plan to give the Gates Foundation the bulk of his personal fortune in annual installments over 20 years.

Charitable giving set a new record in 2006, an estimated $295.02 billion. In 2006, donors gave an estimated $11.97 billion more than they did in 2005. The increase is 4.2 percent (1.0 percent adjusted for inflation) above a revised estimate for 2005 of $283.05 billion.

The 2006 total includes $1.9 billion paid in 2006 by Mr. Buffett as the first installment on his multiyear pledge. The estimate also includes donations from hundreds of millions of other Americans, as well as gifts from charitable bequests, foundations, and corporations.

Record total, but not all charities benefit equally

In *Giving USA*'s survey, 59 percent of responding charities reported an increase in charitable contributions. Among all charities surveyed, the results indicate a total increase of 5.5 percent in the amount raised, before adding disaster relief contributions to 2005 or 2006 results. When disaster relief giving is included in both years, and when foundation and religious organizations estimates are included, the change is growth of 4.2 percent.

The most significant shift in the survey for 2006 is that nearly one-third (32 percent) of charities reported a drop in charitable contributions in 2006, compared with 2005, when 28 percent

FAQ: *Why is giving up 1 percent adjusted for inflation when nearly 60 percent of surveyed organizations report growth in charitable receipts?*

- The rate of change found in 2006 is based on a total for 2005 that incorporated $7.37 in disaster relief giving and a few large bequests.

- When the disaster relief giving is excluded from calculations, giving grew by 6.6 percent (3.2 percent adjusted for inflation). This reflects what most organizations experienced instead of the overall rate of change that includes the unusual giving in 2005 to a relatively small number of charities.

FAQ: *How do I use the rates of change to benchmark for my organization?*
For most subsectors, *Giving USA* conducts a survey of a random sample of nonprofit organizations based on size. Use the survey results in the chapters to benchmark your results against organizations that are similar to yours, based on size and subsector. In every group, some organizations saw increases, and others saw declines.

reported a decline. Some of the declines were very large, even when disaster gifts from 2005 are excluded from the analysis.

The *Giving USA* survey is the only regular study of charitable giving that reaches a randomly selected group of charities that represent the entire nonprofit sector. Other polls reach a nonrandom group of respondents. Two of them also noted that the year saw some charities with growth and others that reported 2006 was a difficult fundraising year.[1] With more than 850 responses, *Giving USA* can present results for a representative sample of U.S. charities, both by size and by subsector (type of recipient).

Individual giving rises 4.4 percent
Individual giving makes up the largest portion of the *Giving USA* estimate. For 2006, individual giving grew an estimated 4.4 percent (1.1 percent adjusted for inflation) when including disaster relief giving, and grew 6.9 percent (3.6 percent adjusted for inflation) when excluding disaster relief giving from the calculations for both 2005 and 2006.

Nearly all of the wealthiest 10 percent of households, those with incomes of $100,000 or more, give to charity. These 11 million households account for approximately 40 to 45 percent of the total individual estimated contributions, according to data released by the IRS, which show only amounts claimed in itemized deductions. The *Bank of America Study of High Net-Worth Philanthropy* surveyed people in the top 3 percent of income and found that high-income/high net-worth households gave an average of $120,651 to charity in 2005.[2] High net-worth households often contribute more than they itemize on tax returns. Donors with high net-worth are very likely to increase their giving in a year such as 2006, with a 10 percent increase (adjusted for inflation) in the stock market.

Average households under financial stress
About 90 percent of households in the United States earn less than $100,000. An estimated 65 percent of those families contribute to charity. These 65 million or so households contribute an estimated 55 to 60 percent of all household or individual donations. Average giving from these households is about $2,000.[3]

As donors confront rising costs, it is likely that they economize, possibly affecting their charitable giving. In 2006, gas prices spiked above $3 per gallon in the summer and fell to about $2.50 per gallon by year-end.[4] Health care costs rose, with employees paying a larger share of their family budget for medical care.[5] Other economic shifts in the year included a weak housing market and high levels of consumer debt. One analysis showed that credit cards were used more for necessities than luxuries, and households dedicated nearly 15 percent of their disposable income to paying off debts.[6]

Corporate giving estimate dips

We estimate a decline in corporate contributions in 2006, to $12.72 billion. While corporate profits increased for the fifth year, it was at a slower rate than in 2005. Corporations reported publicly that they expected their giving in 2006 to slow. One study found a median growth of 6.1 percent in giving among 89 major U.S. corporations.[7] Even in that group, though, a portion

of these respondents did report a drop in their giving.

Giving USA focuses on deductible charitable gifts. On corporate tax returns, noncash donations are limited to the corporation's cost for the product. Other studies count fair market value of noncash donations. The different methods often lead to different results.

Foundation giving rising

Foundation giving increased a robust 12.6 percent in 2006 according to the Foundation Center, climbing to $36.5 billion. About half of the dollars awarded by independent foundations are from "family foundations." This vehicle may be replacing some individual giving.

Charitable bequests drop slightly in 2006 after all-time high in 2005

Charitable bequests reached an exceptional high in 2005 when a few estates of $20 million or more lifted charitable bequests considerably. In 2006, the estimate for charitable bequests shows

---

FAQ: *Why did numbers change from last year?*

Revisions to estimates of charitable giving are made annually to take into account additional information that is incorporated as it is available. In making revisions with new data, *Giving USA* follows the standard practice of nearly all economic estimating. When other organizations release new data, *Giving USA* revises its estimates. For example:

- The Federal Bureau of Economic Analysis updates the Gross Domestic Product each quarter. *Giving USA* uses the GDP in its estimate for corporate giving.

- The Federal Reserve Board conducts The Survey of Consumer Finances (SCF) every three years. *Giving USA* uses SCF data in its estimate for charitable bequests from estates below the federal filing threshold.

a slight decline to $22.91 billion. This reflects a general downward trend in recent years in the bequest amounts from estates valued below $20 million (see Chapter 8) and demographic shifts. Estate tax returns filed in 2006 are likely to be filed by estates where the death occurred earlier, either in 2004 or 2005. Fewer people died in 2005 and 2004 than in prior years. It is likely that fewer estate tax returns were filed in 2006, which translates to a dip in charitable bequests.

Revisions to the historical data for subsectors

This edition of *Giving USA* includes estimates based on newly available information about giving by type of recipient. The Giving USA Foundation™ and the Urban Institute's National Center for Charitable Statistics (NCCS) used NCCS data to re-estimate giving to all subsectors except religion and foundations. The data, which have been prepared by NCCS using IRS Forms 990, offer a consistent series covering 1989 through 2004. This new data series enables *Giving USA* to present more updated information to the philanthropic community and the general public than has been possible previously.

More detailed information about the revisions will be available at www.givingusa.org using the log-in information at the front of this volume.

Research about why people give

More studies are exploring the "science" of giving—whether in the neural bases of altruistic behavior[8,9] or in psychological predispositions to give (and to engage in other helping behaviors),[10] and even whether altruism is genetic.[11] (All seem to play a role.) Scholars have looked at whether social networks shape giving behavior or whether donors are motivated by the desire to reciprocate. (Both are important).[12] Even as researchers explore the biological, psychological, and sociological factors behind charitable giving, each individual donor responds to specific opportunities based on how they are presented.

Conclusion

Chapters in *Giving USA* present the estimates for 2006, share findings from the *Giving USA* survey, and summarize studies released during the year that can help your organization formulate fundraising plans based on the latest knowledge about who gives, to what, and how. We are pleased to present these data to the American public and the philanthropic community so that they can guide readers' charitable activities.

---

1   Guidestar.org released results from its October 2006 online poll, showing 50 percent of charities saw growth, 27 percent said contributions remained the same as in 2005, and 19 percent reported decreases, www.guidestar.org. The Association of Fundraising Professionals surveyed members, and among respondents, 69 percent reported increased charitable revenue; 7 percent raised about the same; and 27 percent said they raised less, www.afpnet.org.

2   The Center on Philanthropy at Indiana University, *Bank of America Study of High Net-Worth Philanthropy*, October 2006, http://newsroom.bankofamerica.com/index.php?s=press_kit&item=63.

3   Center on Philanthropy Panel Study, 2003 and 2005 waves. Information at www.philanthropy.iupui.edu.

4   Wikipedia, U.S. Retail Gasoline Prices, 2005–2007, consulted May 29, 2007.

5   J. Mincer, Health care costs to hit workers, retirees harder, writing about a Milliman and Watson Wyatt Worldwide study. In the article, Mincer writes: "Average annual medical costs for a family of four in a preferred provider organization is $13,382 in 2006, up 9.6% from 2005." *Wall Street Journal*, July 5, 2006, www.wsj.com.

6   K. Downey, Basics not luxuries, blamed for high debt, *Washington Post*, May 12, 2006, writing about an analysis of data collected by the Federal Reserve Board in its Survey of Consumer Finances. The analysis was done by the Center for American Progress, an avowedly "progressive think tank" in Washington, D.C., and released as a May 2007 economic report.

7   Committee Encouraging Corporate Philanthropy, 2006 giving survey, released mid-2007, www.corporatephilanthropy.org.

8   The joy of giving: Donating to charity rewards the brain, *The Economist*, October 12, 2006, reporting about research conducted at the National Institute of Neurological Disorders and Stroke in Bethesda, Maryland and published in *Proceedings of the National Academy of Sciences*. Viewed at www.economist.com.

9   D. Tankersley, C J. Stowe, and S. Huettel, Altruism is associated with an increased neural response to agency, *Nature Neuroscience*, January 21, 2007. Viewed at http://www.nature.com/neuro/journal/.

10   R. Bekkers and M. Wilhelm, Helping behavior, dispositional empathic concern, and the principle of care, working paper posted September 2006, http://www.philanthropy.iupui.edu/Research/WorkingPapers/.

11   H. Briggs, Altruism 'built-in' in humans, a BBC News report covering articles appearing in *Science*, March 3, 2006, viewed at http://news.bbc.co.uk.

12   P. Branas-Garza and M. Espinosa, Altruism with social roots: An emerging literature, working paper posted at a Web site for Research Papers in Economics, RePEc, http://ideas.repec.org.

3 Key findings

Total charitable giving for 2006 is estimated to be $295.02 billion. This is an increase of 4.2 percent compared with the revised estimate of $283.05 billion for 2005. Adjusted for inflation, the increase is 1.0 percent.

Individual contributions reached an estimated $222.89 billion in 2006, an increase of 4.4 percent (1.2 percent adjusted for inflation). Individual donations account for 75.6 percent of total giving in 2006.

Charitable bequests are estimated to be $22.91 billion for 2006, a drop of 2.1 percent compared with the revised estimate of $23.40 billion for 2005. This is a decline of 5.1 percent when adjusted for inflation. Charitable bequests are estimated to be 7.8 percent of total giving for 2006.

Foundation grantmaking rose to an estimated $36.50 billion for 2006, for independent, community, and operating foundations, based on the Foundation Center's survey conducted in January and February 2007. This is an increase of 12.6 percent (9.1 percent adjusted for inflation) compared with the revised amount of $32.41 billion for 2005, which reflects grantmaking reported on IRS forms 990-PF and 990 (for community foundations) filed for 2005 and tabulated by the Foundation Center. Foundation grantmaking is estimated to be 12.4 percent of total giving in 2006.

Corporate giving in 2006 reached an estimated $12.72 billion, counting $4.2 billion in corporate foundation grantmaking as estimated by the Foundation Center, which includes some corporate foundation relief giving. Corporate giving decreased an estimated 7.6 percent from the revised total of $13.77 billion for 2005 (-10.5 percent adjusted for inflation). Corporate contributions are an estimated 4.3 percent of total contributions for 2006.

Gifts to religious organizations rose to an estimated $96.82 billion, an increase of 4.5 percent (1.2 percent adjusted for inflation) over the revised estimate of $92.69 billion for 2005. Giving to religious organizations included in the *Giving USA* study is estimated to be 32.8 percent of total giving in 2006.

Giving to educational organizations is estimated at $40.98 billion for 2006, an increase of 9.8 percent (6.4 percent adjusted for inflation). This estimate is based on a combination of sources, including findings from the Council for Aid to Education through June 2006 and a *Giving USA* survey for all of 2006. Giving to educational organizations is estimated to be 13.9 percent of total giving in 2006.

Giving to grantmaking foundations is estimated by the Foundation Center and *Giving USA* to be $29.50 billion, an increase of 7.4 percent (4.1 percent adjusted for inflation) compared with the $27.46 billion reported by the Foundation Center in gifts to foundations in 2005. For 2006, gifts to grantmaking foundations are approximately 10.0 percent of all giving.

Giving to human services organizations fell to $29.56 billion in 2006. The estimate is 9.2 percent less than the estimate of $32.55 billion for 2005 (-12.0 percent adjusted for inflation). Giving for human services organizations was 10.0 percent of total estimated giving.

Gifts for health organizations are estimated to be $20.22 billion in 2006, a decrease of 2.3 percent (and a decline of 5.4 percent adjusted for inflation) compared with 2005. Gifts to health organizations are an estimated 6.9 percent of total charitable giving for 2006.

Giving for public-society benefit organizations reached an estimated $21.41 billion, an increase of 5.7 percent (2.4 adjusted for inflation). Giving for organizations in this sub-sector, which includes United Ways, Jewish federations, commercially sponsored donor-advised funds, civil rights organizations, and a number of other types of charities, was 7.3 percent of total estimated giving for 2006.

Contributions for organizations in the arts, culture, and humanities subsector increased 9.9 percent in 2006, to $12.51 billion. This is an increase of 6.5 percent adjusted for inflation. Gifts to arts, culture, and humanities organizations were 4.2 percent of total estimated giving for 2006.

Gifts to organizations engaged in international affairs, including international relief and aid, reached an estimated $11.34 billion in 2006. The total in 2006 is a drop of 9.2 percent (-12.0 percent adjusted for inflation). Giving for organizations in the international affairs subsector was 3.8 percent of total estimated giving.

Gifts for organizations in the environment and animals subsector reached an estimated $6.60 billion, an increase of 1.9 percent (-1.3 percent adjusted for inflation) from the 2005 adjusted estimate of $6.48 billion. Giving for organizations in the environment and animals subsector was 2.2 percent of total estimated giving.

Unallocated contributions are estimated to be $26.08 billion, or 8.8 percent of the total. Unallocated giving includes: gifts to newly formed organizations; individual and corporate deductions expected to be claimed in 2006 for gifts made in prior years (carried over); amounts that donors deduct at a value different from what the nonprofit reports as revenue (e.g., corporate deductions at cost and nonprofit receipt at fair market value); gifts and grants to government entities claimed by donors but not reported as received at a 501(c)(3) charity; gifts to organizations treated legally as foundations but not making grants or qualifying as operating foundations; and foundation grants to organizations located in another country.

4 Charitable giving in context

The estimate of total giving in the United States can be rounded up to $300 billion. $300 billion—a 3 followed by 11 zeroes—can be put into perspective in various ways. Here are some equivalencies to help show just how much this amount is.

Time and money

- It would take almost 9.5 years to spend $300 billion if a person spent at the rate of $1,000 per second (spending = $31.56 billion per year).

- It would take 3 million years to reach $300 billion by spending $100,000 per year.

Gross Domestic Product

- The GDP of Poland ($303 billion) is roughly equal to the amount that Americans gave to charitable organizations in 2006.[1]

- The GDP of the world[2] is 148 times the amount given by Americans to charitable organizations in 2006.

U.S. population

- $300 billion is approximately $1,000 per person in charitable contributions.[3]

Comparisons to companies

- Microsoft's market value is $289 billion (Feb. 2007), which is nearly equivalent to the amount Americans donated to charity in 2006.[4]

- The amount given by Americans to charitable organizations in 2006 is about twice the amount that the stock of Google.com is worth.[5]

Federal spending

- The amount donated by Americans to charitable organizations is 40 years of Environmental Protection Agency operations at $7.5 billion per year (2006 budget for that department).[6]

- Since 2003, the U.S. has spent a total of about $290 billion on the war in Iraq, including military operations, indigenous security forces, diplomatic operations and foreign aid.[7]

---

1   Worldbank.org. www.worldbank.org.
2   The World Factbook. Central Intelligence Agency. www.cia.gov/cia/publications/factbook/print/xx.html.
3   The United States' population reached 300 million in October, 2006, www.census.gov.
4   According to the *Forbes* list of the world's 2,000 largest public companies
5   As of February 7, 2006, Google's market value was $144 billion.
6   FY 2006 Budget Protects Public Health and the Environment. EPA Newsroom. 7 Feb 2005. http://yosemite.epa.gov/opa/admpress.nsf/c4ae07c90d1d5453852570210055e370/3d439e2c740183c885256fa1006682c1!OpenDocument.
7   Estimated appropriations provided for Iraq and the war on terrorism, 2001–2006; Iraq amounts only summed here. From the Congressional Budget Office, www.cbo.gov/ftpdocs/75xx/doc7506/GWOT_Tables_2006_08.pdf.

5 | *Giving USA*: The Numbers

2006 contributions: $295.02 billion by source of contributions

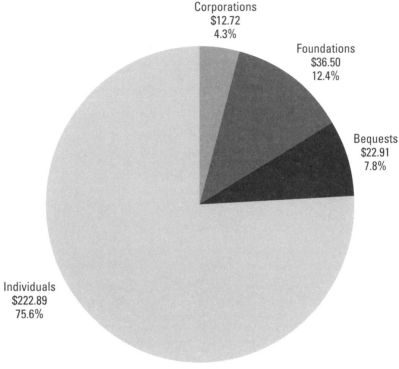

Corporations
$12.72
4.3%

Foundations
$36.50
12.4%

Bequests
$22.91
7.8%

Individuals
$222.89
75.6%

All figures are rounded. Total may not be 100%.

- Total estimated charitable giving in 2006 reached $295.02 billion, which is an increase of 4.2 percent from the revised estimate of $283.05 for 2005.

- The greatest portion of charitable giving ($222.89 billion) was given by individual or household donors. This accounts for 75.6 percent of the total estimated giving.

- Charitable bequests accounted for 7.8 percent of the total giving in 2006 at an estimated $22.91 billion.

- The sum of gifts by living individuals and through charitable bequests is $245.80 billion, which represents 83.3 percent of the estimated total giving for 2006.

- The Foundation Center estimated grantmaking by independent, community, and operating foundations to be $36.50 billion in 2006. This is 12.4 percent of the estimated total.

- Corporate giving is estimated to be $12.72 billion, which is 4.3 percent of the total charitable contributions in 2006.

2006 contributions: $295.02 billion by type of recipient organization

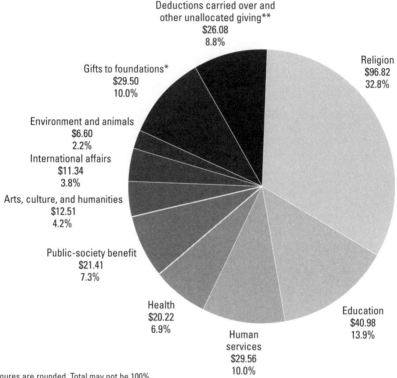

Deductions carried over and
other unallocated giving**
$26.08
8.8%

Gifts to foundations*
$29.50
10.0%

Environment and animals
$6.60
2.2%

International affairs
$11.34
3.8%

Arts, culture, and humanities
$12.51
4.2%

Public-society benefit
$21.41
7.3%

Health
$20.22
6.9%

Human
services
$29.56
10.0%

Education
$40.98
13.9%

Religion
$96.82
32.8%

All figures are rounded. Total may not be 100%.
*Foundation Center and *Giving USA* estimate.
**See last bullet point on following page for definition.

- Religious organizations received the most in charitable gifts in 2006, an estimated $96.82 billion, which is 32.8 percent of the total estimate.

- Donors gave an estimated at $40.98 billion to educational organizations, or 13.9 percent of the total.

- Human services organizations received $29.56 billion, or 10.0 percent of the total.

- Donations to the health subsector totaled an estimated $20.22 billion, which is 6.9 percent of the total.

- Public-society benefit organizations received $21.41 billion, or 7.3 percent of the total.

- Donors gave an estimated $12.51 billion to the arts, culture, and humanities subsector, which is 4.2 percent of the total.

- International affairs organizations received $11.34 billion, or 3.8 percent of the total.

- Gifts made to environment/animals organizations totaled an estimated $6.60 billion, or 2.2 percent of the total.

■ The Foundation Center and *Giving USA* estimate giving of $29.50 billion to foundations in 2006, or 10.0 percent of the total. This includes an estimated fair market value for gifts to patient assistance foundations and gifts to private and community foundations.

■ Contributions to organizations that are not tracked (for example, government entities or scholarship donations to mutual benefit associations), deductions carried over and unallocated giving are estimated at $26.08 billion, or 8.8 percent of the total. This amount represents individual and corporate deductions expected to be claimed in 2006 for gifts made in prior years (carried over), amounts that donors deduct at a value different from what the nonprofit reports as revenue, gifts and grants to government entities, gifts and grants to an entity classified as a foundation but not yet a grantmaking foundation, foundation grants to organizations located in another country, and contributions to new organizations not yet allocated to a subsector.

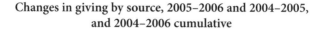

Changes in giving by source, 2005–2006 and 2004–2005,
and 2004–2006 cumulative

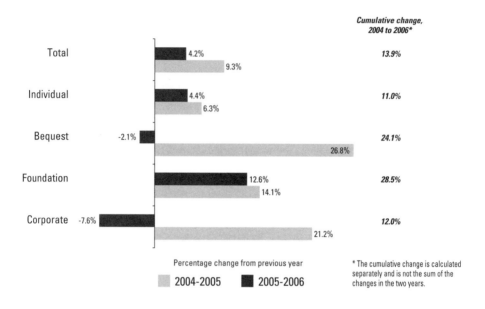

- The sum of estimated giving by all sources is $295.02 billion.

- Total giving between 2005 and 2006 rose by an estimated 4.2 percent. This is a slowed rate of growth compared with 2004 and 2005, when giving rose by an estimated 9.3 percent change, including contributions for disaster relief.

- In 2005, an estimated $7.37 billion was given for disaster relief. In 2006, the disaster relief estimate is $1.17 billion. Without disaster relief giving in 2005 or 2006 included, the estimated change from 2005 to 2006 is 6.6 percent.

- Individual giving increased 4.4 percent from the 2005 revised estimate of $213.47 billion. When an estimated $5.83 billion in disaster relief giving in 2005 and an estimated $0.94 billion in disaster gifts made in 2006 are excluded, the change is 6.9 percent.

- The 2006 estimate for dollars given by charitable bequest has decreased 2.1 percent from last year's revised estimate. The 2005 estimate is revised this year based on IRS tax return data released early in 2007.

- Foundation giving increased 12.6 percent in 2006, compared with the 2005 revised estimate, based on data from the Foundation Center.

- Corporate giving decreased in 2006 by 7.6 percent from the 2005 revised estimate. The 2005 estimate, however, included $1.38 billion for disaster relief giving and the 2006 estimate includes $0.15 billion for disaster relief. When these amounts are excluded, the change in 2006 is growth of 1.5 percent.

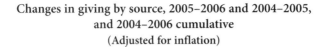

Changes in giving by source, 2005–2006 and 2004–2005,
and 2004–2006 cumulative
(Adjusted for inflation)

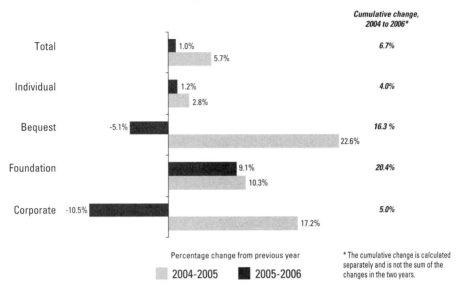

Cumulative change,
2004 to 2006*

Source	2005-2006	2004-2005	Cumulative change, 2004 to 2006*
Total	1.0%	5.7%	6.7%
Individual	1.2%	2.8%	4.0%
Bequest	-5.1%	22.6%	16.3 %
Foundation	9.1%	10.3%	20.4%
Corporate	-10.5%	17.2%	5.0%

Percentage change from previous year

2004-2005   2005-2006

* The cumulative change is calculated
separately and is not the sum of the
changes in the two years.

- When adjusted for inflation, total giving between 2005 and 2006 rose by an estimated 1.0 percent. The slowed rate of growth reflects added giving of $7.37 billion in 2005 for disaster relief and just $1.17 billion in estimated disaster relief giving in 2006. When these amounts are not included, the change is an inflation-adjusted increase of 3.2 percent.

- Individual giving rose an estimated 4.0 percent cumulatively from 2004 to 2006, after adjustment for inflation.

- The 2006 estimate for charitable bequests has decreased 5.1 percent from last year's revised estimate. The change over two years is growth of 16.3 percent.

- Foundation giving increased 9.1 percent in 2006 when compared with the 2005 revised estimate. This is a slower rate of growth than in 2005. From 2004 through 2006, foundation giving rose 20.4 percent cumulatively.

- Corporate giving declined an estimated 10.5 percent in 2006, adjusted for inflation. The 2005 estimate includes increased contributions in 2005 for disaster relief. When they are not included, the change is a decline of 1.7 percent. The net change from 2004 to 2006 is growth of 5.0 percent, with disaster gifts included in 2005 and 2006.

Changes in giving by type of recipient organization, 2005–2006 and 2004–2005, and 2004–2006 cumulative

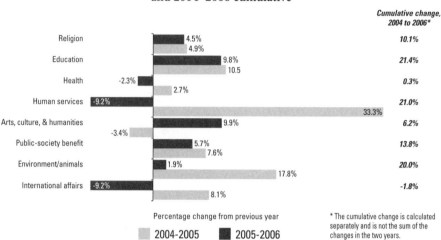

Cumulative change, 2004 to 2006*

Recipient	2004-2005	2005-2006	Cumulative change, 2004 to 2006*
Religion	4.9%	4.5%	10.1%
Education	10.5	9.8%	21.4%
Health	2.7%	-2.3%	0.3%
Human services	33.3%	-9.2%	21.0%
Arts, culture, & humanities	-3.4%	9.9%	6.2%
Public-society benefit	7.6%	5.7%	13.8%
Environment/animals	17.8%	1.9%	20.0%
International affairs	8.1%	-9.2%	-1.8%

Percentage change from previous year

■ 2004-2005   ■ 2005-2006

* The cumulative change is calculated separately and is not the sum of the changes in the two years.

- This page compares changes between 2005 and 2006 and changes in giving between 2004 and 2005 for each subsector, before adjustment for inflation. The following page examines the same years, after adjustment for inflation.

- Giving to religious organizations rose by 4.5 percent in 2006, following a change of 4.9 percent from 2005. In two years, giving to religion increased 10.1 percent.

- Gifts to the education subsector increased by 9.8 percent in 2006, trailing the 10.5 percent increase seen in 2005. In two years, giving to education rose 21.4 percent.

- Giving to health organizations fell by 2.3 percent in 2006, nearly cancelling out the 2.7 percent gain found for 2005. The net result is 0.3 percent increase.

- Giving to human services organizations decreased by 9.2 percent in 2006, much less than the 33.3 percent increase in 2005. That increase in 2005 does include disaster contributions estimated to be about one-half of the gain seen that year. The two-year change is growth of 21.0 percent.

- Gifts to the arts, culture, and humanities subsector increased by 9.9 percent in 2006, compared with a decline of 3.4 percent in 2005. Over two years, the change is 6.2 percent.

- Giving for organizations in the public-society benefit subsector rose by 5.7 percent in 2006, following a gain in 2005 of 7.6 percent (which includes disaster gifts received). The net result is an increase of 13.8 percent from 2004 to 2006.

- Giving to environmental organizations increased by 1.9 percent in 2006, compared with a change of 17.8 percent in 2005. The two-year change is growth of 20.0 percent.

- Giving for organizations in the international affairs subsector decreased by 9.2 percent in 2006, much less than the 8.1 percent increase in 2005. The increase in 2005 includes gifts made for disaster relief and recovery. The two-year change is a drop of 1.8 percent.

Changes in giving by type of recipient organization, 2005–2006 and 2004–2005
(Adjusted for inflation)

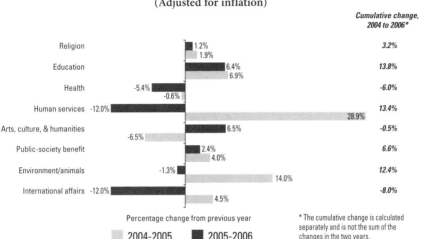

Cumulative change,
2004 to 2006*

	Cumulative change, 2004 to 2006*
Religion	3.2%
Education	13.8%
Health	-6.0%
Human services	13.4%
Arts, culture, & humanities	-0.5%
Public-society benefit	6.6%
Environment/animals	12.4%
International affairs	-8.0%

Percentage change from previous year

2004-2005   2005-2006

* The cumulative change is calculated separately and is not the sum of the changes in the two years.

- Adjusted for inflation, gifts to religious organizations grew by 1.2 percent in 2006, compared with a change of 1.9 percent in 2005. The 2005 contributions include estimated giving for disaster relief if denominations included that in their reports to the National Council of Churches of Christ, in the parish survey, or to the Evangelical Council of Financial Accountability. Over two years, the growth is 3.2 percent.

- Gifts to educational organizations in 2006 rose by an inflation-adjusted 6.4 percent, close to the 6.9 percent rate of growth in 2005. Over two years, the change is 13.8 percent.

- Adjusted for inflation, gifts to the health subsector fell by 5.4 percent, following a small drop of 0.6 percent in 2005. Over two years, the drop is 6.0 percent.

- Gifts to human services organizations experienced a significant decrease of 12.0 percent. This drop follows the healthy growth of 28.9 percent in 2005. The 2006 change reflects a decline following the extraordinary disaster relief gifts of 2005. Over two years, the change is 13.4 percent.

- Gifts to arts, culture, and humanities organizations rose by 6.5 percent in 2006, bouncing back from the decline of 6.5 percent experienced in 2005. The change from 2004 to 2006 is a drop of $0.06 billion, or a decline of 0.5 percent.

- Adjusted for inflation, gifts to the public-society benefit subsector increased by 2.4 percent, up from 4.0 percent growth in the previous year. The two-year change is 6.6 percent.

- Gifts to environment/animals organizations decreased by 1.3 percent, which follows an increase of 14.0 percent in 2005. The cumulative change is 12.4 percent from 2004 to 2006.

- Giving to the international affairs subsector dropped by 12.0 percent after adjustment for inflation, the first decline since 1993. This decline is from a high in 2005 that included disaster relief giving. The cumulative change since 2004 is -8.0 percent.

Total giving, 1966–2006
($ in billions)

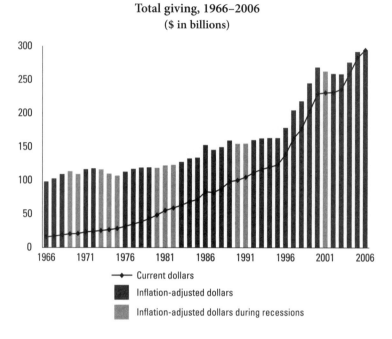

- Current dollars
- Inflation-adjusted dollars
- Inflation-adjusted dollars during recessions

- Giving in 2006 is estimated to be $295.02 billion. In current dollars, before inflation adjustment, estimated giving has increased by $279.23 billion since 1966. More than half of the growth has been since 1996, when giving was an estimated $139.1 billion.

- Adjusted for inflation, giving has increased $196.76 billion between 1966 and 2006, or from an estimated $98.26 billion to an estimated $295.02 billion. The change is more than 200 percent growth, adjusted for inflation, in 40 years.

- In 1996, inflation-adjusted giving was $178.73 billion. Giving has grown by $116.29 billion in 10 years. Adjusted for inflation, the ten-year change is 65.1 percent.

- Giving shows a slowed rate of growth—or even an inflation-adjusted decline—in years of recession.

- Giving showed the most dramatic rates of growth in the late 1990s through 2000, when the stock market was soaring.

- The inflation-adjusted increase in the stock market in 2006 was 10 percent. After removing disaster-relief gifts, giving rose 3.2 percent in 2006.

Total giving by source by five-year spans in inflation-adjusted dollars, 1967–2006
($ in billions)

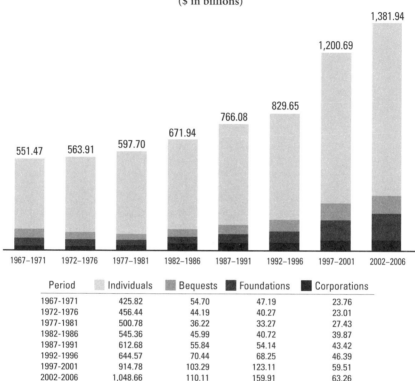

Period	Individuals	Bequests	Foundations	Corporations
1967-1971	425.82	54.70	47.19	23.76
1972-1976	456.44	44.19	40.27	23.01
1977-1981	500.78	36.22	33.27	27.43
1982-1986	545.36	45.99	40.72	39.87
1987-1991	612.68	55.84	54.14	43.42
1992-1996	644.57	70.44	68.25	46.39
1997-2001	914.78	103.29	123.11	59.51
2002-2006	1,048.66	110.11	159.91	63.26

Giving USA uses the CPI to adjust for inflation.

- Individual giving is always the largest portion of the total.

- Adjusted for inflation, individual giving increased by 146.3 percent when comparing the total of $1,049 billion ($1.05 trillion) for 2002–2006 with the $425.8 billion total for 1967–1971.

- Charitable bequests (at $110.11 billion in the 2002–2006 period) have more than doubled since 1967–1971, when they were $54.70 billion (adjusted for inflation).

- Foundation grantmaking has grown the fastest in 40 years, with a change of 238.9 percent from $47.19 billion in 1967–1971 to $159.91 billion in 2002–2006.

- Corporate contributions, including giving by corporate foundations, increased from $23.76 billion in 1967–1971 to $63.26 in the 2002–2006 period. This is growth of 166.2 percent.

Giving by source: percentage of the total by five-year spans, 1967–2006

| 1967–1971 | 1972–1976 | 1977–1981 | 1982–1986 | 1987–1991 | 1992–1996 | 1997–2001 | 2002–2006 |

Period	Individuals	Bequests	Foundations	Corporations
1967–1971	77.2%	9.9%	8.6%	4.3%
1972–1976	80.9%	7.8%	7.1%	4.1%
1977–1981	83.8%	6.1%	5.6%	4.6%
1982–1986	81.2%	6.8%	6.1%	5.9%
1987–1991	80.0%	7.3%	7.1%	5.7%
1992–1996	77.7%	8.5%	8.2%	5.6%
1997–2001	76.2%	8.6%	10.3%	5.0%
2002–2006	75.9%	8.0%	11.6%	4.6%

- Giving by individuals has continued to maintain a 50-year trend of being the single most important source of donations in the United States.

- In the period 2002–2006, the allocation by type of donor reflects the increase in foundation donations, which is becoming one vehicle used by living donors for their contributions. That is, family foundation grantmaking, which accounts for about half of grant dollars distributed, is a form of "individual" giving, at least in part.

Giving by individuals, 1966–2006
($ in billions)

- Charitable giving by individuals and households reached an estimated $222.89 billion in 2006, compared with a revised estimate of $213.47 billion for 2005. This is a growth of 4.4 percent (1.2 percent adjusted for inflation).

- Contributions from individuals are an estimated 75.6 percent of total giving.

- This year's estimate includes $3.9 billion in gifts known to have been transferred, based on reports in the *Chronicle of Philanthropy*.

- The Katrina Emergency Tax Relief Act (KETRA) of 2005 reportedly stimulated some new giving and fulfillment of pledges made earlier. It may have shifted some giving into 2005 that would have occurred in later years. With no official data released by the IRS as of April 2007 about the extent of the impact of the KETRA provision, no adjustment has been made to the *Giving USA* estimate for individual giving in 2005 or 2006.

- The Pension Protection Act of 2006 included provisions that are believed to have resulted in additional gifts, including untaxed transfer of assets (roll-over) from Individual Retirement Accounts held by people age 70½ or more, beginning in August 2006 and in force through December 2007.

- The 2005 and 2006 estimates each include individual contributions made for disaster relief. If those estimated amounts are not included in the totals, charitable giving by individuals and households rose 3.4 percent in 2005 (0.0 percent adjusted for inflation) and 6.9 percent in 2006 (3.6 percent adjusted for inflation).

- Individual giving has increased an average of 2.8 percent per year over the past 40 years, adjusted for inflation. In the past 10 years, individual giving has increased an average of 5.0 percent per year, adjusted for inflation.

Giving by bequest, 1966–2006
($ in billions)

- Charitable bequests are estimated to be $22.91 billion, which is a 2.1 percent decline (-5.1 percent adjusted for inflation) when compared with the revised estimate for 2005. Bequest giving is 7.8 percent of total estimated giving for 2006.

- The revised 2005 estimate for charitable bequests is $23.4 billion. Large estates that filed federal estate tax returns in 2005 included exceptional gifts to charity. Internal Revenue Service data show a 22 percent growth in value for the largest estates (more than $20 million) and a 68 percent increase in charitable bequests from those estates. Nearly the same number of large estates claimed a deduction in 2005 as in 2004 (328 compared with 330). In other estate sizes ($1.5 million to $19.99 million), combined gross estate value in 2005 fell 15.7 percent compared with 2004, and charitable bequests fell 5.3 percent.

- Huge estates skew the amount claimed in charitable bequest deductions. Since 2000, between 200 and 330 donor estates with gross estate value of $20 million or more have accounted for 44 to 64 percent per year of the total itemized charitable bequests.

- This year's estimate includes gifts of more than $4 billion that are anticipated to be made by estates that filed estate tax returns two years after the death of the donor— gifts announced in 2004.

- The federal estate tax filing exemption for 2006 jumped to $2 million (up from $1.5 million in 2004 and 2005).

- Since 1966, bequest gifts have grown an average of 4.5 percent annually, adjusted for inflation. Since 1996, the average annual rate of growth has been 5.5 percent, adjusted for inflation.

Giving by foundations, 1966–2006
($ in billions)

- The Foundation Center estimated $36.50 billion in giving in 2006 by independent, community, and operating foundations. This is 12.4 percent of total estimated giving for 2006.

- This is a 12.6 percent increase in grantmaking by these types of foundations (9.1 percent adjusted for inflation) compared with the final amount of $32.41 billion for 2005.

- According to the Foundation Center, the "principal factors driving growth in foundation giving in 2006 were strong gains in the stock market and a higher level of new foundation establishment than was seen in the early 2000s."

- Giving by foundations has increased an average of 4.4 percent annually since 1966 (adjusted for inflation).

- The annual increase in the past 10 years has averaged 9.3 percent, in spite of the fact that this period includes no growth in 2002 and 2003.

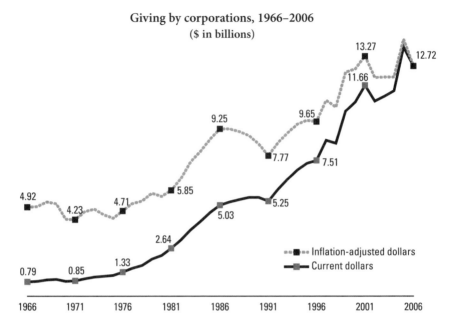

Giving by corporations, 1966–2006
($ in billions)

- Corporate contributions were an estimated $12.72 billion in 2006, a decrease of 7.6 percent (-10.5 percent adjusted for inflation) compared with the revised estimate of $13.77 billion for 2005, which includes $1.38 billion in estimated giving for disaster relief.

- An estimated 4.3 percent of charitable contributions came from corporate giving.

- Corporate giving is associated with changes in corporate profits. The Bureau of Economic Analysis' report of corporate profits before tax showed a growth of 19.2 percent in 2006 (16.0 percent adjusted for inflation). This is a strong rate of growth historically, but follows two years during which profit growth exceeded 20 percent after inflation adjustment.

- Corporate foundation grantmaking is an estimated $4.2 billion, using data collected by the Foundation Center. Corporate foundation grantmaking rose an estimated 6.0 percent in 2006. The grantmaking amount does not include distributions from operating foundations created by corporations that provide pharmaceuticals and medical products. Those foundations are treated by the Foundation Center as operating foundations instead of as corporate foundations.

- The Committee Encouraging Corporate Philanthropy (CECP) collected data from 89 of the country's largest firms. Those companies reported a median change of 6.1 percent increase in charitable contributions for 2006. CECP collects data about the fair-market value of product donations. *Giving USA* estimates the allowed tax deduction for product contributions, which is less than the fair market value.

- The 40-year average annual increase in charitable giving by corporations is 2.7 percent, adjusted for inflation. Since 1996, the average annual rate of change in corporate giving is 3.2 percent, adjusted for inflation.

Total giving as a percentage of gross domestic product, 1966–2006

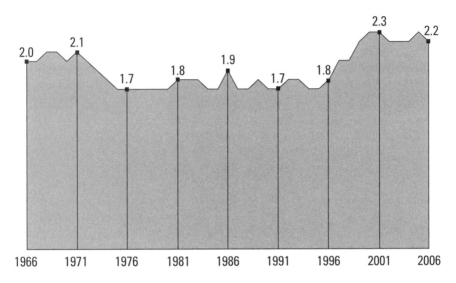

- The 2006 total estimate of charitable giving of $295.02 billion is 2.2 percent of the gross domestic product for 2006.
- The highest percentage of GDP that charitable giving has ever accounted for, 2.3 percent, was in 2000 after several years of rapid growth in the stock market, and again in 2001 and 2005, when disaster relief was part of the total estimate.

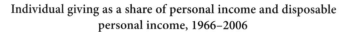

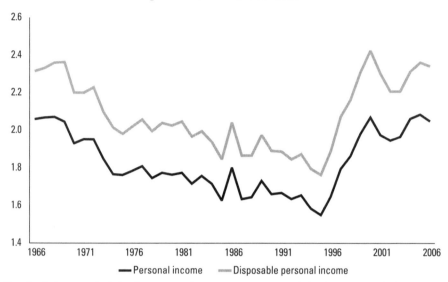

Individual giving as a share of personal income and disposable personal income, 1966–2006

— Personal income   — Disposable personal income

Note: Graph shows actual calculated percentages. In text, percentages are rounded to the nearest 1/10th of one percent.

- Individual giving as a percentage of personal income decreased to 2.0 percent in 2006 compared with 2.1 percent in 2005.

- The 2006 individual giving as a percentage of personal income is above the 40-year average of 1.8 percent.

- Personal income (before taxes) rose in 2006 by 6.3 percent (3.0 percent adjusted for inflation).

- Individual giving as a percentage of disposable personal income decreased to 2.3 percent compared with the 2005 percentage of 2.4.

- Individual giving as a percentage of disposable personal income is above the 40-year average of 2.1 percent.

- Disposable personal income grew by 5.4 percent (2.1 percent adjusted for inflation). After adjusting for inflation, this rate of disposable personal income growth is slower than the 40-year average of 2.7 percent.

Corporate giving as a percentage of corporate pretax profits, 1966–2006

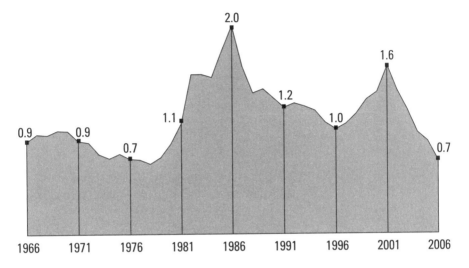

Note: Graph shows actual calculated percentages. In text, percentages are rounded to the nearest 1/10th of one percent.

- Corporate giving as a percentage of pretax profits is estimated to be 0.7 percent in 2006, which is less than the 40-year average of 1.1 percent.

- According to work by the Conference Board, international contributions are growing rapidly. Depending on how such contributions are made, it is possible that not all are counted as charitable donations under U.S. tax law.

- One of the largest sources of corporate philanthropy is pharmaceutical companies. Certain product donations made by these firms are reported at fair market values of more than $3.3 billion for 2005. The fair market value is not included in this estimate. In-kind donations are deductible under U.S. law at the cost of production, which is typically far less than fair market value.

- Between 1981 and 2004, corporate giving as a percentage of pretax profits was 1 percent or more. However, the percentage has dropped in recent years. This reflects rapidly increasing profits, not declining giving.

Giving to religion, 1966–2006
($ in billions)

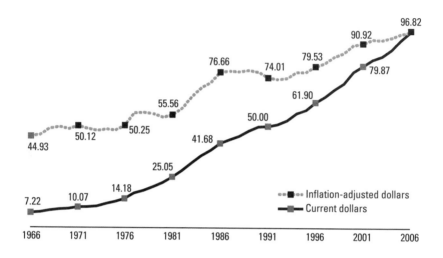

- In 2006, giving to religious organizations reached an estimated $96.82 billion, an increase of 4.5 percent (1.2 percent adjusted for inflation) from the revised estimate of $92.69 billion for 2005.

- Giving to religious organizations represented 32.8 percent of total estimated charitable contributions in the United States in 2006.

- Since 1966, in current dollars, gifts to religion have increased an average of 6.8 percent per year. Adjusted for inflation, the average annual 40-year increase is 2.0 percent. The ten-year average increase is 4.7 percent per year (2.1 percent adjusted for inflation).

- Giving to religion increases over time, but more slowly than does giving to other subsectors. As a percentage of total giving, religion's share has fallen from roughly half (45.7 percent) in 1966 to just under one-third (32.8 percent).

- Countless religious congregations organized volunteers in 2005 and 2006 to go to hurricane-affected communities in the American South to assist with rebuilding. Volunteer hours and expenses that volunteers paid for these trips are not included in the estimate of giving to religion.

Giving to education, 1966–2006
($ in billions)

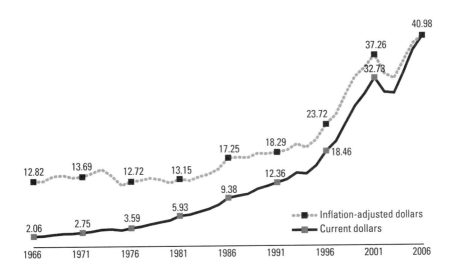

- Giving to educational organizations was estimated to be $40.98 billion in 2006, an increase of 9.8 percent (6.4 percent adjusted for inflation) from the 2005 revised estimate of $37.31 billion for 2005.

- An estimated 13.9 percent of total giving went to educational organizations.

- The education giving estimate is based on data from the Council for Aid to Education for gifts to higher education, from the National Association of Independent Schools for gifts to private K–12 schools, and from the *Giving USA* survey for gifts to other types of educational organizations.

- The new average rate of change of giving to education is 7.6 percent (3.1 percent adjusted for inflation) per year over the last 40 years. In the past ten years, giving to education has increased at an average annual rate of 8.0 percent (5.9 percent adjusted for inflation).

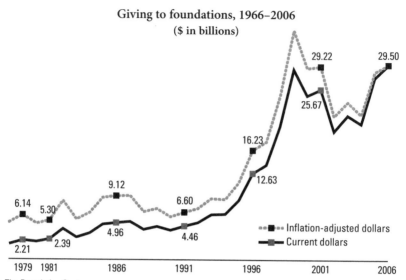

Giving to foundations, 1966–2006
($ in billions)

Data: The Foundation Center.
Excludes gifts to corporate foundations.

- In 2006, giving to foundations reached an estimated $29.50 billion—an increase of 7.4 percent (4.1 percent adjusted for inflation) from the revised estimate of $27.46 billion for 2005.

- Giving to foundations represented 10.0 percent of total estimated charitable contributions in the United States in 2006.

- Gifts to foundations in 2006 include major donations of Warren Buffett ($1.9 billion), Herbert and Marion Sandler ($1.3 billion), and Bernard Osher ($0.7 billion), as well as bequests from the estates of Jim Joseph ($500 million) and Mary Joan Palevsky ($212.8 million).

- FoundationSearch America showed 2,146 newly registered foundations established since January 2006, including trusts and scholarship funds. Many new foundations receive contributions that are not included in the gifts received by grantmaking foundations. For 2006, an unknown amount was given to foundations that are not (yet) grantmaking. The graph above is limited to grantmaking foundations.

- Giving to foundations has grown an average of 13.6 percent a year (9.1 percent adjusted for inflation) since data began in 1978. In the past ten years, giving to foundations has increased an annual average of 11.1 percent (8.4 percent adjusted for inflation).

Giving to human services, 1966–2006
($ in billions)

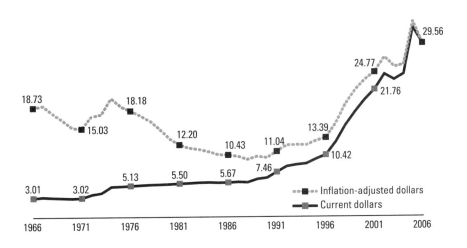

- Giving to organizations in the human services subsector is estimated to be $29.56 billion in 2006. This is 10.0 percent of total estimated giving.

- In current dollars, giving to human services declined by an estimated 9.2 percent in 2006. Adjusted for inflation, this is a drop of 12.0 percent.

- The decline estimated for 2006 follows exceptional growth in 2005 related to contributions for disaster relief and to bequests of $1.3 billion reported by one charitable organization.

- After adjusting for disaster relief gifts estimated for 2005 and 2006, giving to human services is $27.94 billion in 2005 and $28.86 billion for 2006.

- The rate of change without considering disaster relief giving in 2005 or 2006 or the billion-dollar bequest in 2005 is 3.3 percent (0.1 percent adjusted for inflation).

- The 40-year average rate of growth in giving to human services is 5.7 percent (1.5 percent adjusted for inflation). In the past decade (1997–2006), the average growth rate in human services has been 9.9 percent (8.9 percent adjusted for inflation).

Giving to health, 1966–2006
($ in billions)

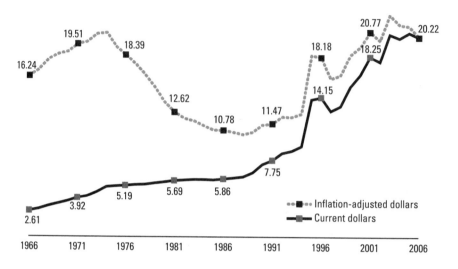

- In 2006, giving to health organizations reached an estimated $20.22 billion, a decrease of 2.3 percent (-5.4 percent adjusted for inflation) from the revised estimate of $20.70 billion for 2005.

- Giving to health organizations represented 6.9 percent of total estimated charitable contributions in the United States in 2006.

- The Bill & Melinda Gates Foundation continued its commitment to world health and made major grants that far surpassed any other single donor's philanthropic support for the subsector.

- The new 40-year average rate of growth for giving to health is 5.9 percent (1.0 percent adjusted for inflation).

- Health giving rose an average 4.2 percent per year (1.4 percent adjusted for inflation) from 1997 through 2006.

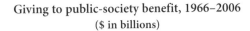

Giving to public-society benefit, 1966–2006
(\$ in billions)

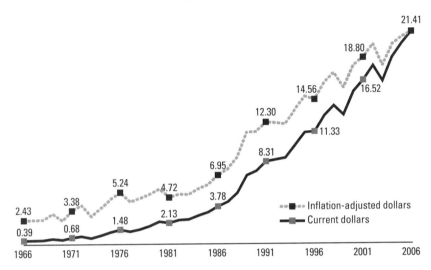

- In 2006, giving to public-society benefit organizations reached an estimated \$21.41 billion, an increase of 5.7 percent (2.4 percent adjusted for inflation) from the revised estimate of \$20.25 billion for 2005.

- Giving to the public-society benefit subsector represented 7.3 percent of total estimated charitable contributions in the United States in 2006.

- Over the past 40 years, the average increase in giving to public-society benefit organizations is 11.4 percent (6.4 percent adjusted for inflation). Since 1996, the average annual rate of change has been 6.6 percent (4.2 percent adjusted for inflation).

- According to the annual Philanthropy 400 rankings, United Way of America was the charity that raised the most money in the United States in 2004 and 2005. This includes gifts to more than 1,300 United Way affiliates.

Giving to arts, culture, and humanities, 1966–2006
($ in billions)

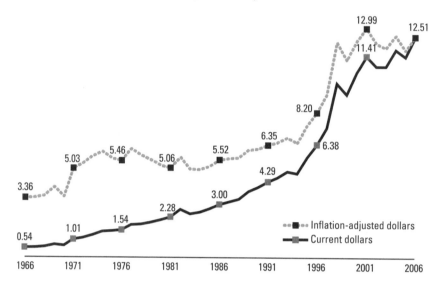

- In 2006, giving to arts, culture, and humanities organizations reached an estimated $12.51 billion, an increase of 9.9 percent (6.5 percent adjusted for inflation) from the revised estimate of $11.38 billion for 2005.

- Giving to the arts, culture, and humanities subsector represented 4.2 percent of total estimated charitable contributions in the United States in 2006.

- The 40-year average increase in gifts to arts, culture, and humanities organizations is 8.5 percent (4.2 percent adjusted for inflation). In the years from 1997 to 2006, the average annual increase is 5.5 percent (4.9 percent adjusted for inflation).

Giving to international affairs, 1966–2006
($ in billions)

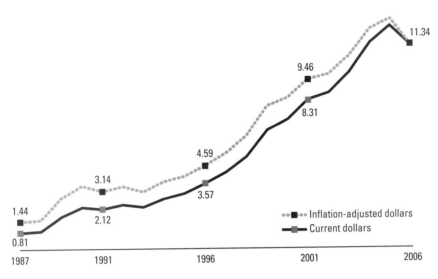

- In 2006, giving to international affairs organizations reached an estimated $11.34 billion, a decrease of 9.2 percent (-12.0 percent adjusted for inflation) from the revised estimate of $12.49 billion for 2005.

- The amount in 2005 includes $1.14 billion in giving for relief after the December 2004 tsunami and the 2005 hurricanes. With disaster gifts excluded, the change in 2006 is a drop of 0.3 percent (-3.3 adjusted for inflation). The decline in 2006 is the first drop in giving for this subsector since 1993.

- Giving to the international affairs subsector represented 3.8 percent of total estimated charitable contributions in the United States in 2006.

- In 1987, *Giving USA* began collecting data on gifts for international affairs, including aid, relief, and development giving, as well as contributions for student exchange programs and organizations working on global peace and security issues. Since 1987, giving for international affairs has increased an average of 16.3 percent annually (12.9 percent adjusted for inflation).

- From 1997 through 2006, giving to this subsector increased at an average annual rate of 12.5 percent (10.0 percent annually, after adjustment for inflation).

- Gifts to international affairs organizations include cash and in-kind contributions. In-kind gifts, often from corporations, include supplies, products, and equipment. U.S. recipient organizations are permitted by law to record those donations at fair-market value, which may exceed the amount allowed in deductions for the donor.

Giving to environment and animals, 1966–2006
($ in billions)

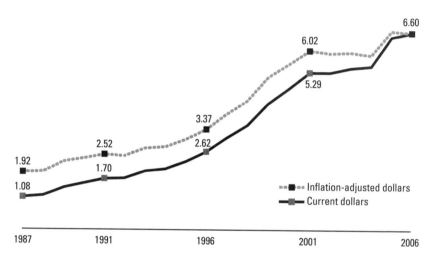

- In 2006, giving to the environment and animals subsector reached an estimated $6.60 billion, an increase of 1.9 percent (-1.3 percent adjusted for inflation) from the revised estimate of $6.48 billion for 2005.

- Giving to environment and animals organizations represented 2.2 percent of total estimated charitable contributions in the United States in 2006.

- Since 1987, when giving to environment and animals organizations began to be tracked separately, the average annual increase has been 8.1 percent (6.9 percent adjusted for inflation).

- From 1997 to 2006, the average annual increase has been 8.1 percent (7.2 percent adjusted for inflation).

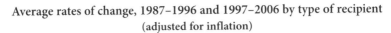

Average rates of change, 1987–1996 and 1997–2006 by type of recipient
(adjusted for inflation)

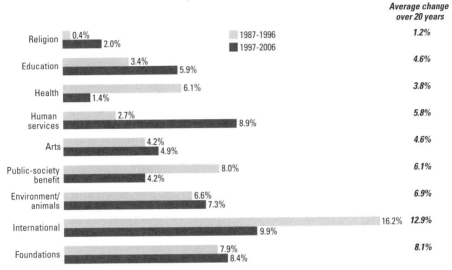

- The graph here compares the inflation-adjusted rates of change for the subsectors for three time periods. The light grey bars indicate the average rate of change for the years 1987 through 1996. The dark grey bars show the average rate of change for 1997 through 2006. The column on the right is the 20-year average for years 1987 through 2006.

- The rate of change is the highest in giving for international affairs in all three periods: 1987 to 1996, 1997 to 2006, and the combined period 1987–2006.

- Over the 20-year span, religion shows the lowest rate of growth. However, the average rate of change from 1997 through 2006, at 2.0 percent, is several times more than the very low rate of 0.4 percent in the years from 1987 to 1996.

- In the most recent decade, from 1997 to 2006, giving to human services has increased an average of 8.9 percent annually, while giving for health increased an average of only 1.4 percent per year.

Giving by type of recipients, five-year spans (adjusted for inflation), 1967–2006
($ in billions)

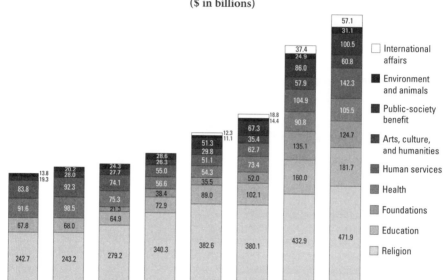

- Giving to religion, which was $242.7 billion in the 1967–1971 period, increased to $471.9 billion for the period from 2002–2006. This is nearly a doubling of giving to religion in 40 years (a 94 percent increase).

- Giving to education rose 168 percent, from $67.8 billion in the 1967–1971 period to $181.7 billion in 2002–2006.

- Giving to foundations rose by 486 percent from the first data in the mid-1970s to the 2002–2006 period.

- Giving to health shows the lowest rate of change of all the types of recipients, growing 15 percent from $91.6 billion in the 1967–1971 period to $105.5 billion in 2002–2006.

- Giving to human services charities was $83.8 billion in 1967–1971 and $142.3 billion in 2002–2006. This is growth of 70 percent.

- Giving to arts, culture, and humanities organizations rose by 216 percent, from $19.3 billion from 1967–1971 to $60.8 billion in 2002–2006.

- Giving to public-society benefit organizations rose from $13.8 billion in 1967–1971 to $100.5 billion in 2002–2006. This is growth of 628 percent.

- Giving to organizations in the environment/animals subsector rose from $11.1 billion in 1987–1991 to $31.1 billion in 2002–2004. This is growth of 181 percent.

- Giving for international affairs increased 363 percent, from $12.3 billion in 1987–1991 to $57.1 billion in 2002–2006.

Giving by type of recipient as a percentage of total giving, 1967–2006
(Five-year spans; does not include "unallocated")

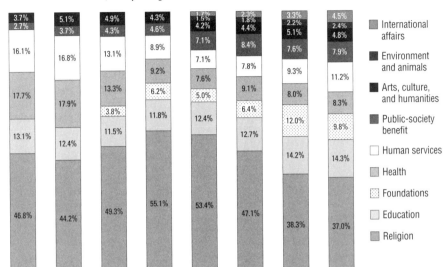

- Giving to religion represents the greatest percentage of total giving across time periods. In the time period 2002 through 2006, religious giving accounted for 37.0 percent of total charitable giving.

- Education has been the second largest portion of giving since the 1982 through 1986 period, when giving to education accounted for 11.8 percent of charitable giving.

- Donations to foundations made up 9.8 percent of all charitable donations between 2002 and 2006.

- The percentage of total charitable contributions that is accounted for by gifts to health has decreased from 1967–1971, when health received 17.7 percent of the total, to 2002–2006, when health organizations received 8.3 percent.

- Human services organizations received 16.1 percent of the total in the 1967–1971 period and 11.2 percent in the 2002–2006 period.

- Giving to public and society benefit has increased as a percentage of total charitable gifts since 1967–1971, when it was 2.7 percent. In 2002–2006, it was 7.9 percent.

- Arts, culture, and humanities gifts account for 4.8 percent of total charitable giving between 2002 and 2006. This is an increased share compared with 1967–1971, when arts, culture, and humanities organizations received 3.7 percent of the total.

- Environment/animal organizations have received around 2.0 percent of the total since they began to be tracked in 1987.

- International affairs organizations received 1.7 percent of the total from 1987–1991 and 4.5 percent in 2002–2006.

Distribution of levels of change in charitable revenue, 2005–2006
(By organizational size category)

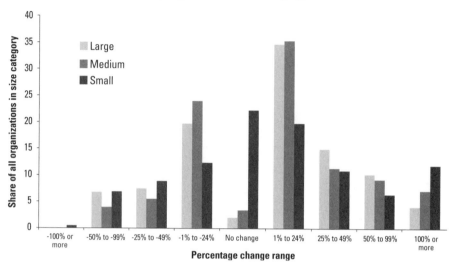

- In the *Giving USA* survey for this edition, more organizations reported an increase in giving than a decrease. This was true for every size group: large, medium, and small. In this analysis, "moderate" organizations are clustered with medium-sized organizations.

  — Large organizations:
    - 64 percent reported an increase
    - 2 percent reported "no change"
    - 34 percent reported a decrease

  — Moderate and Medium-sized organizations:
    - 63 percent reported an increase
    - 3 percent reported "no change"
    - 34 percent reported a decrease

  — Small organizations:
    - 49 percent reported an increase
    - 22 percent reported "no change"
    - 29 percent reported a decrease

  — All organizations:
    - 59 percent reported an increase
    - 9 percent reported "no change"
    - 32 percent reported a decrease

- Among all size groups, small organizations were the least likely to see an increase and most likely to see "no change."

The number of 501(c)(3) organizations, 1996–2006

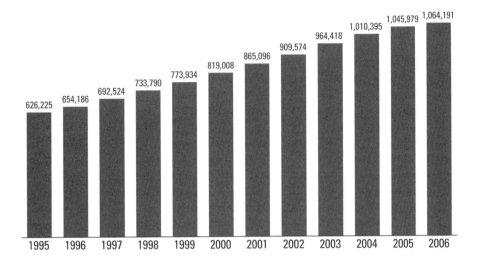

- The number of registered charities increased 1.7 percent between 2005 and 2006.

- Of the registered 501(c)(3) organizations, approximately 250,000 file an IRS Form 990 or IRS Form 990-PF. The other registered organizations either do not have total revenues of $25,000 or more, are defunct, or fail to file.

- Some scholars estimate that there may be as many 300,000 or more charities operating that have not registered with the Internal Revenue Service. They include new organizations, very small grassroots organizations, and organizations that have registered with a state office but have not yet filed paperwork for federal registration.

In addition to registered charities, there are an estimated 300,000 to 400,000 congregations that are not required to register, although some chose to file as a charitable organization under section 501(c)(3) of the Internal Revenue Code.

6 Disaster relief giving recap and 2006 estimates

- Total giving for disaster relief in 2006 is an estimated $1.17 billion. This estimate is based on the best available data, as of early 2007, including cash and in-kind gift amounts received at organizations responding to the *Giving USA* survey for 2006 and, major relief agencies responding to inquiries sent by the Center on Philanthropy at Indiana University, and media reports of major donations by corporations and foundations.

- An estimated $940 million ($0.94 billion) in disaster relief contributions came from individual donors.[1] The estimated individual contributions amount is 80.3 percent of the estimated total.

- Corporate donors gave an estimated $150 million ($0.15 billion) in 2006 for disaster relief, based on reported gifts on the Million Dollar List maintained by the Center on Philanthropy, supplemented with corporate giving information from the recipient agencies polled by *Giving USA*.[2] Corporate donations were 12.8 percent of the estimated total relief giving in 2006.

- Foundation grantmaking for disaster relief is estimated to have been at least $80 million in 2006, based on entries on the Center on Philanthropy's Million Dollar List[3] and news items released in *Philanthropy News Digest* at the Foundation Center. Foundation grantmaking is 6.8 percent of the estimated total.

- The majority of donations were reportedly given to the human service subsector, including $450 million to the American Red Cross in 2006 and $162 million received at the Salvation Army in 2006.

- These estimates estimates include some but not all contributions made through religious congregations, either cash to be sent to the hurricane-affected areas or as contributions in-kind of volunteers and companies that provided products and services.

- All the figures here are estimates based on information available in spring 2007. Many organizations that could not respond to the *Giving USA* survey or to inquiries from the Center on Philanthropy also received disaster relief contributions. Amounts are unknown.

Summary of the extent of damages from Hurricanes Katrina, Wilma, and Rita

The 2005 hurricane season was the most active Atlantic hurricane season in recorded history.[4] Of the 2005 hurricanes, three Category 5 hurricanes hit the American Gulf Coast within a 2-month period, leaving a wake of destruction behind them not soon to be forgotten. The first of these three hurricanes, Hurricane Katrina, formed on August 23, 2005 and hit land first as a Category 1 on August 25 in Florida. It then hit again, after increasing to a Category 5, in Alabama, Mississippi, and Louisiana on August 29.[5] Following Katrina, Hurricane Rita formed on September 17 and hit land in Louisiana as a Category 5 on September 24.[6] Little covered in the U.S. press, Hurricane Stan struck Mexico as a Category 1 storm and is thought to be responsible for more than 2,000 deaths.[7] Finally, Hurricane Wilma formed on October 15 and was a Category 5 storm. It hit land first in Mexico on October 21 and then hit land in Florida, as a Category 3 storm, on October 24.[8]

With total estimated damages from Hurricanes Katrina, Rita, and Wilma reaching $125 billion,[9] and the number of residences affected by the storms reaching an estimated 1,197,499,[10] best estimates for full reconstruction extend 10 or more years.[11] Throughout 2006, Americans raised funds, volunteered, and sent material aid to communities in the regions hardest hit—Louisiana, Mississippi, and Alabama—and to a lesser extent, Florida and Texas. People from those regions who resettled in other states drew upon government aid and some charitable assistance as they rebuilt their lives in new communities.

Summary of total giving for hurricane relief

More than 70 countries (many of which had been helped historically by the U.S.) contributed monetary donations following the Gulf Coast hurricanes. Of these foreign contributors, Kuwait made the largest single pledge by donating $500 million.[12] Qatar ($100 million), India ($5 million), China ($5 million), Pakistan ($1.5 million), and Bangladesh ($1 million) also made large contributions.[13]

Charitable giving is estimated at $6.47 billion, including $1.17 billion in 2006 and $5.30 billion in 2005.[14] While this amount exceeds all previous records for giving following a national disaster in U.S. history, it is nonetheless less than 1.5 percent of total estimated giving in the U.S. for 2005 and for 2006. Of these donations, more than 36 percent went to human service organizations, whereas less than 1 percent went to environment, education, and health-related disaster charities.[15] The majority of this money was used for feeding and sheltering evacuees, and providing direct financial assistance.

An estimated 13 million Americans made donations online to disaster relief efforts following the Gulf Coast hurricanes, and 7 million Americans set up their own hurricane relief efforts using the Internet.[16] Approximately $1 billion of the donated money raised went to new or fledgling charities,[17] $2.3 billion went to the Red Cross,[18] $365 million went to the Salvation Army,[19] and the remaining amount went to other established charities.

Around $170 million of in-kind donations were given in addition to direct monetary contributions. These donations consisted primarily of food, clothing, and medical supplies.[20]

Corporate disaster relief giving played a major role in 2005

A survey conducted by the Foundation Center found that among their respondents, corporations and corporate foundations pledged $358.1 million, or 62 percent, of overall institutional giving in response to Hurricanes Katrina and Rita.[21] Among foundation types (independent, corporate, and community), corporate foundations were the most likely to support disaster relief agencies. The Foundation Center also tracked 81 corporations that provided an additional $227.4 million in in-kind contributions for relief and recovery. Examples include Albertson's $9 million in food and water, General Motors' $6 million in vehicles, and FedEx Corporation's $500,000 in shipping services.

Giving USA, working with the Center for Corporate Citizenship at the U.S. Chamber of Commerce, estimated even more given in 2005 than found by the Foundation Center in its study. The estimated $1.38 billion in 2005 donations for tsunami recovery and hurricane recovery was approximately 10 percent of total estimated corporate giving in 2005, according to *Giving USA 2006.*[22] Despite that strong commitment to disaster relief in 2005 by corporate giving, fewer than one-quarter of Conference Board survey participants listed the costs of responding to natural disasters as one of their top three philanthropic challenges for giving in 2006.[23]

Study of foundation grantmaking for disaster relief

Foundations awarded an estimated $219 million ($0.22 billion) in grants in 2005 and into 2006 for relief, rebuilding, and recovery efforts. The vast majority of this support (59.4 percent) went toward immediate human service needs. Large proportions of this funding also went to housing development (7.3 percent), education and educational reform (6.6 percent), health and mental services (3.2 percent), and economic and community development (2.2 percent).[24]

Almost half (47.7 percent) of independent, corporate, and community foundations surveyed by The Foundation Center provided some type of hurricane-related support. Eighty-two percent of these respondents gave only to immediate relief efforts, while 22 percent gave to long-term recovery efforts (such as housing, or economic and job development).[25]

To estimate foundation giving in 2006, *Giving USA 2007* tracked announced foundation grants and tallied an estimated $80 million awarded in 2006. Some of those grants are multiyear commitments that will be paid in years to come.

Giving continued in 2006, but at a much lower level

Based on available data from business contributions and foundation grants, *Giving USA* estimates that at least $1.17 billion of the total donations were given for hurricane rebuilding in 2006. To that amount must be added donations to religious organizations not participating in the *Giving USA* studies and the amount contributed to organizations not responding to the *Giving USA* survey. The total of those gifts is very difficult to estimate without asking households about their giving. Most religious congregations do not routinely report contributions at a national level, and household surveys are one of the few sources of data available about disaster relief contributions that are made to religious congregations.

The largest recipient of hurricane-related donations, the American Red Cross, announced in February 2006 that after receiving donations exceeding its $2.12 billion projected budget for hurricane relief, it would no longer accept monetary donations for this particular relief effort. The Red Cross planned to use the $2.12 billion raised as follows:

- $1.554 billion in emergency financial assistance;

- $227 million in food and shelter donations;

- $198 million in hurricane recovery/ long-term recovery donations;

- $95 million in fundraising costs/ management and general expenses;

- $32 million in additional Red Cross support (such as the creation of Web sites and toll-free information lines); and the remaining

- $3 million in mental and physical health services.[26]

Documented activity in 2006 to support Gulf Coast rebuilding

Much of the rebuilding effort underway in 2006 was organized through institutions, whether religious congregations, corporations, or other charitable organizations such as Habitat for Humanity or United Way affiliates.

Religious congregations

One central organizing point for reconstruction has been congregations. The Mississippi Commission for Volunteer Service estimated that more than 250 organizations deployed volunteers to areas within that state within one year of the disaster.[27] Many of the teams came from churches or were hosted by churches in the communities served. Many congregations in unaffected regions adopted sister congregations in the hurricane area and sent teams of volunteers, supplies, and other donations.[28]

The General Board of Global Ministries, the mission agency of the United Methodist Church, stated that it expects to be involved in hurricane relief efforts throughout the Gulf Coast area, at least until January 2012. The denomination raised $63.8 million through its United Methodist Committee on Relief (UMCOR), with an additional $7.6 million of relief and emergency supplies shipped from UMCOR's supply depot to the annual conferences in that region.[29] The UMCOR figures are included in the *Giving USA* estimate for 2006.

In March of 2006, the North American Mission Board, which is the mission agency of the Southern Baptist Convention, announced plans for a $10 million reconstruction project called Project NOAH—New Orleans Area Hope.[30] This project, begun in April 2006, relies on volunteers to rebuild damaged houses and Baptist churches during a two-year period. As of January 2007, the church reported that 5,997 volunteers had already participated, tearing down more than 480 damaged churches and homes, actively reconstructing more than 65 structures, and having completed rebuilding on 12.[31] No estimates of time or materials for this project are in the *Giving USA* estimate.

On February 20, 2007, the Presbyterian Disaster Assistance (PDA) advisory committee approved a $1.7 million dollar proposal from the Presbytery of South Louisiana for the recovery work from hurricanes Katrina and Rita. The plan encompasses New Orleans, the North Shore, and the Lake Charles area. The goal of this plan is to rebuild 350 homes each year until recovery is complete. PDA also reported that prior to February 2007 it had already expended more than $7 million and sent more than 18,000 volunteers for relief and recovery work throughout the affected areas.[32] The Presbyterian giving figures are in the *Giving USA 2006* estimate for contributions for hurricane relief, but data for 2006 contributions received was not available at press time.

Not all reconstruction efforts actually occurred in the hurricane region. For example, the Southeast Christian Church in Louisville, KY, a nonde-nominational mega-church, held "Help Build Hope." This four-hour home-building project mobilized more than 6,000 volunteers to frame interior and exterior walls for 33 houses. The church shipped the wall units to New Orleans to be assembled into homes for families displaced by Hurricane Katrina.[33]

Businesses

Wal-Mart, which gave more than $236.1 million in cash to charity in 2005, donated more than $18 million to support Katrina relief and recovery efforts.[34] Recipients included the American Red Cross, the Bush-Clinton Katrina Fund, the Salvation Army, and the Texas Disaster Relief Fund. Through its Associate Disaster Relief Fund, the company also provided another $14.5 million in cash assistance to more than 20,000 of its employees. In addition to cash, Wal-Mart donated 100 truckloads of merchandise—such as water, ice, batteries, blankets, and diapers—valued at upward of $3 million.

GE provided nearly $5 million in cash and $10 million in equipment and services to aid more than 50 New Orleans schools in opening on September 7, 2006. Supplies were donated from GE's Consumer & Industrial business, which provided electrical equipment, lights, ballasts, and appliances.[35]

Some of the other notable corporate donations made to relief and recovery efforts in 2006 came from Shell Oil, ExxonMobil, AT&T, Cisco, Disney, and Wachovia. Cisco pledged $20 million in March 2006 in a three-year commitment to aid the rebuilding of Louisiana schools.[36] ExxonMobil made a similar pledge of $10 million in July 2006 to support mathematics and science education within New Orleans schools.[37] Disney announced a $1.5 million donation in April 2006 to aid in the rebuilding of 16 Boys & Girls Clubs within affected communities.[38] Shell Oil pledged $3.5 million to Louisiana State University to be distributed over 3 years.[39] AT&T donated $1 million to help rebuild Gulf Coast libraries.[40] Wachovia Corp. gave $800,000 to the Gulf Coast Community Foundation for the rebuilding of southern Mississippi.[41]

An article from *Harvard Business Review* points out another emerging trend for corporate giving toward disaster relief. The corporate-charity partnership is becoming important,[42] which was witnessed by several organizations' cases. Examples cited in the article include new alliances with companies such as Lands' End, the mail-order clothing company; Maggie Moo's Ice Cream and Treatery; Kohl's department stores; and Madame Alexander Dolls, which encourages its customers to make cash and product donations to the charity. Wal-Mart stores helped lift fundraising returns for the Salvation Army's western territory, which represents local branches of the charity in 13 states.

Businesses continued to give for reconstruction into 2007. In January 2007, for example, Chevron announced

donations of $18 million for learning programs in more than 20 school districts.[43] In February 2007, UGS Corporation announced a $307 million in-kind grant for software products to three Baton Rouge school districts affected by Hurricane Katrina.[44] Similarly, in February 2007, Microsoft Corp. announced a $1.7 million donation of cash, software, and specialized curricula to several nonprofit organizations in Texas and Louisiana to assist with rebuilding government organizations and the economies of affected communities.[45]

Foundation giving in 2006 for reconstruction efforts

Among the notable foundation grants announced in 2006 are:

- The Ford Foundation's 10-year commitment for rebuilding;[46]

- Grants from the W.K. Kellogg Foundation, including an $8.7 million grant for school-based health centers;[47]

- The Getty Foundation's seven grants, totaling $1 million to New Orleans arts institutions for conservation and transitioning following the hurricanes;[48] and

- The Charles Stewart Mott Foundation's grants totaling $1 million to Dillard and Xavier Universities in New Orleans.[49]

As with corporate giving, foundation giving also continued into 2007. In January 2007, for example, the Gulf Coast Community Foundation announced a $30 million grant to aid in Katrina relief: $15 million of this money was earmarked for rebuilding and repairing homes, and another $6 million was designated to rebuild community centers.[50]

Individuals' donations difficult to track; much giving presumed through religious congregations and schools

Total individual or household giving for Katrina reconstruction and rebuilding in 2006 will be difficult to tabulate entirely. Major institutions receiving funds will, in time, report those through IRS Forms 990, yet uncounted funds were raised informally through religious congregations, civic groups, youth development programs (scouting, for example), and schools. Contributions taken as someone "passes the hat" typically remain undocumented for the donor (no receipt and thus often no way to claim or report the gift) and are uncountable on a major scale for the recipients.

One study, *Individual Giving in Illinois*, found that 48 percent of households that contributed for Katrina relief in 2005 gave through a church; 28 percent gave through a school or a workplace.[51] Informally collected donations are often passed along to recipients who do not report income through charitable donations on an IRS Form 990, either because the entity is not required to report (being a small charitable organization, a government entity such as a school or fire department, or a religious group such as a congregation) or because the funds are given to individuals or a group not registered with the IRS as a charitable organization. Contributions to help specific, named families, for example, would not be tax deductible contributions under law but may count as charity in the hearts and minds of the donors.

Volunteering

In addition to cash and resources, relief also came in the form of continued volunteering throughout 2006. Volunteerism has been an unprecedented force for change all along the Gulf Coast. A recent report by The Corporation for National and Community Service states that more than 500,000 volunteers have served in recovery and relief efforts. Louisiana and Mississippi state government offices recruited volunteers through online sites, as did numerous churches, charities, and civic associations.[52]

The Red Cross estimates that following Hurricanes Katrina, Rita, and Wilma, it sent more than 244,000 workers to the Gulf Coast, 95 percent of whom were unpaid volunteers.[53] In total, the Corporation for National and Community Services estimated that nearly 600,000 Americans volunteered in the Gulf Coast following the hurricanes and identified 45 different charitable organizations that are helping in the gulf.[54]

Tens of thousands of volunteers were college students, many of whom sacrificed their spring or summer breaks to help with relief and rebuilding. Many of these volunteers came from the United Way's "Alternative Spring Break" program. This program, supported by funding and donations from FedEx, MTV, Gamestop, & EB

Games, sent (and continues to send) 18–24-year-old volunteers to the Gulf Coast to help in projects such as roofing houses, repairing homes, and clearing and rebuilding parks and trails.[55]

Another large group of student volunteers came from Habitat for Humanity's "Collegiate Challenge" alternative spring break program. Within this alternative spring break program, students spend their time performing all aspects of building a home. Habitat for Humanity estimates that by mid-summer 2007 it will have completed more than 1,000 homes for Hurricanes Katrina, Rita, and Wilma victims.[56]

Many companies, both large and small, organized teams of employees to assist with rebuilding efforts. These companies include: Rejuvenation Lighting Company in Portland (OR),[57] AT&T,[58] and Dow.[59]

Entire towns have "adopted" storm-ravaged communities. Aiken, Georgia adopted Waveland, Mississippi;[60] Carmel, Indiana adopted Long Beach, Mississippi;[61] Belmar, New Jersey adopted Pass Christian, Mississippi;[62] and so on.

Conclusion

The immediate philanthropic response to the tsunami and hurricane disasters led to unprecedented amounts contributed for relief work. The recovery and rebuilding period is expected to be 10 or more years in both disaster regions (Indian Ocean and U.S. Gulf Coast). Charitable organizations and intermediaries such the Corporation for National and Community Service and others will be working to sustain interest in the gulf and the immense rebuilding tasks there.

1   This amount is considered "over and above" the estimate that *Giving USA* would develop without a disaster and is added to individual giving.

2   This amount is added to the estimate of corporate giving over and above *Giving USA*'s usual estimating procedure.

3   The foundation grantmaking amount is included in the estimate of total giving from the Foundation Center for *Giving USA 2007*. No adjustment is made for giving with and without disaster relief contributions for foundations.

4   Staff writer, *Hurricane Katrina: One Year Later*, Charity Navigator. Retrieved on April 9, 2007.

5   R. D. Knabb, J. R. Rhome, and D. P. Brown, *Tropical Cyclone Report: Hurricane Katrina*, NOAA. Retrieved on April 9, 2007.

6   Ibid.

7   No author, Hurricane names "retired" from list of storm names, *NOAA Magazine*, April 6, 2006, viewed at www.magazine.noaa.gov.

8   R. J. Pasch, E. S. Blake, H. D. Cobb III, and D. P. Roberts, *Tropical Cyclone Report: Hurricane Wilma*, NOAA. Retrieved on April 9, 2007.

9   Associated Press, *Katrina Damage Estimate Hits $125B*, USA Today, September 9, 2005.

10 Department of Housing and Urban Development Office, February 12, 2006.

11 R. W. Kates, C. E. Colten, S. Laska, and S. P. Leatherman, *Reconstruction of New Orleans After Hurricane Katrina: A Research Perspective*, Proceedings of the National Academy of Sciences of the United States of America, 30(140), October 3, 2006, pages 14653–14660.

12 Staff Writer, *Asian nations offer U.S. assistance*, BBC News, September 5, 2005.

13 Ibid.

14 The Center on Philanthropy at Indiana University, *Giving USA 2006* (Glenview, IL: Giving USA Foundation).

15 Charity Navigator report, as in note 4.

16 Charity Navigator report, as in note 4.

17 E. Altpowell, *Katrina Provided Lessons About Charities*, Charity Navigator, August 23, 2006.

18 2006 Red Cross Annual Report, www. redcross.org.

19 Press release, *The Salvation Army's National Response to Hurricane Katrina,* The Salvation Army. See www.salvationarmyusa.org.

20 Charity Navigator report, as in note 4.

21 L. Renz, S. Lawrence and J. Diaz, *Giving in the Aftermath of the Gulf Coast Hurricanes,* The Foundation Center, August 2006.

22 The Center on Philanthropy at Indiana University, *Giving USA 2006*, (Glenview, IL: Giving USA Foundation).

23 S. Muirhead, *2006 Corporate Contributions Report*, Conference Board, www.conference-board.org.

24 L. Renz, S. Lawrence, and J. Diaz, *Giving in the Aftermath of the Gulf Coast Hurricanes*, The Foundation Center, August 2006.

25 M. North, *New Foundation Center Report: Foundations and Corporations Have Committed More Than $577 Million for Katrina Recovery*, The Foundation Center, August 9, 2006.

26 Press release, *Turning Compassion into Action: Donor Dollars at Work*, American Red Cross. See www.redcross.org.

27 Q. Smith, Volunteers reach out to get South Mississippi on its feet, *Mississippi Sun Herald*, August 28, 2006, viewed at Philanthropy News Digest, www.foundationcenter.org.

28 For a list of several such partnerships, see J. Patton, Hurricane relief works will last for years, *Patriot News* (Harrisburg, PA), June 23, 2006, viewed at www.lexis-nexis.com.

29 J. Patton, *Hurricane Relief Work Will Last for Years*, Patriot News, June 23, 2006.

30 J. H. Price, *Southern Baptist Mission to Rebuild Big Easy Homes*, The Washington Times, March 16, 2006.

31 Press release, *Operation NOAH Rebuild*, North American Mission Board, February 22, 2007. See www.namb.net.

32 Press release, *Presbytery of Southern Louisiana 2007 Relief Plan*, Presbyterian Church, February 20, 2007. See www.pcusa.org.

33 Personal communication with author Len Moisan, The Covenant Group, Louisville, KY, December 2006.

34 N. Barton and C. Jones, *Wal-Mart Makes Disaster Relief a Central Part of Its Operations, Chronicle of Philanthropy*, August 17, 2006.

35 No author, *GE Grant Helps Schools Reopen in N.O. for Fall*, The Advocate, September 29, 2006.

36 Press release, Cisco Pledges $20 Million to Rebuild Louisiana Schools Damaged by Katrina, viewed at Philanthropy News Digest at http://foundationcenter.org.

37 Press release, ExxonMobil Announces $10 Million Commitment to New Orleans Area Schools for Mathematics and Sciences Education: ExxonMobil Donations to Hurricane Katrina Relief and Recovery Increase to More Than $23 Million. Viewed at http://home.businesswire.com.

38 Press release, Disney Awards $1.5 Million to Rebuild Hurricane Devastated Boys & Girls Clubs. Viewed at Philanthropy News Digest at http://foundationcenter.org

39 Press release, Louisiana State Receives $3.5 Million for Coastal Studies, Business Recovery. Viewed at Philanthropy News Digest at http://foundationcenter.org.

40 Press release, AT&T Foundation provides $1 million grant to restore Gulf Coast school libraries destroyed by hurricanes, August 29, 2006, www.att.com.

41 Press release, Wachovia Establishes Fund to Rebuild South Mississippi. Viewed at Philanthropy News Digest at http://foundationcenter.org.

42 A. Thomas and L. Fritz, "Disaster Relief, Inc.," *Harvard Business Review,* November 2006.

43 S. Maloney, $18M Chevron Donation Helps Fuel Recovery for Schools, New Orleans City Business, January 22, 2007.

44 Press release, Three School Districts in Baton Rouge Directly Impacted by 2005 Hurricanes Katrina and Rita Receive $307 Million Software Grant from UGS. Viewed at Philanthropy News Digest at http://foundationcenter.org.

45 No author, Microsoft Donates $1.7 Million to Support Rebuilding of Gulf States, PR Newswire US, February 26, 2007. Viewed at Lexis-Nexis academic.

46 No author, *Ford Foundation "Katrina Update,"* Ford Foundation Report Online, Number One, 2007.

47 Press release, Kellogg Foundation Awards $8.7 Million for School-Based Health Centers in New Orleans. Viewed at Philanthropy News Digest at http://foundationcenter.org.

48 Press release, Getty Foundation Awards Grants to New Orleans Arts Institution, J. Paul Getty Trust. Viewed at Philanthropy News Digest at http://foundationcenter.org.

49 Press release, $1 Million in Mott Grants Aid Katrina-Ravaged Black Colleges, Charles Stewart Mott Foundation. Viewed at Philanthropy News Digest at http://foundationcenter.org.

50 Associated Press, Gulf Coast Community Foundation to Award $30 Million in Katrina Aid, viewed at Philanthropy News Digest at http://foundationcenter.org.

51 Center on Philanthropy, *Individual Giving in Illinois,* Donors Forum of Chicago, released April 2007, www.donorsforum.org.

52 See Web sites of Mississippi Commission for Volunteer Service, http://www.mcvs.org; Hurricane Katrina Information for Louisiana.gov, http://katrina.louisiana.gov/ volunteer.htm; Presbyterian Volunteer Village Youth Program, www.pcusa.org; Southern Medical Association, www.sma.org; and Volunteer Match, www.volunteermatch. org. All sites were active as of May 29, 2007.

53 No author, *A Year of Healing: The American Red Cross Response to Hurricanes Katrina, Rita, and Wilma,* American Red Cross, August, 2006. www.redcross.org.

54 No author, *The Power of Help and Hope after Katrina by the Numbers: Volunteers in the Gulf,* Corporation for National and Community Service, September 18, 2006, http://www.nationalservice.gov/pdf/ katrina_volunteers_respond.pdf.

55 Press release, United Way announces Alternative Spring Break 2007, United Way, March 1, 2006. See www.unitedway.org.

56 Press release, Habitat's Hurricane Recovery on the US Gulf Coast, Habitat for Humanity, retrieved on April 13, 2007 at www.habitat.org.

57 Sales catalog, 2007 and see www.rejuvenation. com under "Extra Mile" and then "Hurricane Katrina." "In 2006, Rejuvenation supported the clean-up and rebuilding efforts in New Orleans by sending a team of employees to the city for a week of demolition and food distribution. … we plan on doing something similar again."

58 No author, AT&T Wins 2006 Page Principles Award for Role in Reuniting Families After Hurricane Katrina, PR Newswire US, October 2, 2006. Viewed at lexis-nexis.com.

59 Press release, Dow volunteers take part in Habitat Blitz Build, June 14, 2006, www. news.dow.com.

60 No author, A Team that Delivers: Aiken Group Helps Katrina-Ravaged Mississippi Town on Road to Recovery, *Augusta Chronicle,* March 20, 2006. Viewed at lexis-nexis.com.

61 Press release, Mayor Skellie of Long Beach No Longer Able to Serve as Parade Marshal, Carmel City Hall, June 27, 2006. See www. ci.carmel.in.us/government/newsrelease/ 06-27-06.htm.

62 *Shore to Shore, Hand to Hand, Belmar to Pass Christian.* Viewed at www.belmar.com.

7 Giving by individuals

- Charitable giving by individuals and households reached an estimated $222.89 billion in 2006, compared with a revised estimate of $213.47 billion for 2005. This is a growth of 4.4 percent (1.2 percent adjusted for inflation).

- Contributions from individuals are an estimated 75.6 percent of total giving.

- This year's estimate includes $3.9 billion in gifts known to have been transferred, based on reports in the *Chronicle of Philanthropy*.

- The Katrina Emergency Tax Relief Act (KETRA) of 2005 reportedly stimulated some new giving and fulfillment of pledges made earlier. It may have shifted some giving into 2005 that would have occurred in later years. With no official data released by the IRS as of April 2007 about the extent of the impact of the KETRA provision, no adjustment has been made to the *Giving USA* estimate for individual giving in 2005 or 2006.

- The Pension Protection Act of 2006 included provisions that are believed to have resulted in additional gifts, including untaxed transfer of assets (roll-over) from Individual Retirement Accounts held by people age 70½ or more, beginning in August 2006 and in force through December 2007.

- The 2005 and 2006 estimates each include individual contributions made for disaster relief. If those estimated amounts are not included in the totals, charitable giving by individuals and households rose 3.4 percent in 2005 (0.0 percent adjusted for inflation) and 6.9 percent in 2006 (3.6 percent adjusted for inflation).

- Individual giving has increased an average of 2.8 percent per year over the past 40 years, adjusted for inflation. In the past ten years, individual giving has increased an average of 5.0 percent per year, adjusted for inflation.

Giving USA findings

The *Giving USA* estimate is based on a projection that uses historical trends in itemized giving, taking into account income growth, stock market growth, and recent changes in personal income tax rates and in itemized deductions for charitable gifts.[1]

- Just over one-quarter (26 percent) of the estimated change of $6.8 billion predicted in the itemized deductions for charitable giving is attributable to growth in household assets, as measured by the Standard & Poor's 500 Index, which rose 13.6 percent (10.6 percent adjusted for inflation) in 2006.[2]

- Approximately 65 percent of the estimated growth of $6.8 billion in itemized giving is attributed to a 6.4 percent (3.6 percent adjusted for inflation) jump in personal income.[3]

WHAT THIS MEANS TO YOU

Individual giving follows the economy, especially tracking disposable income and the stock market. But economic growth does not automatically translate into more giving distributed equally across all organizations.

The organizations that receive larger gifts in times of economic growth are those that have succeeded in building relationships with donors, that provide good stewardship, and that have developed strategically managed and well-organized solicitation programs.

- About 7 percent of the estimated growth of $6.8 billion in itemized giving is associated with the trend of a growth in contributions claimed in recent years.[4]

- None of the estimate reflects changes in tax rates because there are no differences in tax rates for 2006 compared with 2005.

- A portion of the estimate is for households that do not itemize charitable deductions. The estimate of charitable contributions for 2006 includes an increase of $1.96 billion (5.2 percent) in donations from the 70 percent of households that do not itemize contributions. An estimated 54 percent of nonitemizing households do contribute to charity. Among these donor households, the average gift is about $1,100.[5]

- In addition to the modeling procedure that *Giving USA* implemented in 2002, this year's estimate includes $3.9 billion in gifts reported by the *Chronicle of Philanthropy* as made (assets transferred to the organization) in 2006. This takes into account Warren Buffett's initial installment to the Bill & Melinda Gates Foundation and other contributions listed on the *Chronicle*'s list of the Top 60 donors for 2006.[6]

High international investment returns in 2006 not part of Giving USA *estimate*
As more households hold investments in overseas capital markets, investment returns are likely to change with fluctuations unrelated to the U.S. stock market. The estimates for giving in *Giving USA* are based in part on U.S. stock market performance, and to the extent that global capital markets perform better, *Giving USA*'s initial estimate (this year's estimate for 2006) may not fully incorporate the earnings of some investors and the giving that follows higher earnings.

Billion-dollar gifts announced
Warren Buffett stunned the world with the summer 2006 announcement that he would donate the bulk of his personal fortune, reported by year-end to be $43.5 billion.[7] More than $30 billion will go in 10 installments to the Bill & Melinda Gates Foundation, and the rest of the gift will be split among four foundations created by members of the Buffett family.[8] Mr. Buffett's wealth comes from stock in his investment firm Berkshire Hathaway. This year's estimate for *Giving USA* includes $1.9

billion, reported by the *Chronicle of Philanthropy* as paid in 2006,[9] in addition to the estimated change of $6.8 billion that results from the estimating model developed for *Giving USA*.

Herbert and Marion Sandler gave $1.3 billion to the Sandler Family Supporting Foundation, using proceeds from their sale of Golden West Bank to Wachovia.[10] Their business partner, Bernard Osher, also contributed a portion of his sale proceeds, $723 million, to the Bernard Osher Foundation.[11] These amounts are also included in the *Giving USA* estimate for individual giving in 2006 and are above the amount projected by the estimating model.

Inter vivos *(lifetime) giving on the rise*

A number of wealthy individuals announced contributions in 2006 that transfer their wealth to charities during their lifetime, often to foundations. This appears to be a trend that follows a few years of very high contributions made through bequests. In the early part of the decade, the estates of William Hewlett, Walter Annenberg, Joan Kroc, Susan Buffett, and others formed the bulk of the $1 billion or more gifts. In 2006, gift commitments

from at least three living individuals reached those heights.

In addition to Mr. Buffett, several others announced their intent to give their fortunes away during their lifetimes. They include T. Boone Pickens, who contributed to a foundation that will handle his giving;[12] Sandy Weill of Citigroup;[13] and (in early 2007) Henry (Hank) Paulson, U.S. Secretary of the Treasury and former head of Goldman Sachs.[14]

Gifts of $100 million or more increase in number

The *Chronicle of Philanthropy* noted an increase in the number of gifts from individuals of $100 million or more, compared with 2005 and 2004.[15] Chapter 21 of this edition lists gifts of $5 million and above and includes donations tracked in the *Chronicle* and by the Center on Philanthropy on its Million Dollar List.

Rapid increase in wealth among fund managers leads to giving

Hedge funds, a type of investment partnership, made news in 2006 with reportedly high returns and the use of high-risk investment strategies. This type of investment fund, which

WHAT THIS MEANS TO YOU

Much of the philanthropic "wealth transfer" giving tracked in the media is to institutions that donors have established themselves (foundations, new organizations) or those with which they have a long history.

Fundraisers at many charities need to avoid falling into the "Forbes 400" trap of thinking that they can appeal to the wealthiest. Fund-raising needs to be directed to people now close to the organization. Those are the people most likely to create connections with new prospective donors and enlarge the circle of constituents who support the nonprofit organization.

typically sets a high minimum investment amount,[16] is marketed privately (not through public offerings) to sophisticated investors[17] and is not subject to Securities and Exchange Commission oversight.

The hedge-fund industry publication *Absolute Return* found that the top 10 hedge funds in the United States, by size, had an estimated $250 billion under management in 2006.[18] In its survey, *Absolute Return* found 241 funds, each managing at least $1 billion, with a combined total of $1.2 trillion under management.

Many founders and investment managers of hedge funds have become very wealthy, and some have created private foundations or made major gifts to other institutions. Bruce Kovner, Paul Tudor Jones II, and George Soros are three such donors, and the *Chronicle of Philanthropy* profiled a number of others in early 2007, reporting that foundations created by people in this industry had $1.6 billion in assets in 2005.[19]

The *New York Times* profiled at least two hedge funds that are structured to generate fees that the fund creators then use for charitable purposes: London (England)–based Children's Investment Fund and Blue Orchid

Capital. The *Times* noted that creators of hedge funds have also been personally charitable, including Paul Tudor Jones II, founder of Tudor Investment Corporation and the Robin Hood Foundation; and Arthur Samburg, founder of Pequot Capital Management, who gave $25 million in 2006 to Columbia University.[20]

Record bonuses on Wall Street not likely to affect giving much

Research has shown in the past that one-time changes in income are not likely to affect charitable giving.[21] That didn't stop charitable organizations in New York City and other financial centers from hoping that at least some of an estimated $36 billion dollars in bonuses paid by investment firms in 2006 would be donated.[22] While certainly some charitable gifts resulted, the media covered other types of expenditures by employees of investment firms, who reportedly bought real estate, luxury goods, and cars.[23]

"Typical" households reported little increase in giving in 2006 in online polls

Harris Interactive, an online market research enterprise, conducted repeated polls in 2006 in the company's quarterly survey, called *DonorPulse*. Early in the

WHAT THIS MEANS TO YOU

Hedge funds in the mid-2000s are a rapidly growing industry, with fortunes to be made (or lost) at an equally fast pace.

Many people who earn substantial amounts through hedge funds are relatively new to wealth and to philanthropy. Although the highest profile gifts thus far have been made by senior managers with lengthy careers in investment, it appears that younger hedge fund managers are also gaining access to significant wealth at an early age.

year, the *DonorPulse* study found that of those who were considering making contributions in 2006, 68 percent said they expected to give about the same amount they did in 2005, whereas 17 percent said they expect to give more, and 16 percent said they expect to give less.[24] Key findings from several quarters' results were presented at the American Marketing Association Conference and summarized by the *NonProfit Times*.[25]

Giving methods/vehicles

Each year, *Giving USA* tracks some of the latest findings about different giving vehicles. For 2006, new research appeared about giving circles, direct mail, and online giving. Each study is summarized briefly as follows with additional information about its source as available.

Target Analysis Group finds challenges for donor retention in 2006 after "high" of 2005 giving for disasters
Donor counts dropped in all five subsectors studied in Target Analysis Group's direct mail-based "Quarterly Index of Fundraising Performance," as of the third quarter of 2006. Donors who gave first after the disasters of late 2004 and in 2005 did not uniformly renew, which was anticipated.[26] Two types of entities—relief and animal welfare organizations—saw first-year donor retention rates fall by more than 15 percent in 2006, after each gained many new donors in 2005.

Median revenues tracked by Target Analysis returned to levels that fit the historical growth pattern by the third

quarter of 2006, after reaching highs in the fourth quarter of 2005. This return to a trend line suggests that the disaster-giving effect lasted six to nine months. This is consistent with other studies of disaster giving.[27]

Growth projected for online giving
An analysis conducted by Network for Good covering about $100 million in charitable donations between 2001 and 2006 found that online giving is following the pattern set by online shopping and banking and is expected to continue to expand.[28] The study noted 30 percent of the giving tracked by Network for Good was in response to disasters.

In a separate study, Target Analysis Group worked with DonorDigital to recruit 12 organizations that shared information that the firms analyzed to create online donor benchmarks.[29] In the 12 participating organizations, a relatively small percentage of donors (less than 15 percent) gave online, yet the number of online givers had increased by more than 100 percent over three years, compared with 6 percent growth in the number of direct mail donors at the same organizations. Online donors were younger and had higher income than donors not giving online. They also gave more, even when they had the same income as other donors. The median gift amount online was $57, compared with a median of $33 for gifts from all other channels. Note that online donation is a frequent "first time" donor approach, and the online donors had a lower renewal rate in this study than donors through other means. However, when online donors renew, their gifts are higher, on average, which means the results for the organization are improved.

2006 pilot study looking at data from 2004 and 2005 shows donor attrition a major issue in a wide range of charities
A new measure of donor retention, the Fundraising Effectiveness Project, launched a pilot study in late 2006, collecting data from any organization that chose to participate. Among 275 responses, the overwhelming trend was increased donation amounts of about 60 percent more in 2005 than in 2004 from renewing or upgrading donors; offset by about 50 percent declines in the amounts contributed by donors who lowered their gift or who lapsed.[30]

Giving circles engage new donors; highly likely to provide general support for relatively new charities
Giving circles are defined as a cross between an investment club (everyone puts in a specified amount of money) and a book group (all participants have a chance to contribute to the discussion of how the money will be given). New Ventures Philanthropy (NVP), a project at the Forum of Regional Associations of Grantmakers, found active circles in at least 45 states.[31] The second NVP scan of giving circles includes a description of who participates in giving circles, how the circles work, and what attracts members. People of all ages and wealth levels, interests, and preferences participate in giving circles. However, some general trends found in the NVP study include the following:

- 59 percent of participants are between the ages of 40 and 65;
- 28 percent of members are between the ages of 25 and 40;
- 11 percent are over the age of 65; and
- The remaining members are under 25.

The average donation requested of members in a circle per year was $2,809, and the most common donation level was $1,000. Donors to a giving circle frequently give beyond their commitment to the pooled fund and include gifts of their time and expertise for the agencies selected.

Angela Eikenberry at Virginia Tech studied giving circles as part of a 2006 project funded by the Association of Fundraising Professionals. She found that giving circles tend to favor local charities, which are often new or have a strong, comparatively young, executive director.[32] Organizations reported that the circles usually gave only once. Donations tended to be for general operating support, although many supported projects. Organizations valued the "multidimensionality" of the support provided by giving circles: cash, volunteers, and other resources. Some organizations said that giving circle members donated individually beyond the collective gift. An important caveat offered in the report is that giving circles can be focused on different agendas than the issue of the charity they support. One interviewee said "…they don't understand the work we do and they…barely know what is going on."

Giving USA estimates for 2004 surpassed by itemized deductions

Tax data from 2004, released in fall 2006, show an exceptionally high level of individual giving claimed on tax returns, at $165.56 billion (compared with the estimate from *Giving USA* released in summer 2005 of $149.28 billion for itemized gifts). The IRS data show an increase that exceeds projections for several reasons:

- Nearly 2 million more tax returns included itemized gifts in 2004 than in 2003.

- A higher percentage of returns itemized deductions (30.7 percent, up from 29.6 percent in 2003).

- The amount claimed in "carry-over" donations increased by 29.6 percent compared with 2003, the highest increase in carry-over since 2000.

- In the highest-income group (those with $10 million or more), income in 2004 rose by 61 percent, deductions claimed for charitable giving increased by 57 percent; and the carry-over amount rose by 255 percent. This group of fewer than 3,500 tax returns makes up 10 percent of total giving and accounts for nearly one-third (31 percent) of the growth in giving in 2004 compared with 2003.

It is also possible that 2004 saw a one-time "bump" with car donations made to qualify for a deduction after legislation passed that made some vehicle donations nondeductible after January 1, 2005. Numerous nonprofits promoted this at the end of 2004.

Table 1 shows, by income group, how income and giving compare as a percentage of the national total. Households with income of $200,000 and above are just over 2.3 percent of the tax returns filed, yet account for 30.5 percent of all estimated giving (when an estimate is included for households that do not itemize deductions, as *Giving USA* does in its estimate of individual giving).

Table 1
Charitable gifts by income range, 2004
Based on deductions claimed and a nonitemizer estimate

Income range	% of tax returns	% of income from this group	% of itemized gifts from this group, per IRS data	% of all individual giving in *Giving USA* estimate, including nonitemizer estimated amount
< $75,000	82.7%	42.6%	30.2%	25.1%
$75,000 under $100,000	7.7%	12.9%	12.5%	10.4%
$100,000 under $200,000	7.4%	19.0%	20.7%	17.2%
$200,000 and up	2.3%	25.5%	36.7%	30.5%
Nonitemizer returns Income range unknown				16.9%
	100.0%	100.0%	100.0%	100.0%

*Total percentages may not equal 100% due to rounding.

IRS reports on non-cash charitable contributions, 2003

According to the Internal Revenue Service's (IRS) report on individual non-cash donations, $6.7 billion was donated in non-cash charitable contributions during 2003.[34] Non-cash donations include securities, real estate, art works, and other appreciated assets, as well as clothing, household goods, and items that are likely to have depreciated in value with use.

Generally speaking, donation types varied with age. People 45 to 55 years of age tended to give more food, clothing, household items, and vehicles while older donors (age 65+) tended to give stock and other securities, real estate, and art and collectibles.

Studies of household or individual charitable giving

Many organizations and scholars study charitable giving. This section summarizes key findings from some of the major studies appearing in 2006. Each study is summarized briefly as follows with additional information about its source as available.

Bank of America High Net-Worth Household study

The Center on Philanthropy conducted a survey of high net-worth households in 2006 for Bank of America.[35] The key points of the 2006 report are:

Among these households, giving is nearly universal (98 percent gave). Donations averaged $117,488 from high net-worth household donors, compared with an estimated $1,917 among all U.S. donor households. The median gift amount for donors in the Bank of America study was $15,500; for typical households, the median was $700.

The report covers giving preferences, motivations, and barriers—or conditions under which donors thought they would give more. *Giving USA* has focused only on the barriers. Households selected from a list of possibilities in response to the question, "I would give more if...." The responses fell into four types:

- Improved perceptions of nonprofit operations, especially efficiency, with the most frequent choice being "less were spent on administration;"

- Greater personal financial capacity;

- More information available about nonprofit and giving options; and

- Personal preferences about time allocation and information-sharing.

Center on Philanthropy Panel Study, data collected in 2005 about 2004

The University of Michigan's Panel Study of Income Dynamics released data from the third Center on Philanthropy Panel Study in March

2007.[36] The nationally representative study covered household income and finances in 2004 with a survey reaching more than 8,000 households. Overall, 68 percent of households reported making a charitable contribution in 2004. The average total amount contributed was $2,064. The median gift amount from donor households in 2004 was $775.[37]

Nationwide study confirms social and economic factors affecting giving

Using IRS tax return data on charitable giving, and without adjusting to reflect estimates of giving by nonitemizing households, Ross Gittell and Edinaldo Tebaldi of the University of New Hampshire confirmed previous findings about income, wealth, religious affiliation, age, volunteering, and educational attainment and their positive associations with household giving. The study also found that states with higher percentages of African American residents tended to have higher average giving, and that no other major racial group had any statistically significant association with level of giving.[38]

This work is replicated in a slightly different approach in *Giving USA Update #3* from 2004. The *Giving USA* work includes maps that show states in which giving is higher or lower than might be expected, given the demographic composition of the state's population.

Who Really Cares?

Arthur Brooks, a public administration professor at Syracuse University's Maxwell School, released *Who Really Cares: America's Charity Divide* in 2006.[39] In this book, he argues that people who attend worship services regularly (once per week) give more to religion and give more to secular causes than do people who attend less often. He analyzed a number of different data sets that included questions about charitable giving. Another

WHAT THIS MEANS TO YOU

Be consistent in your messages to demonstrate the impact of your organization's work. People need to see your case for support repeatedly and in different forms before it "sinks in." Report the percentage of funds received that is spent on program work often and clearly.

Explain fairly the ways in which administration supports program work through hiring and supervising staff, accounting for funds, processing gifts and sending receipts, and so on. Explain that administrative activities are important functions for transparency and accountability.

If your organization spends "too much" on administration, examine where the costs are, develop a plan to reduce administrative expenses, and report your work publicly to show progress. This is one of the most important things you can do to reassure donors that you are a responsible steward of their money.

conclusion Brooks reaches is that people who believe the government should do more to create income equality give and volunteer for charitable organizations less than do people who believe government does not have a role in income redistribution. And, not surprisingly, charitable giving is learned within families, especially within families with two adults.

Fidelity Charitable Gift Fund^{sm}: Boomers plan higher gifts this year; Gen X looking toward higher lifetime giving than parents

In an online poll conducted among 1,015 households that met criteria about their giving ($1,000 for those over 30; $250 for those under 30), Fidelity Charitable Gift Fund found that Baby Boomers participating in the study planned to give more in 2006 than others of that generation had planned to give in 2005.[40] The poll also found that Generation X participants (age 25 to 39 in 2006) were very likely

(73 percent) to say that they planned to "give more of their paycheck to charity over their lifetimes than their parents did."[41]

Generational differences (or similarities) in giving

People born between 1964 and 1981 or so, Generation X, began entering their peak earning years (usually ages 40 to 65) in the mid-2000s. Data from the Center on Philanthropy Panel Study show that through 2003, this generation was giving a lower share of its income to charity than the preceding generations did at the same age. This was most notable for religious giving and it was also true for donations to secular causes.[42] There are few studies with enough data about the charitable giving of people in Generation Y (also called the Millennial Generation—those born since 1981) to compare with prior generations. However, other indicators suggest that for this generation, social causes and volunteering are important.[43]

WHAT THIS
MEANS TO YOU

Repeated studies have found that income, net worth, and education level are all linked to higher levels of giving.

Engaging people at all levels of income and education is still appropriate because people with lower income still give and often give proportionately more (in comparison with their incomes).

Several reports have suggested that at all ages, social interaction matters for giving: volunteers give more; people who attend worship services often give more; for some types of gifts, having school-aged children is associated with more giving.[44]

1   P. Deb et al., Estimating charitable giving for Giving USA, *Nonprofit and Voluntary Sector Quarterly*, December 2003.

2   Prior research has shown that giving is closely tied to household income and to assets, as measured by the stock market. The stock market growth in 2006 was the fastest rate of growth in the Standard & Poor's 500 Index since 2003, when the market rose 26.4 percent (24 percent adjusted for inflation) after its slide from early 2000 through 2002. By December 2006, the Standard & Poor's 500 Index, at 1418.3, was still below its year-end high of 1469.25 from 1999.

3   This rate of growth in personal income is the highest rate seen since 2000, when adjusted for inflation, personal income rose by 5.4 percent. Income rose by 3.4 percent (adjusted for inflation) in 2004.

4   In 2004, itemized deductions on tax returns increased by 13.6 percent, largely driven by a 42 percent increase in the amount of "carry-over." Households that had made gifts in earlier years could not claim them because of caps on deductions limited to 50 percent (or for stock gifts to foundations, 30 percent) of income. With a growth in income, households could claim deductions for cash gifts made in the previous five years (three years for gifts of securities) that were not allowed earlier. A jump in giving is one factor that is used in estimating this year's donations.

5   Center on Philanthropy Panel Study, 2003 and 2005 waves, www.philanthropy.iupui.edu.

6   America's most generous donors, *Chronicle of Philanthropy*, February 22, 2007, www.philanthropy.com.

7   Di Mento, M. and Lewis, N., Record-breaking giving, *Chronicle of Philanthropy*, February 22, 2007, www.philanthropy.com.

8   How Warren Buffett's gift will work, *Chronicle of Philanthropy*, July 20, 2006, www.philanthropy.com.

9   America's most generous donors, *Chronicle of Philanthropy*, February 22, 2007, www.philanthropy.com.

10 Ibid.

11 Ibid.

12 Ibid.

13 In June 2006, the newsletter *Financial News* reported that Citigroup's Sandy Weill intends to give away his $1.4 billion fortune before he dies in what he called a "deal with God."

14 H. Moore, Paulson plans to give away fortune, *Financial News Online*, January 15, 2007, www.financialnews-us.com.

15 America's most generous donors, *Chronicle of Philanthropy*, February 22, 2007, www.philanthropy.com.

16 Investorwords.com. http://www.investorwords.com/2296/hedge_fund.html.

17 Hedge Funds: Implications for Growth, Securities and Exchange Commission, 2003, www.sec.gov/news/studies/hedgefunds0903.pdf.

18 A. Barr, J.P.Morgan is largest U.S. hedge-fund firm, MarketWatch, March 5, 2007, reporting a study conducted by *Absolute Return*.

19 N. Lewis, Betting on hedge funds: Charities seek to tap into fast growing source of wealth, *Chronicle of Philanthropy*, January 25, 2007, www.philanthropy.com.

20 J. Anderson, A hedge fund with high returns and high-reaching goals, *New York Times*, November 13, 2006, viewed at lexis-nexis.com.

21 W. Randolph, Dynamic income, progressive taxes and the timing of charitable contributions, *Journal of Political Economy*, August 1995.

22 K. Crow, Giving back, *Wall Street Journal*, December 29, 2006.

23 J. Anderson, Wall St. bonuses: So much money, too few Ferraris, *New York Times*, December 20, 2006.

24 The Harris Poll # 33, April 27, 2006, http://www.harrisinteractive.com/harris_poll/index.asp?PID=657.

25 The *NonProfit Times* in its Instant Fundraising Feature, November 9, 2006.

26 M. Nobles, What a disaster: Donor counts declined, *NonProfit Times*, February 5, 2007, about the Target Analysis index.

27 See *Giving USA 2003* for a summary of some other studies of giving in the wake of disasters.

28 The Young and the Generous: A Study of $100 Million in Online Giving to 20,000 Charities, www.networkforgood.org.

29 Target Analysis, 2006 donorCentrics™ Internet Giving Benchmarking Analysis, www.targetanlysis.com.

30 Fundraising Effectiveness Project, summary report presented at the conference of the Association of Fundraising Professionals, Dallas, Texas, March 26, 2007. See www.urban.org or www.afpnet.org for a copy.

31 New Ventures in Philanthropy, *More Giving Together: A Second National Scan of Giving Circles and Shared Giving in the United States*, Forum of Regional Associations of Grantmakers, June 2007.

32 A. Eikenberry, 2006, with funding from the Association of Fundraising Professionals. See report at http://afpnet.org/ka/ka-3.cfm?content_item_id=23967&folder_id=2326.

33 Center on Philanthropy Panel Study, 2003 data set, analyzed at the Center on Philanthropy at Indiana University, www.philanthropy.iupui.edu.

34 J. Wilson and M. Strudler, *Individual Noncash Charitable Contributions*, 2003, Internal Revenue Service, www.irs.gov/pub/irs-soi/03inccart.pdf.

35 The Bank of America Study of High Net-Worth Philanthropy is the first scientific study (using a random sample) of high net-worth households and their philanthropy. Prior studies had been based on samples from client lists. This study defined high net-worth households as those with income of $200,000 or more or net worth of $1 million or more. More than 1,400 surveys were returned. The first report, released in October, 2006, included about 1,000 respondents. Later reports appeared in 2007.

36 See summary information at the Center on Philanthropy at Indiana University, www.philanthropy.iupui.edu.

37 These differ from the estimated amounts used in the Bank of America (BOA) study. The BOA findings appeared in October 2006, before the 2004 data from COPPS. The BOA report used COPPS data for giving in 2002 and adjusted the 2002 values for inflation to estimate giving in 2005.

38 R. Gittel and E. Tebaldi, Charitable Giving: Factors Influencing Giving in U.S. States, *Nonprofit and Voluntary Sector Quarterly*, 2006, Vol. 35: 721-736.

39 A. Brooks, *Who Really Cares: America's Charity Divide: Who Gives, Who Doesn't, and Why It Matters*, (New York: Basic Books), 2006.

40 Press release, Boomers on track to give 20% more to charity than average donor, Fidelity Charitable Gift Fund[sm] reveals, December 7, 2006, www.fideltiy.com.

41 Ibid.[fidelity press release]

42 M. Brown and M. Wilhelm, Generation X: Less generous than expected, paper presented at ARNOVA, November 16, 2006, Chicago, IL, and available at www.arnova.org in the area for conference papers.

43 P. Gogoi, Welcome to the Gen Y Workplace, *Business Week*, May 4, 2005.

44 T. Yoshioka, Patterns of Giving in COPPS, 2003, Center on Philanthropy mimeo, 2006, www.philanthropy.iupui.edu.

8 Giving by bequest

- Charitable bequests are estimated to be $22.91 billion, which is a 2.1 percent decline (-5.1 percent adjusted for inflation) when compared with the revised estimate for 2005. Bequest giving is 7.8 percent of total estimated giving for 2006.

- The revised 2005 estimate for charitable bequests is $23.4 billion. Large estates that filed federal estate tax returns in 2005 included exceptional gifts to charity. Internal Revenue Service data show a 22 percent growth in value for the largest estates (more than $20 million) and a 68 percent increase in charitable bequests from these estates. Nearly the same number of large estates claimed a deduction in 2005 as in 2004 (328 compared with 330). In other estate sizes ($1.5 million to $19.99 million), combined gross estate value in 2005 fell 15.7 percent compared with 2004, and charitable bequests fell 5.3 percent.

- Huge estates skew the amount claimed in charitable bequest deductions. Since 2000, between 200 and 330 donor estates with gross estate value of $20 million or more have accounted for 44 to 64 percent per year of the total itemized charitable bequests.

- This year's estimate includes gifts of more than $4 billion that are anticipated to be made by estates that filed estate tax returns two years after the death of the donor—gifts announced in 2004.

- The federal estate tax filing exemption for 2006 jumped to $2 million (up from $1.5 million in 2004 and 2005).

- Since 1966, bequest gifts have grown an average of 4.5 percent annually, adjusted for inflation. Since 1996, the average annual rate of growth has been 5.5 percent, adjusted for inflation.

Giving USA 2006 survey

Giving USA sent a survey to 4,765 nonprofit organizations, and 764 returned the survey. Of those, 300 (49 percent) included data about charitable bequests received. Using this information, *Giving USA* generated averages and medians for bequest receipts by different types and sizes of charitable organizations. *Giving USA* includes only realized bequests in its estimates, not planned commitments.[1]

The survey results are not used to develop the estimates of charitable bequests.[2]

Table 1 summarizes findings from the 2006 survey of nonprofits, which asked about realized bequests.[3] On average, the largest amount per bequest was for large public-society benefit organizations. The largest average number of bequests was received at health-related charities.

Table 1
Average number and amount per bequest for organizations that
reported bequest receipts, by size and subsector, 2006

	Large		Moderate		Medium		Small	
	Average number of bequests	Average amount per bequest ($)	Average number of bequests	Average amount per bequest ($)	Average number of bequests	Average amount per bequest ($)	Average number of bequests	Average amount per bequest ($)
Arts	9	267,102	7	35,229	4	27,968	4	500,051
Education	65	142,278	4	200,800	2	170,215	**	
Environment	66	48,073	16	98,231	4	102,992	2	90,613
Health	209	55,673	98	122,364	8	58,623	14	12,277
Human Services	26*	40,118	21	90,704	13	48,048	3	11,820
International	43	47,867	10	100,364	21	38,236	**	
Public-society benefit	13	125,822	15	168,615	2	171,035	**	

*Two large human services organizations reported receiving more than 2,500 bequests each. They are not included in the average number of bequests here. If they were, the average would be 434. These organizations are included in the average amount per bequest because their averages per bequest were not exceptionally high.
**Too few organizations responded with bequest data for analysis.

WHAT THIS MEANS TO YOU

Table 1 presents benchmarks from organizations based on their size and subsector. Use the table as a point of comparison.

Ask: Is your organization receiving close to the average number of bequests for your size and subsector? Do you have a planned giving program? Are you working with donors to create planned gifts? If this is not something your organization can do on its own, is there a community foundation or other entity in your region that can help?

The benchmarks can assist your staff and volunteers in determining realistic goals for your organization's bequest receipts.

Four estate gifts make "Top 60" for 2006

Four estates were announced in 2006 with charitable gifts of $100 million or more, and six were on the "Top 60" list for amounts less than $100 million.[4] The *Chronicle of Philanthropy* showed these top estate gifts in 2006:

- Jim Joseph Estate, $500 million to the Joseph Foundation to benefit Jewish causes.[5]

- Hector and Doris Di Stefano, $264 million, split among eight charities.[6]

- Mary Joan Palevsky, $212.8 million to California Community Foundation.[7]

- Arthur Zankel, $141 million to at least nine charities representing Mr. Zankel's lifetime interests and the work of his wife, illustrator Judith Zankel.[8]

It is expected that these and other large estate gifts announced in 2006 are likely to appear on estate tax returns filed in 2008 or even later. The IRS reports that while most estate tax returns are filed the year after the decedent's death,[9] complex estates or those with assets that take time to distribute usually take longer.

At least since 2002, there has been a steady flow of large charitable bequests (more than $25 million apiece). Table 2 summarizes the number and amount of bequest gifts reported on the *Chronicle of Philanthropy*'s Top 60 donor list.

Table 2
Distribution of charitable bequests, 2002–2006
Total $ in billions

	Number of charitable bequests in size range*					Total $ Amount
	$25–$100 M	$100–$500 M	$500–$1 B	$1 B +	Total gifts	
2002	2	2	0	1	5	$1.79
2003	6	2	0	1	9	$2.58
2004	3	2	0	1	6	$3.40
2005	8	1	0	0	9	$0.76
2006	6	3	1	0	10	$1.32

*Estates with multiple charitable beneficiaries are counted as one bequest with the combined reported value. Data: The *Chronicle of Philanthropy*, Top 60 donors, bequest amounts of $25 million or more.

The *Chronicle* captures major gifts announced during a year. The IRS reports amounts deducted in charitable bequest gifts from estate tax returns for the year the return is filed. Figure 1 shows the amounts claimed based on gross estate value for estates valued from $1 million ($1.5 million for 2004 and 2005) to $19.99 million and for estates valued at $20 million or more, from 2002 through 2005.

The lower values in 2003 and 2004 reflect a much lower percentage of gross estate value left to charity by estates with value of $20 million or more in those two years. In the highest-valued estates, average estate value in 2003 was 1 percent less than the prior year, and in 2004 it was 2 percent less.[10] When estate values decline, even a small percentage, the amount remaining for charity also declines.

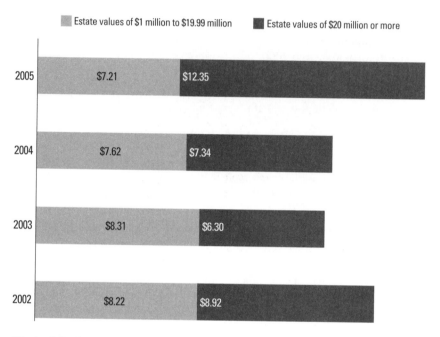

Figure 1
Sum of charitable bequest amounts claimed,
estates above and below $20 million in gross estate value*
($ in billions)

*Number in bar is amount reported on estate tax returns for charitable bequests claimed by estates filing in the year.

Data: Internal Revenue Service, Estate tax returns by year filed, 2002 through 2005.

WHAT THIS
MEANS TO YOU

Don't let the fluctuations in the really large estates—those of $20 million or more—distract you. The vast majority of estates are valued below $1 million and do not even appear in the estate tax data.

The "bread and butter" for most charities is in estates valued below $20 million and more likely in estates below $1 million. For the past four years, charitable bequests from estates of $1 million to $19.99 million have been trending slightly downward. The "mega-gifts" in the $20 million and up category are atypical and might not be as helpful as benchmarking information.

Lawsuits demonstrate need for careful gift planning and precise wording in wills

Warren Buffett, when announcing the transfer of his assets to five foundations, reportedly said about planning an estate, "It's a much tougher problem, frankly, than amassing the money."[11] A number of lawsuits in the news in 2006 illustrate that the difficulties can persist for heirs and beneficiaries. Some key questions for those who write bequests emerge when reviewing these reports. By coincidence, three of them are from Texas.

1) Who is responsible for taxes due? A Texas museum and university received $24 million from an estate, which also left a ranch to a family member. The family member reportedly did not have cash to pay generation-skipping taxes and argued that the money should come from charitable beneficiaries because the will read "any taxes due shall be paid by the estate."[12]

2) How much discretion is appropriate to give a trustee? In a lawsuit about the $100 million in the Sybil B Harrington Living Trust,[13] the Texas Assistant Attorney General argued that too much money has been directed by trustees to one of the 30 counties Mrs. Harrington named (which happens to be in Arizona) and not enough to Texas charities. A court previously had instructed trustees to mirror the giving habits Mrs. Harrington followed during her life. The case rested in part on definitions of whether to mirror geographic giving

patterns or be true to the types of causes that Mrs. Harrington supported. The judge who heard the case determined, "Any attempt to devise a formula, geographic or otherwise... would not be in keeping with Mrs. Harrington's expressed desires."[14]

3) What steps can be taken to prevent conflicts of interest? A bank and a Houston law firm were fined a combined total of $65.5 million when a jury found that the attorneys, who represented a family foundation—one beneficiary of a $130 million estate—and a bank that was executor of the estate, undertook to also represent the decedent's widow in her own estate planning. The lawyers advised the widow to put her share of the estate into the family foundation, of which a bank officer was the chairman.[15] The jury agreed with the widow, whose case included arguments that she had not been adequately informed of her estate planning options and that there were conflicts of interest among the attorneys, the bank, and the individual who worked at the bank and chaired the family foundation.

4) What can be done to make sure that the charitable organization can use the gift without going to court? Bequests to institutions that are not involved when the gift is planned may require the beneficiary to file court documents in order to be used. One university fundraising officer said, "The risk...is the money may unintentionally be targeted to a

program that doesn't exist…we have to go to the courts and ask permission to redirect the money."[16]

5) What can or should be done to notify family members of a charitable bequest? Numerous estates are contested by family members who believe that a charitable organization should not receive some portion of the estate. Various reasons are provided in different cases. One of the common grounds is that the person making the will is not capable of making decisions, as was advanced in a Wilmington, North Carolina case, in which nieces and nephews of the decedent received little in comparison to a church named as the principal beneficiary and caregivers who were residual beneficiaries.[17] The case was resolved after three weeks of trial, and the will was upheld.[18]

Philanthropy organizations receive half of the charitable dollars on estate tax returns, 2005

David Joulfaian, a researcher at the U.S. Department of the Treasury, analyzed the types of recipients of charitable bequests reported on estate tax returns for 2005.[20] Philanthropy and voluntarism, which include private foundations, community foundations, Jewish federations, and United Ways, received 50.5 percent of the total dollar amount claimed. No further breakout among those types of recipients is available. Figure 2 shows the distribution of dollars claimed as deductions for charitable bequests on estate tax returns.

This is the first time since 2002 that foundations and other philanthropy and voluntarism organizations have received more than 50 percent of the total amount claimed on estate tax returns.

The large share for human services, at $2.68 billion, likely reflects a single large deduction claimed for the gift of $1.3 billion from Joan Kroc's estate to the Salvation Army. *Giving USA* does not have exact information about which estates filed tax returns in which years, but this subsector has received approximately $1 billion a year from bequests over several years. To jump suddenly in one year to $2.68 billion, in the same year that the Salvation Army reported receiving $1.3 billion,[21] strongly suggests that Mrs. Kroc's estate may be included in the data for 2005. She died in 2003.

A paper by Kathryn Miree presented at the 2005 National Conference on Gift Planning highlighted specific issues for wording planned gifts, with a special focus on donor intent.[19]

WHAT THIS MEANS TO YOU

Gift planners have a responsibility to work with donors to think through a number of possible scenarios and how the language for the gift can be worded clearly to safeguard the donor's intent and fulfill the beneficiary organization's needs.

Figure 2
Amount by type of recipient, charitable bequests on estate tax returns, 2005
($ in millions)

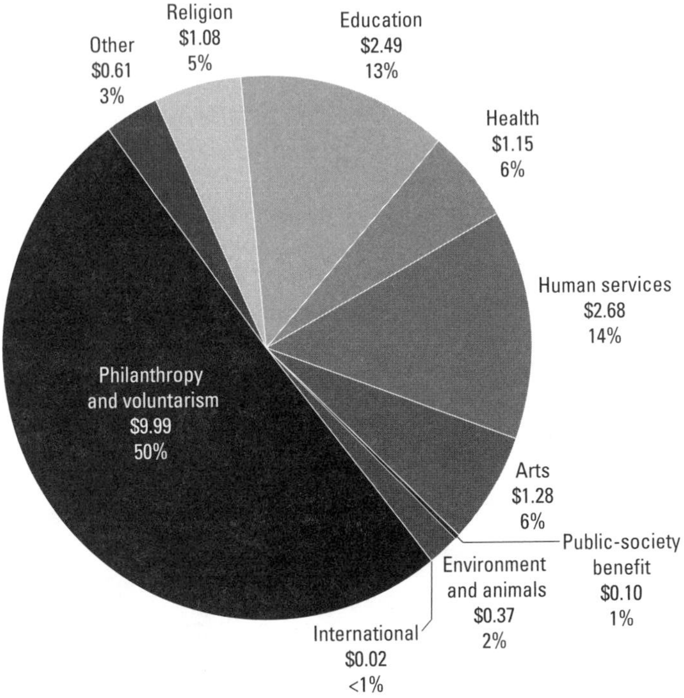

Other
$0.61
3%

Religion
$1.08
5%

Education
$2.49
13%

Health
$1.15
6%

Human services
$2.68
14%

Philanthropy
and voluntarism
$9.99
50%

Arts
$1.28
6%

Public-society
benefit
$0.10
1%

Environment
and animals
$0.37
2%

International
$0.02
<1%

Bequest donors emphasize the impact a bequest gift can have

Adrian Sargeant, Toni Hilton, and Walter Wymer researched bequest giving motivations by conducting focus groups with donors to a number of different charities in the United States. The study recruited participants from among the members of bequest clubs (those who indicated to the organization they made a will naming that charity as a beneficiary).[22] The researchers explored the perceptions and beliefs of the donors who chose to participate. Overall, three broad-based categories emerged: organizational characteristics; individual attributes

and belief; and legacy-specific motivations. Among the organizational traits these donors identified are:

- Performance. Donors wanted to be sure their legacies would be well-used to address the issue or problem.

- Professionalism. These legacy donors gave to more organizations annually than they intended to support through a charitable bequest. The organizations likely to receive bequests were those that could demonstrate in every detail a high level of professional capacity, down to getting people's names right.

■ Communications. High-quality communications are timely and convey relevant information about organizational work and finances. The organization does not burden the donor, either in the quantity of communications or in their content.

Participants in these discussions also "expressed considerable negativity toward the approaches to legacy fundraising adopted by many organizations."[23] They did not want to be counseled to make a will—they already had wills. They wanted materials that make a stronger case for the importance

of the organization's work and the potential impact a bequest can have. One participant said, "…leave the legal jargon to the lawyers."[24]

Reports appearing annually summarized

Key findings of the most recent data available from annual studies are summarized in Table 3. These findings include data about planned gift instruments other than charitable bequests. *Giving USA* provides the Web site addresses to help readers more easily access the complete reports.

Table 3
Key findings from studies of bequest and deferred giving

Internal Revenue Service Estate tax returns filed, data available at www.irs.gov			
	2003	2004	2005
Federal estate tax filing threshold. Based on death date, not return date	$1 million	$1.5 million	$1.5 million
Total number of estate tax returns filed*	66,044	62,718	39,481
Number with charitable deduction (from analysis by U.S. Department of the Treasury)	13,400	11,861	8,074
Charitable deductions itemized on returns (from analysis by U.S. Department of the Treasury), in billions	$14.77	$14.97	$19.56

*Estate tax returns are based on the value of the estate at the time of death. The number of returns filed in 2004 includes those for people who died earlier when the filing threshold was $1 million or less.

Charitable remainder unitrust Tax returns filed Data available at www.irs.gov			
	2003	2004	2005
Number	91,371	93,329	94,779
Assets (per Form 5227, book value, in billions)	$81.56	$77.37	$79.84
Assets (year-end, estimated fair market value, in billions)	$84.70	$89.57	$95.05

Charitable remainder annuity trust Tax returns filed Data available at www.irs.gov			
	2003	2004	2005
Number	22,783	22,626	21,667
Assets (book value, in billions)	$9.60	$9.46	$9.54

Charitable lead trusts Tax returns filed Data available at www.irs.gov			
	2003	2004	2005
Number	5,481	5,658	6,168
Assets (book value, in billions)	$12.78	$12.32	$15.50

1   Planned gift commitments are **not** included in estimates of giving by bequest. The value of a planned gift commitment that is claimed as a deduction by a living donor appears in the estimate of giving by individuals. All, or a portion of the value of charitable remainder trusts and certain other planned gifts that terminate in a given year, are included as part of the charitable bequest figures reported by the IRS and therefore indirectly affect the amount of bequests reported each year.

2   For the estimates of giving by bequest, *Giving USA* relies on federal reports of charitable bequests claimed on estate tax returns and on estimates for estates that fall below the federal filing threshold. The estimates for giving by estates below the

federal estate tax filing threshold rely on:
- Data obtained from the U.S Treasury's analysis of estate tax returns showing the percentage of net estate value donated by donor estates, which increases with the age at death;
- IRS income tax return data for the percentage of estates that make charitable contributions (4.6 percent in 2005, the most recent year for which this analysis is available); and
- Estimates of household net worth by age, developed by the Federal Reserve Board.

3   Estate tax returns, on which the IRS data are based, are filed for the year in which an estate is closed. That is, for 2005 returns, the returns might be for individuals who

died much earlier (as is likely the case for people of great wealth) or for people who died in 2005 (which is more likely for relatively small estates). Estate tax returns, however, do not tell us when the bequest was actually distributed to the recipient, only when it was reported to the Internal Revenue Service. *Giving USA*'s survey of nonprofit organizations tracks when organizations receive the gifts. Some distributions are made far in advance of the date of filing the estate tax return. Because of these differences in timing between payment of the gift and reporting of the gift, there will sometimes be a discrepancy between *Giving USA*'s estimate of gifts by charitable bequest in a given year and the amount reported later in estate tax returns.

4   *Chronicle of Philanthropy*, February 22, 2007.

5   Ibid.

6   Ibid.

7   Ibid.

8   Ibid.

9   IRS, Tax Stats Issue 2007–08, Revised filing year estate tax tables, received March 28, 2007.

10 *Giving USA* analysis.

11 J. Peters, He is not only smart, but careful, too, *New York Times*, July 2, 2006. Viewed at lexis-nexis.com.

12 J. Tedesco, Charities call gift grandson's tax burden, *San Antonio Express-News*, May 9, 2006.

13 K. Welch, Court battle over Amarillo, Texas, philanthropist's charitable intent begins, *Amarillo Daily News*, November 2, 2006. Viewed at lexis-nexis.com.

14 K. Smith Welch, Ruling in Texas favors Harrington trustees, *Amarillo Daily News*, November 3, 2006.

15 R. Gertner, Law firm, bank must pay $65.5M to widow in estate planning case, *Lawyers Weekly USA*, January 16, 2006. Viewed at lexis-nexis.com.

16 Mary Anna Dunn, California State University, Fresno, quoted in D. Boyles, Surprise bequests to colleges not uncommon, *Fresno Bee*, March 27, 2006. Viewed at Lexis-nexis.com.

17 K. Little, Family and church in dispute over $5 million, *Star-News*, April 12, 2006. Viewed at Lexis-nexis.com.

18 K. Little, Agreement ends trial contesting Smith will, StarNewsOnline, April 25, 2006, http://wilmingtonstar.com.

19 Contact the National Center on Planned Giving, www.ncpg.org for information about how to obtain a copy.

20 D. Joulfaian, Brief facts on charitable giving, mimeo, May 2007. Posted to the Social Science Research Network, www.ssrn.org.

21 Salvation Army, 2006 annual report available at www.salvationarmyusa.org.

22 A. Sargeant, T. Hilton, and W. Wymer, Bequest motives and barriers to giving: The case of direct mail donors, *Nonprofit Management and Leadership*, Fall 2006.

23 Ibid, page 61.

24 Ibid, page 61.

9 Giving by corporations

- Corporate contributions were an estimated $12.72 billion in 2006, a decrease of 7.6 percent (-10.5 percent adjusted for inflation) compared with the revised estimate of $13.77 billion for 2005, which includes $1.38 billion in estimated giving for disaster relief.

- An estimated 4.3 percent of charitable contributions came from corporate giving.

- Corporate giving is associated with changes in corporate profits. The Bureau of Economic Analysis' report of corporate profits before tax showed a growth of 19.2 percent in 2006 (16.0 percent adjusted for inflation). This is a strong rate of growth historically, but follows two years during which profit growth exceeded 20 percent (after inflation adjustment).

- Corporate foundation grantmaking is an estimated $4.2 billion, using data collected by the Foundation Center. Corporate foundation grantmaking rose an estimated 6.0 percent in 2006. The grantmaking amount does not include distributions from operating foundations created by corporations that provide pharmaceuticals and medical products. Those foundations are treated by the Foundation Center as operating foundations instead of corporate foundations.

- The Committee Encouraging Corporate Philanthropy (CECP) collected data 89 of the country's largest firms. Those companies reported a median change of 6.1 percent increase in charitable contributions for 2006. CECP collects data about the fair-market value of product donations. *Giving USA* estimates the allowed tax deduction for product contributions, which is less than the fair market value.

- The 40-year average annual increase in charitable giving by corporations is 2.7 percent, adjusted for inflation. Since 1996, the average annual rate of change is 3.2 percent, adjusted for inflation.

Corporate profits remain strong in 2006, but slower growth than in 2004 and 2005

In 2006, corporate profits rose by 19.2 percent (16 percent after adjusting for inflation), according to the U.S. Bureau of Economic Analysis. This marks the fifth consecutive year during which an inflation-adjusted increase in corporate profits above 8 percent has occurred.[1]

Unprecedented disasters in late 2004 and 2005 and a growing economy prompted the nation's largest corporations to increase their giving in 2005, according to a *Chronicle of Philanthropy* poll.[2] *Giving USA* estimated a 21 percent increase in giving for that year, the fastest rate of growth for corporate giving on record.[3] However, firms responding to the *Chronicle's* poll overwhelmingly said that 2006 giving would fall or remain close to the 2005 levels. Of 72 companies in the poll, 34 (47.2 percent) said their giving would remain steady, and 11 (15.2 percent) said it would decline. Just 27 companies (37.4 percent) said their philanthropy would grow by more than 3 percent in 2006.

While companies reported plans to maintain the level of giving, fundraisers felt successful about raising funds from corporations during 2006. The Philanthropic Giving Index, which is released twice a year by the Center on Philanthropy at Indiana University, showed that as of December 2006, nearly 60 percent of fundraisers on the panel reported success with corporate giving. This is a large gain compared with 40 percent having success with corporate giving in December 2003.[4]

Major donations in 2006 from companies

As companies focused their philanthropy, 2006 saw an increased number of significant gifts from corporations and corporate foundations.[5] According to the Million Dollar List, compiled by the Center on Philanthropy at Indiana University, at least 229 gifts of $1 million or more were announced by corporations in 2006, which is less than half of the gifts recorded in 2005 (464 announced corporate gifts).[6] Among the largest gifts of 2006 are in-kind and cash contributions from technology firms:

- UGS Corporation made an in-kind software grant with a commercial value of $289 million to enhance

engineering programs of the University of Cincinnati,[7] the largest grant in the university's history. This grant was also the largest corporate gift in 2006.[8] Another notable UGS in-kind gift valued at $60 million was made to Hampton University.[9]

- AT&T pledged $100 million to One Economy Corporation for AT&T AccessAll, a three-year program to provide equipment, training, and Internet access for people in economically distressed areas. AT&T Pioneers, company employees, and retirees volunteer to provide the technology instruction.[10]

- Microsoft Corporation donated $40 million in software to organizations that are part of NetHope and $1 million in cash to the Interagency Working Group on Emergency Capacity Building Project to help international aid and development organizations improve their ability to communicate and collaborate during disasters.[11]

- Enterprise Rent-A-Car gave $50 million to the National Arbor Day Foundation to help plant trees in national forests in areas damaged by fire, storm, or disease.[12]

- CVS/pharmacy Charitable Trust launched a five-year, $25 million initiative—CVS All Kids Can—to help make life easier for children with disabilities.[13]

- General Electric pledged $20 million to the public schools in Cincinnati to create a world-class science and math curriculum.[14]

- Carnival Corporation, operator of cruise ships, donated $20 million to the Miami Performing Arts Center Foundation.[15]

Largest companies divided; some increase giving, others report drop

According to the Committee Encouraging Corporate Philanthropy (CECP), companies were split in their 2006 total giving, with 56 percent giving more than in 2005 and 44 percent giving less. These preliminary findings are based on 89 matched-set companies from 2005 and 2006, part of CECP's annual survey across 113 companies, including 44 of the Fortune 100.[16]

While the median total giving rose 6.1 percent in 2006 compared with 2005, this masks wide variability across companies: 25 firms of 89 in the matched set saw total giving increase by more than 15 percent while 16 saw giving decrease by more than 15 percent. Among those that gave less, many cited a return to more typical levels of giving following disaster relief contributions in 2005. For those that gave more, this was attributed to a boost in budgets due to strong profits and more accurate measurement of previously unrecorded giving.

Despite the split, overall median total giving among the surveyed companies increased from $31.35 million in 2005 to $33.25 million in 2006. Giving as a percentage of pre-tax profit among these firms fell slightly from 1.01 percent to 0.98 percent, attributable to a median 12.1 percent increase in profits.

CECP recorded a total of $10.6 billion in cash and non-cash giving in the 113 companies participating for 2006. CECP includes fair-market valuation of in-kind donations. Year-round benchmarking from CECP's extensive database of comparative data is available online to participating companies.

Foundation Center estimates $4.2 billion in corporate foundation giving for 2006

Based on survey responses received in early 2007, the Foundation Center estimated that corporate foundations paid grants of $4.2 billion in 2006. This amount is added to *Giving USA*'s estimate of itemized corporate charitable contributions. *Giving USA* subtracted an estimate of $4 billion given to corporate foundations by their corporate donors to avoid double-counting gifts. Without this adjustment, gifts to the corporate foundation would be counted first when claimed as deductions by corporations and again in the amount of corporate foundation grants paid. While some corporate foundations are endowed and make grants from interest earnings, most are "pass-through" funders, receiving funds and paying grants from that amount within the same year.

Corporate-charity partnership is a component of corporate giving

Corporate giving in the past decade has become more complex for charities to navigate as companies link their business strategic goals with their giving. Corporate support for charities increasingly involves creating opportunities for employee volunteerism, marketing arrangements, and sponsorship of events, as well as grants and products and service donations.[17] According to a Conference Board survey in 2006, corporate grantmakers say their most important concern is how best to align their giving with their business needs.[18] Fifty-one companies in the study said that using their philanthropy to further business goals was one of their top three priorities in 2006.

In a separate study based on records of corporate earnings and corporate giving, a research team led by Professor Baruch Lev at Stern School of Business of New York University concluded that corporate philanthropy boosts the company bottom line.[19] These authors found that giving preceded growth in profits and used statistical techniques to isolate whether giving influenced profits, or profits influenced giving. They report that the contributions stimulated the revenue increase and not that both profits and giving were a result of a third cause (such as a management philosophy or specific market conditions).

Early in this decade, the Committee Encouraging Corporate Philanthropy

WHAT THIS MEANS TO YOU

Companies' heightened emphasis on performance evaluation is likely to put charities under a constraint, especially as many companies now encourage their employees to spend a portion of their business life volunteering for the charities. Some companies also want charities to provide metrics of the benefits that result for the nonprofit when the company's employees volunteer.[20] Be prepared to respond to a company's request that your partnership demonstrate "return on investment" for the firm, either in products sold, people involved, or other measures.

Many nonprofits receive more than 5 percent of their funding from corporations. For these groups, the funding environment is more competitive than ever. Focus on corporations that have some business-driven linkage or connection with your organization's mission. Engage companies first around their expertise in providing solutions to the types of problems your organization confronts. Then build on that involvement and ask for cash and in-kind expertise or products to solve the issue and fund it.

To benefit from new corporate giving strategies, be savvy about how you manage relationships. Habitat for Humanity International has certified project managers who ensure that logistical details of revenue-generating partnerships with companies are handled well.

Consider forming a partnership with other nonprofits to approach corporate sponsors collectively. A national consortium of cancer centers formed the Cancer Research Alliance, a separate nonprofit organization that raises funds through marketing promotions with companies that have a national reach.[21]

spearheaded the creation of a "Corporate Gold Standard" (CGS) reporting system for its member firms. A report released in 2006 based on 2004 data in the CGS shows that for the 57 firms participating that year:

- 36.0 percent of the total amount of giving was "strategic," aligned with the company's business strategy, for which the company expects to see (and measure) some type of impact. This giving is usually through the corporate affairs office or corporate foundation.

- 48.5 percent was "charitable," often distributed in relatively small individual amounts—either as matching gifts for employee contributions or general grants to nonprofits in the company's operating communities. This giving is often through local operating units.

- 15.5 percent was "commercial," including cause-related marketing, event sponsorships, and other giving that is used to support business relationships. Giving in this area occurs in business departments throughout the company.[22]

Diversity is a growing focus for corporate giving

The Conference Board found that a significant number of companies reported that giving to civil-rights organizations and groups that focus on racial equality is a growing priority.[23] Forty-two percent of 231 companies that responded to a 2006 survey said "diversity" is gaining importance as a grantmaking program. What's more, 22 percent of the survey participants ranked giving to Latino organizations as the highest priority among various giving programs related to diversity, perhaps as a result of the debate in Congress about immigration laws in the United States. This trend is witnessed by the new philanthropic initiative by Pfizer, which in 2006 started an effort to help disadvantaged Hispanics along the U.S.-Mexico border.[24]

Companies increasingly interested in international philanthropy

A survey conducted by the Committee Encouraging Corporate Philanthropy with its member companies[25] found that two-fifths (42 percent) of companies reported they have an international philanthropic presence. Almost one-half (46 percent) of the companies with an international philanthropic program were developing strategic plans to further increase and refine their international support for nongovernmental and nonprofit work. Not surprisingly, with the heavy American corporate investment in China, giving internationally was mainly for organizations in that nation, while giving to the Middle East ranked as the region with the lowest priority.[26] In its studies, the Conference Board found that 9 out of 10 multinational companies said they recognize that supporting charitable and other community programs represents a potential source of business for them.[27]

Operating foundations for patient assistance are a growing form of corporate giving

One key form of in-kind giving to emerge in the past decade has been contributions to patient-assistance programs that companies have incorporated as operating foundations. At least a dozen such foundations distributed medications and medical care products in 2005 and reported more than $3.35 billion in contributions made. This amount is not included in the estimate of corporate giving because it represents the fair-market value of the product donations to the operating foundation. Corporations claim a charitable deduction, as allowed by law, for the cost of production on their corporate tax returns. That is included in the estimate of corporate giving.

Table 1 shows the giving history from 2000 through 2005 of some of the largest operating foundations that pharmaceutical and medical products firms have created.

Companies deduct their contributions to these foundations as a corporate contribution, at a deduction amount that reflects the company's cost for manufacturing or purchasing the product, as required by law. In 2004, a total of 48 pharmaceutical and medicine manufacturing companies, each with assets of more than $500 million, claimed $1.79 billion in deductions for charitable contributions.[28] That is, the total claimed in deductions by 48 firms was LESS than the fair-market value reported as gifts-in-kind received by 12 company-sponsored operating foundations. The U.S. Tax Code permits operating foundations to record contributions received at fair market value. Many of the distributions of the medicines from the operating foundations go to recipients outside of the U.S.

Table 1
Distributions or grants awarded,* 2000–2005 by company-sponsored operating foundations providing patient assistance or access to care
($ in billions)

Company sponsor	Year founded*	2000	2001	2002	2003	2004	2005
Bristol Myers Squibb	1998	0.09	0.18	0.30	0.40	0.51	0.58
Merck	2001		0.04	0.24	0.38	0.52	0.53
GlaxoSmithKline	2003				< 0.01	0.01	0.43
AstraZeneca	1993	0.07	0.11	0.26	0.38	0.31	0.40
Janssen Ortho	1997	0.08	0.10	0.16	0.21	0.29	0.39
Wyeth	2002			0.07	0.16	0.18	0.25
Genentech	2002			0.02	missing	0.06	0.19
Roche	2002			0.07	0.11	0.17	0.17
Eli Lilly & Company	1996	0.09	< 0.01	0.01	0.11	0.15	0.17
Boehreinger Ingelheim	2001			0.02	0.04	0.09	0.15
Merck-Schering-Plough	2003				0.01	0.02	0.05
Genzyme	1996	< 0.01	0.01	< 0.01	0.04	0.04	0.04
Total		0.33	0.44	1.14	1.85	2.35	3.35

*This amount is the entire distributions or grant awards.

The Conference Board survey finds 18.3 percent increase in giving for 2005

In its 2006 *Corporate Contributions Report*, the Conference Board released findings about 130 companies that it surveyed about their 2005 giving and that had provided responses for the prior year. The firms responding in both 2005 and 2006 to the survey are among the country's largest and reported giving to U.S.-based charities of $6.83 billion,[29] or half of the estimated $13.77 billion estimated by this edition of *Giving USA* for corporate giving in 2005. Figure 1 shows the cash and non-cash amounts by type of recipient organization. The Conference Board asks for information about in-kind donations at the tax-deductible value. The Conference Board sends its survey to Fortune 500 and Fortune 1000 companies. It is not limited to members.

Figure 1
Corporate giving, cash and non-cash by type of recipient
n=209
Total = $7.74 billion

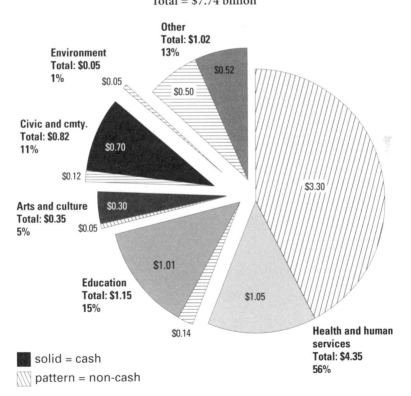

solid = cash
pattern = non-cash

Data: The Conference Board, *2006 Corporate Contributions Report.* Total here is not what was reported in this study as the total but it is the sum of the values shown in Tables 18 to 23.

- Health and human services received the largest share of corporate contributions, with $4.05 billion reported to the Conference Board, including an estimated $3.2 billion in in-kind contributions from pharmaceutical firms. Education received $1.15 billion, which included $140 million in non-cash gifts.

- Arts and culture received just over $350 million, and $50 million was non-cash.

- Civic and community organizations received $820 million, with $120 million in non-cash gifts.

Excluding pharmaceutical firms, just over one-quarter (27 percent) of corporate donations are in-kind. About three-quarters (73 percent) are cash contributions, either from companies or company foundations. Figure 2 shows the type of donation made by companies in the Conference Board study (except pharmaceuticals).

Figure 2
Charitable giving by companies other than pharmaceutical firms, 2005
($ in billions)

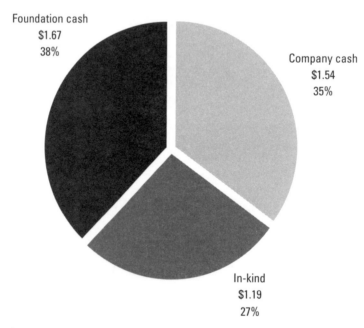

Foundation cash
$1.67
38%

Company cash
$1.54
35%

In-kind
$1.19
27%

Data: The Conference Board, 199 companies

Corporate in-kind giving dominated by pharmaceutical companies

The Conference Board reports that $2.93 billion of the donations it tracked in surveys from more than 200 companies were in-kind donations[30] from 10 pharmaceutical companies.[31] Among these companies, in-kind donations were 86.6 percent of reported total contributions. The Conference Board asks its survey participants to provide giving information that matches what the firm claims in tax deductions (in-kind gifts deducted at amounts allowed by the tax code, not at fair market value). Figure 3 illustrates the importance of in-kind contributions at pharmaceutical firms.

Figure 3
Pharmaceutical company giving, 2005
($ in billions)

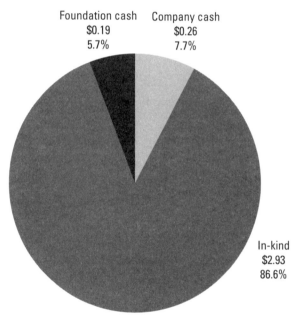

Foundation cash
$0.19
5.7%

Company cash
$0.26
7.7%

In-kind
$2.93
86.6%

Data: The Conference Board, n=10

Corporate foundation grantmaking priorities, 2005

The Foundation Center surveys corporate foundations annually and gathers information about the purposes for which grant dollars are paid. Figure 4 shows the allocation of corporate foundation funding for 2005. The total granted by the surveyed corporate foundations was $1.83 billion.

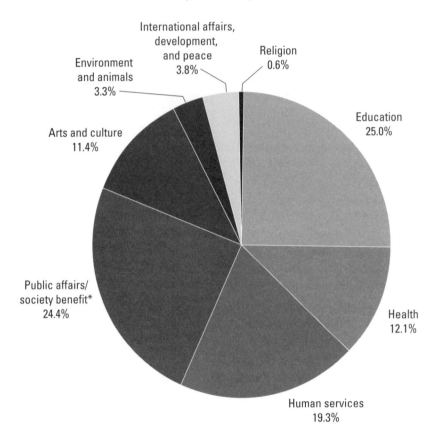

Figure 4
Corporate foundation funding priorities, 2005
($ in millions)

Data: The Foundation Center, *Update on Foundation Giving Priorities*, Table 35.

*Includes civil rights and social action, community improvement and development, public affairs, science and technology research, social science research.

Key findings from annual studies summarized

Table 2 summarizes key findings from studies that appear annually. Three years of data are presented, the most recent available. Web site addresses are provided to help readers get access to the full reports.

Table 2
Key findings from annual studies about corporate giving

$5 Million Dollar List Center on Philanthropy at Indiana University, www.philanthropy.iupui.edu			
	2004	2005	2006
Largest publicized corporate gift	$208 million, from PACE, the Partners for the Advancement of Collaborative Engineering Education, consortium of four firms, to Georgia Institute of Technology	$265 million, Google to its foundation ($90 million) and other to-be-named nonprofit groups ($175 million)	$289 million, in-kind software grant from UGS Corporation to University of Cincinnati as reported (fair market value)

The Corporate Contributions Report The Conference Board, www.conference-board.org			
	2003	2004	2005
Percentage growth in giving over prior year among firms that responded two years in a row to the survey	24 134 firms	21.8 133 firms	18.3 209 firms
U.S. contributions as a percentage of U.S. pretax income (median)	1.7	1.6	1.0
U.S. contributions as a percentage of consolidated (U.S. and international operations) pretax income (median)	0.90	0.85	0.71
Donations per employee, worldwide (median)	$360	$392	$434
Share from corporate cash	24	23	23
Share in-kind (largely pharma)	49	54	53
Share from foundation grants	27	23	24

Foundation Center report about corporate foundations *Foundation Yearbook*, various editions The Foundation Center, www.foundationcenter.org			
	2003	2004	2005
Number of corporate foundations	2,549	2,596 billion	2,607 billion
New gifts received	$3.23 billion	$3.667 billion	$4.008 billion
Grants made	$3.47 billion	$3.443 billion	$3.996 billion

Charitable giving at major corporations, August 5, 2004, August 4, 2005 and August 17, 2006 *Chronicle of Philanthropy*, www.philanthropy.com (Note: 2006 data not available in April 2007)			
	2003	2004	2005
Corporate donor identified as largest cash donor and amount contributed in cash	Wal-Mart $153 million	Wal-Mart $198 million	Wal-Mart $236.1 million
Company reported with the highest amount in cash and product donations	Merck & Company $843 million	Pfizer $1.26 billion	Pfizer $1.6 billion

Business Committee for the Arts, Inc. survey of corporate arts funders Poll of 100 or more prominent corporate funders of the arts Fall surveys project direction of change in giving for the next year, www.bcainc.org (Note: 2006 report not available in April 2007)			
	2003	2004	2005
Percentage who expected their arts giving to:			
Remain stable	58	67	70
Increase	8	13	19
Decrease	19	11	5
Don't know	15	9	6

Sponsorships (includes for-profit and nonprofit) IEG Sponsorship Report, www.sponsorship.com $ in billions (% change)			
	2004	2005	2006
Sports	7.67 (8.3)	8.30 (8.3)	9.9 (10.8)
Entertainment	1.06 (21.7)	1.17 (10.4)	1.6 (16.2)
Fairs, events, festivals	0.48 (n/a)	0.52 (7.9)	0.70 (15.1)
Causes	0.99 (7.2)	1.11 (12.3)	1.44 (10.5)
Arts	0.61 (0.3)	.65 (6.4)	0.82 (10.4)
Associations/membership groups	0.31 (n/a)	.34 (11.1)	0.47 (15.3)

Note: Associations and membership groups were separated in 2004 from fairs, events, and festivals; n/a indicates that percentage change cannot be calculated for 2004.

---

1   Bureau of Economic Analysis, U.S. Department of Commerce, www.bea.gov, downloaded March 30, 2007.

2   I. Wilhelm, A surge in corporate giving, *Chronicle of Philanthropy*, August 17, 2006, http://philanthropy.com.

3   Adjusted for inflation, the 2005 estimated rate of growth is 17.2 percent, the second-highest inflation-adjusted increase on record, after the 18.4 percent jump found for 1999.

4   Center on Philanthropy, Philanthropic Giving Index, December 2006, www.philanthropy.iupui.edu.

5   Besides the cash and in-kind donations that are treated by the tax code as tax-deductible charitable gifts, charities receive other types of support from companies. These other forms of support can include direct services, use of space, collaborative purchasing, and so on. *Giving USA* does not estimate the value of these other forms of corporate support, including expenditures from a marketing budget for activities such as advertising or sponsorship that benefit a charity, time volunteered by company employees, or services provided at a discount.

6   Million Dollar List, Center on Philanthropy, 2006, www.philanthropy.iupui.edu.

7   Press release, University of Cincinnati receives $289 million software grant from UGS, April 19, 2006. Viewed at /www.ugs.com/about_us/press/press.shtml?id=4631.

8   See the list compiled by the Center on Philanthropy at Indiana University, www.philanthropy.iupui.edu.

9   UGS company press release, as in note 7.

10 Press release, AT&T AccessAll: AT&T's largest-ever philanthropic commitment delivers technology resources to families and communities, June 14, 2006, viewed at http://att.sbc.com/gen/press-room?pid=7914..

11 Press release, Microsoft gifts $41 million in software and cash to help groups better collaborate in times of crisis, February 22, 2006, www.microsoft.com/presspass/features/2006/feb06/02-22NGOCollaborate.mspx.

12 E. Hand, Gift will help reforest thousands of acres: Enterprise's $50 million donation comes on the day Laura Bush is to attend a ceremonial planting in Forest Park, *St. Louis Post Dispatch*, October 12, 2006. Viewed at www.factiva.com.

13 PR Newswire, March 30, 2006. http://phx.corporate-ir.net/phoenix.zhtml?c=197786&p=about_all_kids_can.

14 Press release, GE announces record $20 million 'college bound' grant for Cincinnati public schools, October 19, 2006, http://www.geaviation.com/aboutgeae/presscenter/other/other_20061019.html.

15 Press Release, Miami Performing Arts Center Foundation accepts multimillion-dollar naming gift from Carnival Corporation and Knight Foundation, July 19, 2006, www.carnivalcenter.org/_inc/press/releases/pressRelease.aspx?rid=10081.

16 M. Coady, program manager at CECP, personal communication with *Giving USA* research staff, May 18, 2007, based on analysis of the Committee Encouraging Corporate Philanthropy data received spring 2007 about giving in 2006.

17 M. Porter and M. Kramer, Strategy and society: The link between competitive advantage and corporate social responsibility, *Harvard Business Review*, December 2006.

18 I. Wilhelm, Linking charity to company's bottom line is top concern, *Chronicle of Philanthropy*, June 1, 2006, www.philanthropy.com.

19 G. Epstein, Charity has its rewards for generous companies, *Chronicle of Philanthropy*, January 7, 2007, www.philanthropy.com.

20 December 25 article posted to the online magazine, *Red Herring*.

21 As reported in N. Barton and H. Hall, A year of big gains, *Chronicle of Philanthropy*, October 26, 2006, www.philanthropy.com.

22 Committee Encouraging Corporate Philanthropy, with analysis by the Center on Corporate Citizenship at Boston College, Adding it up 2004: *The Corporate Giving Standard, 2006*, www.corporatephilanthropy.org.

23 S. Muirhead, *Philanthropy and Business: The Changing Agenda*, 2006, The Conference Board, www.conference-board.org..

24 I. Wilhelm. A Surge in Corporate Giving, *Chronicle of Philanthropy*, August 17, 2006, www.philanthropy.com.

25 Committee Encouraging Corporate Philanthropy. Exploring Corporate Philanthropy. January 2006, www.corporatephilanthropy.org.

26 Ibid.

27 S. Muirhead, *Philanthropy and Business*, as in note 23.

28 *IRS Corporate Source Book*, 2004, www.irs.gov.

29 S. Muirhead, *The 2006 Corporate Contributions Report*, The Conference Board, www.conference-board.org.

30 The U.S. tax code permits corporations a "limited deduction for charitable contributions made in cash or other property." Non-cash donations are often reported in the media at fair market value, but the amount allowed as a deduction is fair market value minus the income and capital gains that would be earned if the product were sold at fair market value. In effect, corporations can deduct their cost for purchasing or manufacturing assets. In-kind donations have a value to the recipient charity that equals whatever the charity saves by receiving an item that it would otherwise pay for.

31 S. Muirhead, *The 2006 Corporate Contributions Report*, p. 20, www.conference-board.org.

10 Giving by foundations

- The Foundation Center estimated $36.50 billion in giving in 2006 by independent, community, and operating foundations. This is 12.4 percent of total estimated giving for 2006.

- This is a 12.6 percent increase in grantmaking by these types of foundations (9.1 percent adjusted for inflation) compared with the final amount of $32.41 billion for 2005.

- According to the Foundation Center, the "principal factors driving growth in foundation giving in 2006 were strong gains in the stock market and a higher level of new foundation establishment than was seen in the early 2000s."

- Giving by foundations has increased an average of 4.4 percent annually since 1966 (adjusted for inflation).

- The annual increase in the past 10 years has averaged 9.3 percent, in spite of the fact that this period includes no growth in 2002 and 2003.

Foundation grantmaking in 2006

Giving USA reports the Foundation Center's estimates of foundation grantmaking for the year just concluded.[1] The Foundation Center figure of $40.7 billion is adjusted by *Giving USA* to move $4.2 billion of corporate foundation grantmaking to the corporate giving estimate for *Giving USA*. The estimate here for 2006 is for grantmaking by independent, community, and operating foundations. The largest foundation grants announced in 2006 are shown in Table 1.

Table 1
Top five announced grants by foundations, 2006

Funder	Amount	Recipient
Bill and Melinda Gates Foundation[2]	$500,000,000	Global Fund to Fight AIDS, TB, and Malaria (one of many grants from this funder to this recipient in 2006)
Robert W. Woodruff Foundation[3]	$261,500,000	Emory University
Jerome L. Greene Foundation[4]	$200,000,000	Columbia University
Leon Levy Foundation[5]	$200,000,000	New York University
Lucasfilm Foundation[6]	$175,000,000	University of Southern California, School of Cinematic Arts

Source: Center on Philanthropy Million Dollar List.

Foundation response to the Gulf Coast hurricanes

The Foundation Center released a study in August 2006, presenting its findings about foundation giving for hurricane relief and recovery after the storms of fall 2005.[7] That report is summarized in this volume in Chapter 6 about disaster recovery giving.

Stock market performance, and therefore foundation giving, exceeded expectations

The Foundation Center's survey conducted in early 2006 asked funders to indicate the likely direction of change in their grantmaking during the year.[8] In early 2006, foundations projected slow growth in assets and were concerned about fuel and energy costs, the continuing war in Iraq, and increasingly high national debt. These uncertainties led 32 percent of foundations to project declines in their grantmaking for 2006, with 16 percent saying no change and 52 percent anticipating growth.

Community foundations were more likely than independent or corporate foundations to anticipate a growth in giving in 2006. Nearly 6 in 10 (59 percent) of community foundations surveyed expected their grantmaking to increase in 2006, compared with 2005, and 11 percent said no change.[9]

By the end of the year, which saw an unanticipated increase in the stock market, foundation giving increased a strong 12.3 percent, exceeding the early predictions. The Foundation Center summarized the following trends as important to foundation grantmaking in 2006:

- Unexpectedly strong growth in assets from investment returns, given the bull market in 2006;
- Faster rate of foundation establishment and new giving to foundations, with a 35.0 percent increase between 2004 and 2005 in gifts received at foundations;
- Higher levels of grantmaking than the minimum required by law (5 percent of asset value must be used in grantmaking activities), due in part to the number of relatively new foundations that function as vehicles for giving by living donors and are not endowed (pass-through); and
- A dozen or so operating foundations created by pharmaceutical corporations and distributing more than $3 billion in fair-market value of medicines and products to help patients in need.[10]

Donor-advised funds that are housed at community foundations are included in foundation grantmaking estimates because the community foundation reports those distributions on an IRS Form 990 that is tabulated by the Foundation Center.

Commercially sponsored donor-advised funds, which also "grant" funding to charities, are not considered foundations and are not treated as foundations under current law. They are classified, as are United Ways and Jewish federations, as "community funds and federated giving" organizations and are discussed in Chapter 16, Public-Society Benefit. Other types of institutions also house donor-advised funds, including universities, the Humane Society,

World Vision, and others. Contributions to those funds are part of the total for giving to that type of charity. Disbursements from donor-advised funds are NOT considered "new" money for philanthropy but "pass-through" funding.

Twenty-two percent growth in number of family foundations, 2001 to 2005

An increasing number of donors are creating funds and foundations as a vehicle for making gifts. The Foundation Center's early 2007 report about family foundations showed that from 2001 to 2005, the number of family foundations rose from 27,804 to 33,994, which is a growth rate of 22.3 percent. All independent foundations (including family foundations) increased from 55,120 in 2001 to 63,059 in 2005, which is a growth of 7,939 foundations and a 14.4 percent growth rate.

In 2005, family foundations accounted for 54 percent of all independent foundations. In 2001, family foundations were 50 percent of all independent foundations.

In 2005, half of the family foundations granted less than $50,000 each. Approximately 6 percent of family foundations reported grantmaking of $1 million or more for 2005, and the remaining 44 percent granted between $50,000 and $1 million, with most in that group giving between $100,000 and $500,000. In general, family foundations were more likely than independent foundations overall to make grants for education, health, the environment (including animal protection), and religion.

Foundation giving priorities in 2005 differ somewhat from 2001

The Foundation Center releases an annual study of foundation giving priorities, which is based on a sample of grants. Figure 1 shows the dollar amounts and percentages of grant dollars supporting different areas in 2005, as reported by the participating foundations.[11]

WHAT THIS MEANS TO YOU

An increasing amount of "individual" giving is actually being made through family foundations. This formalizes the request process, but does not eliminate the need for good cultivation and stewardship. Family foundations need just as much time or more to get to know your organization before entertaining a proposal as an individual major donor does.

Building a funding relationship with a donor who gives through a family foundation requires the same process and careful fundraising as working with an individual donor—with some consideration of the family interests and pressures.

Be attentive in your community to trends. For example, hedge funds are currently an important investment vehicle. Many people—even those in their 30s—who are earning millions as fund managers have created foundations. Chapter 7 in this volume contains a brief summary of this trend.

Figure 1
Foundation funding priorities, 2005
($ in millions)

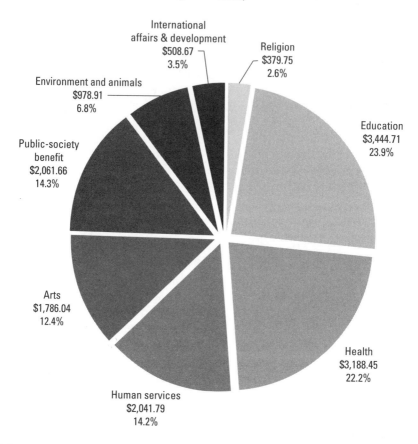

International
affairs & development
$508.67
3.5%

Religion
$379.75
2.6%

Environment and animals
$978.91
6.8%

Education
$3,444.71
23.9%

Public-society
benefit
$2,061.66
14.3%

Arts
$1,786.04
12.4%

Health
$3,188.45
22.2%

Human services
$2,041.79
14.2%

Includes amounts for science and technology and for social science, reported separately by the Foundation Center. Data: The Foundation Center, *Foundation Giving Trends*, 2007 edition, page 69. Based on a sample of foundations.

The amounts of grant dollars awarded to different types of charities in 2005 differ from the amounts found for grants paid in 2001. Figure 2 illustrates the declining amount for education and the increased grantmaking for international affairs and development.

Figure 2
Amounts granted, sample of independent and community foundations,
2001 and 2002

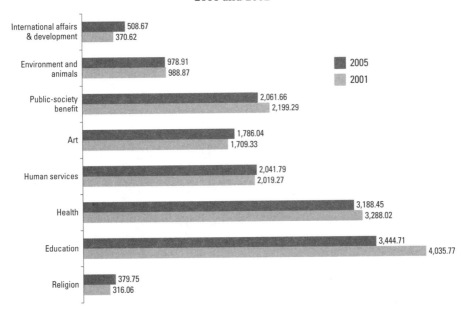

Foundation funding, especially because it is typically short-term program funding, is not a funding strategy for significant portions of an organization's budget. Foundation grants are appropriate for ideas that can be identified and worked out with some lead time, to allow for the cultivation and application process. It is appropriate for projects that can be funded through other means after the initial idea is tested and refined.

**WHAT THIS
MEANS TO YOU**

Community foundation giving grows more than 300 percent from 1990 to 2005

The Foundation Center studied community foundations and reported that they are 1 percent of all foundations, but account for 10 percent of all foundation giving (including giving by corporate foundations, which *Giving USA* considers as corporate donors, not foundation donors).[12] In 2005, community foundations gave $3.2 billion, setting a new record after growth from 2004 of 10.9 percent in grant dollars awarded.

Community foundations house donor-advised funds that are distributed in consultation with the fund creators. Community foundations also have unrestricted funds for grantmaking by program officers.

If your community has a community foundation, it can be helpful to introduce your organization to the program staff. Even if the community foundation does not itself give grants to your type of charity, occasional contact with the program officers can be a helpful source of information and networking opportunities.

Giving by community foundations has more than quadrupled since 1990 (adjusted for inflation). The growth rate of community foundation giving, at a cumulative total of 336 percent from 1990 to 2005, surpassed that of independent foundation giving, which rose 146 percent in that same period.

The Columbus Foundation survey of 641 community foundations in 2005 reported $3.2 billion in grantmaking that year. Of that amount, $995 million,

or nearly one-third (31.1 percent), was from the 10 community foundations that paid out the largest totals in grants for 2005.[13]

Key findings from other studies summarized

Table 2 presents three years of findings from studies released annually about foundations. Web site addresses are provided to help readers get access to the full report.

Table 2
Key findings from other studies about foundation giving

Foundation Yearbook, 2005, 2006 and 2007 editions The Foundation Center, www.foundationcenter.org			
	2003	2004	2005
Number of active independent and community grantmaking foundations	59,690	60,731	63,766
Number of all active grantmaking foundations (including corporate and operating)	66,398	67,736	71,095
Assets in independent and community foundations	$400.00 billion	$463.89 billion	$500.15 billion

Foundation Giving Trends, 2005, 2006 and 2007 editions
The Foundation Center, www.foundationcenter.org

	2003	2004	2005
Average grant amount, surveyed foundations	$118,649	$122,355	$125,442
Median grant amount, surveyed foundations	$25,000	$25,000	$26,000

Columbus Foundation Survey of Community Foundations 2005, 2006 and 2007 editions
Columbus Foundation, www.columbusfoundation.org

	2003	2004	2005
Number of community foundations in the survey	645	636	641
Assets in community foundations	$34.90 billion	$39.40 billion	$44.90 billion
Grants made	$2.60 billion	$2.97 billion	$3.20 billion

1   S. Lawrence et al., *Foundation Growth and Giving Estimates*, April 2007, The Foundation Center, www.foundationcenter.org.

2   Global Fund Press Release, viewed at http://www.gatesfoundation.org/GlobalHealth/Pri_Diseases/HIVAIDS/Announcements/Announce-060809.htm.

3   Emory University Press Release, viewed at http://news.emory.edu/Releases/WoodruffFoundation1163709557.html.

4   Columbia University News, viewed at http://www.columbia.edu/cu/news/06/03/science_center.html.

5   New York University Press Release, viewed at http://www.nyu.edu/public.affairs/releases/detail/1001.

6   University of Southern California News, viewed at http://www.usc.edu/uscnews/stories/12754.html.

7   L. Renz and S. Lawrence, *Giving in the Aftermath of the Gulf Coast Hurricanes:* *Report on the Foundation and Corporate Response*, The Foundation Center, www.foundationcenter.org.

8   L. Renz et al, *Foundation Growth and Giving Estimates*, April 2006, www.foundationcenter.org.

9   J. Atienza, *Key Facts about Community Foundations*, September 2006, www.foundationcenter.org.

10 S. Lawrence et al. as in Note 1.

11 J. Atienza and J. Altman, *Foundation Giving Trends: Preview*, released in December 2005 with 2004 data, The Foundation Center, www.foundationcenter.org.

12 J. Atienza, *Key Facts on Community Foundations*, September 2006, The Foundation Center, www.foundationcenter.org.

13 Columbus Foundation Community Foundation Survey, 2005, www.columbusfoundation.org.

11 Giving to religion

- In 2006, giving to religious organizations reached an estimated $96.82 billion, an increase of 4.5 percent (1.2 percent adjusted for inflation) from the revised estimate of $92.69 billion for 2005.[1]

- Giving to religious organizations represented 32.8 percent of total estimated charitable contributions in the United States in 2006.

- Since 1966, in current dollars, gifts to religion have increased an average of 6.8 percent per year. Adjusted for inflation, the average annual 40-year increase is 2.0 percent. The ten-year average increase is 4.7 percent per year (2.1 percent adjusted for inflation).

- Giving to religion increases over time, but more slowly than does giving to other subsectors. As a percentage of total giving, religion's share has fallen from roughly half (45.7 percent) in 1966 to just under one-third (32.8 percent).

- Countless religious congregations organized volunteers in 2005 and 2006 to go to hurricane-affected communities in the American South to assist with rebuilding. Volunteer hours and expenses that volunteers paid for these trips are not included in the estimate of giving to religion.

Giving USA findings about giving to religion, 2006

The 2006 *Giving USA* estimate of giving to religion[2] includes:

- Contributions to religious congregations, including nondenominational congregations; and

- Giving to other entities for organized religious practice, including:
  - Offices of faith groups;
  - Missionary societies;
  - Religious media; and
  - Other organizations formed for religious fellowship, worship, or evangelism.

It does not, however, include contributions made to separately incorporated, faith-based organizations (FBOs) that provide education, healthcare, or other services. Thus, giving to St. Elizabeth's Hospital, the Reform Jewish Academy, or Lutheran Social Services and similar organizations appears in health, education, and human services, respectively. This chapter includes some news items related to funding for FBOs because that topic is often of interest to people who work in or volunteer for religious organizations.

WHAT THIS MEANS TO YOU

Contributions to religion are predominantly from individuals.

To consider giving without including religious giving, take $96.82 billion out of individual giving (as an approximation). The result is $126.07 billion in individual giving for nonreligious (secular) causes. With other types of giving, the adjusted total is $198.20 billion, and individuals still contribute 64 percent.

Million-dollar gifts awarded to religious organizations

At least seven gifts of $2 million or more each were given to religious organizations in 2006 and publicly announced in the media:

- An anonymous gift of $30 million was given to the Catholic Diocese of Memphis to support its inner-city Jubilee Schools effort.[3]

- The Estate of Henry William Edwards, Jr. gave $18 million to Grace Cathedral in San Francisco, California, to be used to maintain and restore the building.[4]

- $8.17 million from the Lilly Endowment went to the Indianapolis Center for Congregations for operating support.[5]

- Donald Saltz gave $5 million to the Adas Israel Congregation in Washington, D.C., to bolster the congregation's endowment for future programs; the gift was given in honor of his late wife, Mozelle.[6]

- The Rollie Boreham, Jr. Estate gave $4.8 million to the First Presbyterian Church of Fort Smith in Arkansas to provide support for outreach and benevolence, support the church's Center for At-Risk Youth, and provide scholarships and program development for its Hobson Preschool.[7]

- Pew Charitable Trusts granted $3 million to the Billy Graham Evangelistic Association to support construction of the Billy Graham Library, featuring multimedia presentations, films, memorabilia, and the restored Graham family homestead.[8]

- An anonymous donor gave $2.45 million to the Faith First Baptist Church in Indiana for the purpose of creating a new residential center for girls and young women.[9]

One other significant gift will have an impact on religion, although the recipient is a foundation. Jim Joseph bequeathed at least $500 million to The Jim Joseph Foundation, which focuses on helping Jewish children and improving education in the religion's traditions and history.[10]

Multimillion dollar fundraising campaigns for churches and missions

A number of major campaigns for religious organizations were covered in the media in 2006 or early 2007. While not a comprehensive list of all campaigns and fundraising efforts under way, this selection shows the range of goals and purposes.

An article in *Church Executive* reported that 7,000 donors contributed or pledged $105 million to Calvary Chapel in Fort Lauderdale for expansion of its ministry, which already reaches 20,000 people in attendance weekly.[11] The Catholic Diocese in Biloxi announced a rebuilding campaign for $14 million to raise funds needed for expenses not covered by insurance.[12] Other Catholic dioceses launched campaigns for growth and outreach, including a $100 million initiative in Santa Clara County, California, announced in fall 2006.[13]

The Lutheran Church Missouri Synod World Mission launched a six-year effort in 2004, called "Ablaze!," with the goal of raising $100 million in new mission dollars (above church operations). In 2006, that campaign began working in a limited number of districts within the denomination to contact potential donors one at a time. By December 2006, the campaign report showed a combined total of $10 million from the first three districts to participate in the "Fan into Flame" program.[14] The "Fan into Flame" component is just one portion of the overall $100 million goal.

Congregational membership shifts see growth in churches that are more likely to expect tithing; people with no religion also increase as percentage of population

The National Council of Churches of Christ maintains historical records of church membership going back to 1916. In the *Yearbook of American and Canadian Churches* released in 2006, many mainline Protestant denominations reported a decline in membership in 2004, while the Mormon, Pentecostal, and Catholic churches reported an increase.[15] Of the 25 largest churches in the U.S., those showing the largest increases in membership were:

- Assemblies of God, a Pentecostal denomination, up by 1.8 percent to 2.8 million individuals;

- Church of Jesus Christ of Latter Day Saints, up by 1.7 percent to 6 million individuals; and

- Roman Catholic Church, up by 0.8 percent to 67.8 million individuals.

Several studies released in 2006 found different percentages of the population who reported no religious affiliation. A survey by the Gallup organization and Baylor University, a faith-based higher education institution affiliated with the Baptist General Convention of Texas, found that 10.8 percent of the U.S. population is unaffiliated with a religion, which is lower than the 14 percent stated in previous studies.[16]

A separate study published in *USA Today* reported that Americans who say they "consider themselves part of a Christian tradition" fell 6 percentage points (from 80 percent to 74 percent) from 1999 to 2006. The number of people who say they are not part of any religious tradition rose from 13 percent to 18 percent in the same period.[17] It is likely that different wording on the questions in the two studies accounts in part for the difference found in the Baylor and the *USAToday* results.

Conflicts over social issues rock some faith groups

Religious beliefs and values shaped how Americans responded in 2006 to a number of issues. Some donations made to religious groups may have increased or decreased as individuals "voted" with their support (or withdrawal of support) based on their position about the social concern.

An issue that might have spurred giving concerns the state referenda banning same-sex marriage. Same-sex marriage has been constitutionally banned in 19 states.[18] In another example, the Episcopal Church in the U.S. was divided after a General Convention decision affirmed support for gays and lesbians, and opposed state or federal constitutional amendments that prohibit same-sex civil marriages. Also within the Episcopal Church, election of Katharine Jefferts Schori as Episcopal Presiding Bishop led several Episcopal dioceses to refuse recognition of her leadership. Some of these dioceses sought to align themselves with Anglican communions in other countries.[19]

Muslims face challenges for giving in the post-9/11 world

Zakat (giving alms), the third of the five fundamental pillars of Islam, is an annual obligation to donate 2.5 percent of savings and higher percentages of other assets to specific types of charitable causes (the poor and the needy are listed first).[20] Since 2001, many American Muslims have felt they cannot give to organizations such as private Muslim foundations that they previously supported because they might be accused of giving to terrorist organizations.[21] Muslims have been looking for alternative ways to fulfill their religious duty.

In the 2006 book, *Islamic Perspective on Charity: A Comprehensive Guide for Running a Muslim Nonprofit in the US,*[22] Khalil Jassemm, head of the Michigan-based Muslim charity Life for Relief and Development, presents information about:

- How Muslim charities operate; and
- The concept and significance of charity in Islam in a comparative context, among other topics.

Dr. Jassemm, formerly a university professor of surveying and measurement sciences, spoke in 2006 at a forum organized by the U.S. Department of State about issues related to Muslim integration into U.S. society.[23] The organization he now heads, Life for Relief and Development, has consultative status with the United Nations and is reportedly the largest Arab-American nongovernmental charity.

Bankrupt donors may still tithe

President Bush signed a law allowing people who file for bankruptcy to tithe.[24]

WHAT THIS MEANS TO YOU

It is important to remember faith-based giving is more about faith and transformation than it is about politics. Too much politics either way can obscure the mission of the institution, polarize followers, and restrict donations.

The law allows households to continue to tithe and to make charitable contributions even as their debts exceed their assets. Approximately 2.04 million households filed bankruptcy in 2005,[25] but legal reform to bankruptcy-filing regulations lowered that number to about 500,000 in 2006.[26] If 45 percent[27] of those 500,000 households give an average of $1,884 to religion (the national average for giving to religion in 2005), this would equal about $423 million in contributions to religion that might otherwise not have been made before passage of the law. Even under the assumption that all households facing bankruptcy who would otherwise give to religion continue to do so at the national average amount, the total is less than .5 percent of all giving to religion.

Congregations promote giving through technology and theology

A number of trends in religious belief and fundraising practice may influence contributions to religious organizations. For example, churches have put ATMs in their buildings to make it easier for worship participants to contribute.[28]

Giving to religion is an important component of many faith traditions. A *TIME* magazine poll found that 31 percent of those surveyed agreed that if people give their money to God, God will bless them with more money.[29]

Faith-based organizations (FBOs) benefiting from federal and private funds

Faith-based organizations are eligible for federal funding under the Charitable Choice Act, which was extended through 2010. This provision of the Deficit Reduction Act of 2005 allows faith-based groups providing social services to receive federal funding without altering their religious identities or changing their hiring practices.[30]

A March 2006 report showed that nearly $2.1 billion was awarded to FBOs through seven federal agencies in Federal Fiscal Year 2005.[31] (This is about 2 percent of all charitable contributions to churches.) From 2003 to 2005, the Office of Faith-Based and Community Initiatives saw a 38 percent increase in the number of grants to faith-based groups from five federal agencies and a 21 percent increase in the amount of grant money awarded.[32]

In a first-ever look at five grant programs that provide federal dollars to be allocated at the state and local level, it was revealed that FBOs receive a small amount of funding, ranging from 1.7 percent to 5.5 percent, from state and local government funding decisions. This funding level is disproportionately low compared with the number of FBO grant applicants. By 2006, 32 governors and more than 115 mayors had established either an office or a liaison for faith-based and community initiatives. In part to increase the state and local funding allocations made to FBOs, the White House Office of Faith-Based and Community Initiatives held a series of regional conferences in 2006.[33]

The Center for Faith-Based and Community Initiatives was created by

WHAT THIS MEANS TO YOU

The Office of Faith-Based and Community Initiatives created in 2001 within the White House may or may not endure into 2009, when the next president is inaugurated. The related offices at the state and local level are likely to continue in some form, especially if the executive order extending charitable choice to 2010 is not countermanded by the next president so that federal funding continues to remain an option for faith-based organizations.

Disaster relief funding, when next needed, may be accessed through the Department of Homeland Security, which is also seeking to make it available to faith-based organizations in a more streamlined process than was the case in the past.

President Bush's executive order in March 2006 within the Department of Homeland Security (DHS). According to President Bush, the Center "coordinates DHS's efforts to remove regulatory, contracting, and other programmatic obstacles to the participation of faith-based and community organizations in its provision of social and community services, including disaster relief and recovery services."[34]

Court rulings benefit FBOs

Two federal courts upheld AmeriCorps grant recipients' right to teach faith-based subjects in religiously affiliated schools.

- In the October 2005 case of *Lown v. Salvation Army*, the Federal District Court for the Southern District of New York ruled that churches and religious organizations must retain their hiring autonomy when receiving federal financial assistance. The court recognized that FBOs do not become an arm of the government merely by receiving funding to provide social services.

- In the January 2006 case of *American Jewish Congress v. Corporation for National and Community Service,* the District of Columbia Court of Appeals upheld the right of AmeriCorps to grant recipients to teach religious and secular subjects in religiously affiliated schools.

Bank of America Study of High Net-Worth Philanthropy finds widespread support for giving to religion

The study finds that those in high net-worth households are more likely to give to religion than the general population (72 percent versus 45.4 percent). Also, religious beliefs motivate 57 percent of high net-worth respondents.[35] This mail survey was a random sample drawn from neighborhoods in which the households' invested net worth was $3 million or more, and included respondents with an annual household income over $200,000 and/or a net worth over $1 million. The study was conducted and analyzed by the Center on Philanthropy at Indiana University.

Religious conservatives more generous than liberals, study says

In *Who Really Cares: The Surprising Truth about Compassionate Conservatism,* author Arthur C. Brooks concludes that religious conservatives donate far more money than secular liberals to charitable activities, after controlling for income. He cites extensive data analysis to demonstrate that values advocated by conservatives—from church attendance and two-parent families to the Protestant work ethic and a distaste for government-funded social services—make conservatives more generous than liberals.[36] Dr. Brooks is a professor of public administration at Syracuse University.

Religiously committed citizens are exemplars of civic responsibility

Dr. Stephen Monsma's study, *Religion and Philanthropic Giving and Volunteering: Building Blocks for Civic Responsibility,* asserts that people who want to understand and strengthen giving and volunteering in the United States need to take religion into account.[37] Monsma found that Americans who attend religious services on a weekly basis are more likely to give money to charities, both religious and secular, and are more likely to volunteer than those who seldom or never attend church.

Mainline Protestants tended to be more likely to give to charity than were people in the other traditions, although they were closely followed by evangelical Protestants. Respondents who gave money to charity or volunteered for charitable organizations also showed higher levels of political involvement than those who neither gave nor volunteered, suggesting that religiously committed people who give and volunteer are also active citizens in other areas of civic life.

A study of Catholic giving shows overall growth in 2005, but decline in the South

The International Catholic Stewardship Council (ICSC) continued a multiyear research program on Catholic giving to parishes and dioceses. The Center for Applied Research in the Apostolate (CARA) at Georgetown University annually surveys members of the ICSC on levels of Catholic giving. The ICSC data for 2005 contain replies from 60 percent of the dioceses and archdioceses in the 50 states and the District of Columbia. Joseph Claude Harris, an independent research analyst, used the ICSC data to create an estimate of

WHAT THIS MEANS TO YOU

People are motivated to give where the work is the outgrowth of a spiritual mission. In some cases, people might want to do targeted appeals to individuals who are likely to share a faith motivation and call upon the faith origins of the nonprofit where appropriate.

As disposable income rises, households give more money to a wider range of causes and types of organizations. Among the wealthiest households, gifts to religion are fewer than one-quarter (22.6 percent) of the total estimated dollars given, even though more than three-quarters of high net-worth households contribute to religion. The high net-worth donors are giving higher amounts to secular causes.

giving to all parishes in the country. His analysis, which was prepared for *Giving USA*, includes data from 2005, a year which was affected by reported scandals of abuse by priests.

Harris found that average household donations were the lowest in the Pacific ($172) and Northeast ($227) regions. These two regions had the largest number of estimated households per parish of any region in the

country. The Midwest, with the smallest average number of households per parish (458), had the largest average household donation of $630. Harris' data underscore the finding that the cost of operating a parish does not substantially increase when more Catholics register as members. The exercise of religion tends to be a fixed cost endeavor. Table 1 summarizes parish offertory collections by region.

Table 1
Estimated offertory collections for the Roman Catholic Church, 2005

Region	Number of parishes	Total offertory collection ($ in millions)	Estimated Catholic households*	Average household donation ($)	Average parish collection ($)	Average number of estimated households per parish	Percentage of dioceses reporting
Northeast	5,003	$1,660	7,303,281	$227	$331,801	1,460	56%
South Atlantic	1,506	$826	1,851,682	$446	$548,473	1,230	61%
South	2,463	$855	2,850,848	$300	$347,138	1,157	58%
Great Lakes	3,907	$1,448	3,516,620	$412	$370,617	900	62%
Midwest	2,722	$784	1,245,315	$630	$288,024	458	64%
Mountain	876	$364	1,018,410	$357	$415,525	1,163	33%
Pacific	1,641	$665	3,871,480	$172	$405,241	2,359	76%
Unted States	18,118	$6,602	21,657,636	$305	$364,389	1,195	60%

Notes to table:

*The estimate of Catholic households in this edition is based on work done at the Center for Applied Research on the Apostolate (CARA) at Georgetown University. It differs from previous editions of *Giving USA*. This change affects the average donation per household, but not the total or average parish collection (although there are also changes in the number of parishes).

Northeast	Connecticut, Maine, Massachusetts, New Hampshire, New York, New Jersey, Pennsylvania, Rhode Island, Vermont
South Atlantic	Delaware, District of Columbia, Florida, Georgia, Maryland, North Carolina, South Carolina, Virginia, West Virginia
South	Alabama, Arkansas, Kentucky, Louisiana, Mississippi, Oklahoma, Tennessee, Texas
Great Lakes	Illinois, Indiana, Michigan, Ohio, Wisconsin
Midwest	Iowa, Kansas, Nebraska, Minnesota, Missouri, North Dakota, South Dakota
Mountain	Arizona, Colorado, Idaho, Montana, Nevada, New Mexico, Utah, Wyoming
Pacific	Alaska, California, Hawaii, Oregon, Washington

Data from: Joseph Claude Harris, sharris7@earthlink.net

Over time, Harris has found that Catholics continued to give more money to support parish programs. Total Catholic offertory collections increased by $254 million, or 4 percent, between 2004 and 2005. Collections increased by $208 million between 2003 and 2004. The increased funding for 2005 probably came from two sources: the estimated number of Catholic households increased by 415,900, and the average annual gift increased from $298 to $305 for all estimated Catholic households.

There was a significant decline in offertory contributions in the South region. Hurricane Katrina devastated the heavily Catholic area of southern Louisiana. Offertory collections in the South region declined by $77.9 million, or 8.4 percent, between 2004 and 2005. The fact that Catholic New Orleans has only half of the prehurricane population is likely a major factor in the loss of donation revenue.

1   The *Giving USA* estimate for religion in 2006 includes a revised estimate for giving to religion in 2005. To form the revised estimate, the following data were used: the National Council of Churches giving to Protestant churches in 2005; Catholic giving in 2005; and contributions to other religious organizations, such as media ministries. The revised estimate for giving to religion in 2005 is $92.69 billion, or a growth rate of 4.9 percent (1.9 percent adjusted for inflation) from 2004 to 2005.

2   The 2006 estimate is based on data from 29 Protestant denominations reporting contributions to the National Council of Churches' *Yearbook on American and Canadian Churches*. It also includes surveys from religious organizations found on the *Chronicle of Philanthropy*'s list of "The Philanthropy 400," released in fall 2006 for contributions in 2005. The estimate also includes financial information from additional large religious organizations, including some religious denominations whose contribution information is publicly available through the Evangelical Council for Financial Accountability.

3   S. Drake, 'Isn't God good?'—$30 million donation is another giant step for inner-city Jubilee Schools, *The Commercial Appeal*, January 7, 2006.

4   The Living Church Foundation Press Release, www.livingchurch.org.

5   Recent Grants, *Chronicle of Philanthropy*, March 23, 2006, www.philanthropy.com.

6   M. Boorstein, Synagogue gets a surprise with $5 million gift, *The Washington Post*, B1 (Metro), October 5, 2006, www.washingtonpost.com.

7   D. Hughes, $24 million added to Boreham legacy: Baldor founder's trust makes 6 gifts, *The Arkansas Democrat Gazette*, December 22, 2006.

8   Religion in the public life, *The Pew Charitable Trusts*, November 2006, www.pewtrusts.org.

9   D. Shaw, Faith Baptist awarded $2.45 million grant, *Journal and Courier*, May 15, 2006.

10 C. Preston, Bequest Worth at Least $500 Million to Support Jewish Causes, *Chronicle of Philanthropy*, February 23, 2006, www.philanthropy.com.

11 R. Keener, Ministry expansion campaign sets $105 million national giving record, *Church Executive*, February 2007, www.churchexecutive.com.

12 Catholic Faith for Tomorrow, A future with promise, www.biloxidiocese.org.

13 St. Lawrence the Martyr, Catholic Parish and Education Center, News, November 2006, www.saintlawrence.org.

14 Fan Into Flame, Lutheran Church Missouri Synod, Campaign News Bulletin Vol. 1, No. 3, December 2006, www.lcms.org.

15 C. Herlinger, 'Non-mainline' Protestant churches gaining membership in United States, *Worldwide Faith News Archives*, April 3, 2006, www.wfn.org.

16 J. Carolson, Losing My Religion? No, Says Baylor Religion Survey, *Baylor University*, September 11, 2006, www.baylor.edu.

17 C. Grossman, The Episcopal church's new dawn, *USA Today*, February 21, 2007, www.usatoday.com.

18 D. Chen, New Jersey Court Backs Full Rights for Gay Couples, *The New York Times*, October 26, 2006, viewed at the Human Rights Campaign, www.hrc.org.

19 C. Grossman, The Episcopal Church's new dawn, *USA Today*, February 21, 2007, www.usatoday.com.

20 No author, Zakat (Almsgiving or Charity): The Third Pillar of Islam, in *IIssues*, Vol. V, No. 1, December 10, 2002, published by the Islamic Institute, www.islamicinstitute.org/Zakat.pdf.

21 R. Abdelkarim. After year of uncertainty, American Muslim charitable donations rebound. *Washington Report on Middle East Affairs*, January 2004, www.thefreelibrary.com.

22 K. Jassemm, Islamic perspective on charity: a comprehensive guide for running a Muslim nonprofit in the US, AuthorHouse.

23 K. Jassemm, Muslim Integration and Community Outreach in America, *International Information Programs*, April 11, 2006, www.usinfo.state.gov.

24 A bill to clarify the treatment of certain charitable contributions under title 11, United States Code, *The Library of Congress*, September 9, 2006, http://thomas.loc.gov.

25 Personal bankruptcies hit record high, *CNNMoney.com*, January 11, 2006, http://money.cnn.com.

26 D. Lundquist, One-year anniversary of bankruptcy law enactment marks lower but increasing filings, *Lundquist Consulting*, October 24, 2006, www.lundquistconsulting.com.

27 The percentage of the general U.S. population that contributes to religion is 45 percent, The Center on Philanthropy Panel Study, 2001 and 2003 editions.

28 N. Potter and Z. Fannin, An ATM for God, *ABC News*, February 20, 2007, http://abcnews.go.com.

29 T. Regan, Wealth and Theology, at Schulman, Ronca & Bucuvalas, Inc. (SRBI), September 2006, www.srbi.com.

30 President Signs S.1932, Deficit Reduction Act of 2005, The White House, February 8, 2006. www.whitehouse.gov.

31 Fact Sheet: Compassion in Action: Producing Real Results for Americans Most in Need, *Office of the Press Secretary*, March 9, 2006, www.whitehouse.gov.

32 Ibid.

33 "In 2006, the White House Office of Faith-Based and Community Initiatives hosted nine conferences, providing training, legal and technical assistance to over 5,500 new and potential Federal grantees," WHOFBCI Accomplishments in 2006, *The White House Faith-Based and Community Initiative*, www.whitehouse.gov.

34 Statement by Homeland Security Secretary Michael Chertoff on the Creation of a Center for Faith-based and Community Initiatives, *U.S. Department of Homeland Security*, March 8, 2006, www.dhs.gov/xnews/releases.

35 The Center on Philanthropy at Indiana University, *The Bank of America Study of High Net-Worth Philanthropy*, October 2006, http://newsroom.bankofamerica.com.

36 A. Brooks, *Who Really Cares: The Surprising Truth about Compassionate Conservatism*, Basic Books.

37 S. Monsma, Religion and philanthropic giving and volunteering: Building blocks for civic responsibility, presented at the Third Biennial Symposium on Religion and Politics, Calvin College, Grand Rapids, Michigan, April 27–29, 2006.

12 Giving to education

- Giving to educational organizations was estimated to be $40.98 billion in 2006, an increase of 9.8 percent (6.4 percent adjusted for inflation) from the 2005 revised estimate of $37.31 billion.

- An estimated 13.9 percent of total giving went to educational organizations.

- The education giving estimate is based on data from the Council for Aid to Education for gifts to higher education, from the National Association of Independent Schools for gifts to private K–12 schools, and from the *Giving USA* survey for gifts to other types of educational organizations.

- The new average rate of change of giving to education is 7.6 percent (3.1 percent adjusted for inflation) per year over the last 40 years. In the past ten years, giving to education has increased at an average annual rate of 8.0 percent (5.9 percent adjusted for inflation).

Giving USA survey findings

Notes located at the end of this chapter explain what types of organizations are included in the education subsector and what gift types are counted in the annual *Giving USA* survey.[1]

Tables 1 through 3 summarize key findings from the *Giving USA* survey in 2007.[2]

Table 1 shows that among large organizations in the education subsector, average and median amounts received in charitable gifts rose in 2006 compared with 2005. Among the moderately sized and medium-sized organizations, charitable gifts increased. In small educational organizations, both the average and the median declined.

Table 1
Charitable revenue received by educational organizations
in 2005 and 2006, by organizational size

Organizational size	Number of completed surveys	2005 average ($)	2005 median ($)	2006 average ($)	2006 median ($)
Large	41	88,506,304	47,153,579	99,554,163	56,240,757
Moderately sized	14	3,512,846	2,917,137	4,493,699	3,830,063
Medium-sized	25	1,857,284	1,241,239	2,066,760	1,564,033
Small	26	128,676	12,000	127,341	7,455

Large denotes organizations that receive $20 million or more in charitable revenue; *moderately sized* organizations have charitable revenue between $5 million and $19.99 million; *medium-sized* is used for organizations having charitable revenue between $1 million and $4.99 million, and *small* is for organizations that have charitable revenue of less than $1 million.

Table 2 summarizes the average and median increases or decreases in charitable revenue reported for 2006 by organizational size. In large, moderate, and medium-sized organizations, more than 70 percent of the responding organizations reported growth in charitable revenue in 2006 compared with 2005. In large and moderate organizations, the average increase exceeded the average decline. In medium-sized organizations, the organizations that reported a drop in charitable revenue saw a larger decline than the increase reported, on average, by those groups where charitable revenue rose. The

average increase was typically around 20 percent in these three size groups.

In small organizations, half reported growth in charitable revenue, but that increase was overshadowed by the size of the average drop in the 15 percent of small educational organizations where charitable revenue fell. The average percentage drop was 8 percent.

In all sizes of educational organizations considered together, 67 percent saw an increase, 20 percent saw a decline, and 13 percent had charitable revenue in 2006 that was within 1 percent of the amount received in 2005.

Table 2
Increases or decreases in charitable revenue of educational organizations, 2006

Organizational size	Number	Percentage of organizations in size group	Average change ($)	Average change (%)	Median change ($)	Median change (%)
Large						
Increase	30	73	20,120,085	39	15,072,157	30
Decrease	10	24	-14,986,652	-32	-8,099,698	-27
No Change	1	2		<1		<1
Total*	41	100				
All large organizations			11,047,860	21	6,887,227	19
Moderately sized						
Increase	10	71	1,430,409	41	682,682	16
Decrease	2	14	-286,077	-23	-286,077	-23
No Change	2	14	0	0	0	0
Total*	14	100				
All moderately sized organizations			980,853	26	264,066	9
Medium-sized						
Increase	18	72	452,177	35	277,606	18
Decrease	5	20	-579,550	-20	-123,393	-2
No Change	2	8	-2,256	0	-2,256	0
Total*	25	100				
All medium-sized organizations			209,477	21	109,556	14

Organizational size	Number	Percentage of organizations in size group	Average change ($)	Average change (%)	Median change ($)	Median change (%)
Small						
Increase	13	50	52,756	40	20,120	22
Decrease	4	15	-180,131	-68	-12,873	-77
No change	9	35	0	0	0	0
Total*	26	100				
All small organizations			-1,484	-8	0	0

*Total does not always equal 100 due to rounding.

Table 3 shows bequest receipts by organizational size. In large organizations, bequest revenue, on average, declined in 2006 compared with 2005, both as an average and a median. In moderate organizations, bequest receipts increased. In medium-sized organizations, the average rose slightly, and the median declined somewhat. The small organizations with bequest revenue are too few to use to make generalizable statements.

Table 3
Bequest receipts by organizational size, 2005 and 2006

Organizational size	Percentage with bequest revenues	2005 average ($)	2005 median ($)	2006 average ($)	2006 median ($)
Large	88	10,723,761	6,924,756	9,868,346	5,283,082
Moderate	33	279,564	110,000	635,662	238,035
Medium	67	247,999	99,000	254,639	86,619
Small*	11	251,864	48,301	88,234	128,702

*For 2006, only three small educational organizations provided bequest information. The values are reported here, although the number of responses is too low to use in making statistical inferences about all small educational organizations.

Announced gifts to education increase in 2006

Several institutions raised record amounts in 2006. The Council for Aid to Education reported that the top 10 higher education institutions in its survey of more than 1,000 raised $4.56 billion.[3] The top three listed are Stanford University, Harvard University, and Yale University, which raised a combined total of $1.9 billion.

Major contributions to education announced in 2006 included the following pledges and paid gifts, tracked by the *Chronicle of Philanthropy* in its list of the Top 60 donors.[4]

■ Phillip H. Knight, chairman of Nike Corporation, pledged $105 million to Stanford University's Graduate School of Business for a new management center campus.

- Peter B. Lewis, chairman of the Progressive Corporation, pledged $101 million to Princeton University to support creative and performing arts.

- Ronald P. Stanton, chairman of Transammonia, pledged $100 million to Yeshiva University in New York.

- Johns Hopkins University received a pledge of $100 million from an anonymous donor to fund programming in the humanities, medicine, and public health.

- John Arrillaga, co-founder of Peery Arrillaga, gave $100 million to Stanford University for unspecified purposes.

Several large grants made in 2006 by foundations supported education, including:[5]

- The Jerome L. Greene Foundation gave $200 million to Columbia University to fund a neuroscience center for brain research.

- The Robert W. Woodruff Foundation granted to $261.5 million to Emory University to build a model patient-centered health care system and for other purposes at the Atlanta institution.

Council for Aid to Education reports 9.4 percent increase in 2005-2006

Alumni and other individual donors to education gave just over half of the estimated $28 billion going to colleges and universities, according to the Council for Aid to Education's annual survey, Voluntary Support for Education.[6] Alumni giving increased by 18.3 percent in the 2005–2006 fiscal year, and gifts from individuals who are not alumni rose by 14 percent. Figure 1 shows the share of total estimated higher education giving from each source of donation, over a 10-year period.

Figure 1
Sources of voluntary support of higher education
1996–1997 to 2005–2006
($ in billions)

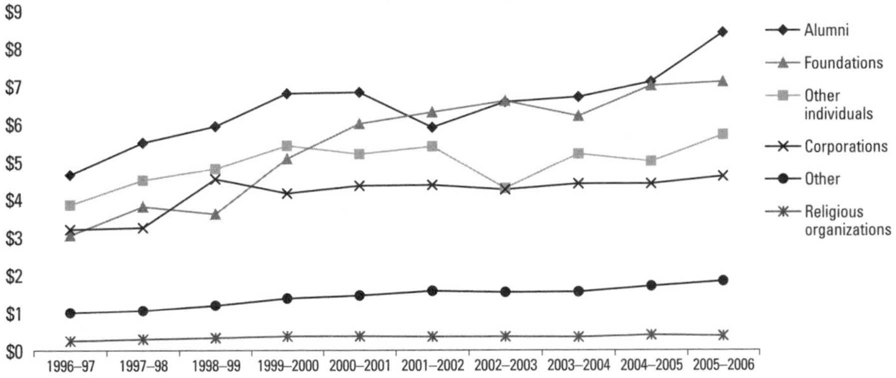

Source: Council for Aid to Education

The Council for Aid to Education noted in its report that nearly 30 percent of foundation grants to institutions of higher education were from family foundations. Families are using foundations as a vehicle for contributions that previously would have been considered donations from their personal assets and counted in the "individuals" category. The trend toward increasing support from foundations can be seen in Figure 2, which compares the percentage of the total estimated contributions to higher education by type of donor over 10 years. Foundation gifts in 2005–2006 were just over 23 percent of the total. In 1998–99, they were 17.7 percent.

Figure 2
Percentage of voluntary support for education from each type of donor

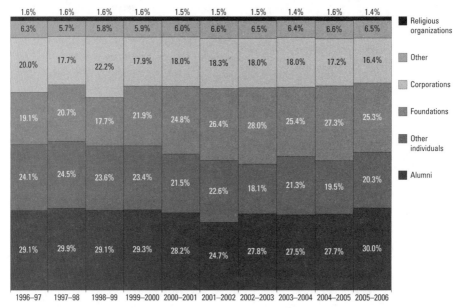

Data: Council for Aid to Education

Giving to university-based hospitals or schools of medicine is included in giving to education

Funding for programs to develop cancer treatment was prominent in 2006. Among the largest gifts were:

- Dan L. Duncan, chairman of Enterprise Products, and his family pledged $100 million to Baylor College of Medicine to support faculty recruitment, research, and the cancer center.[7]

- Melvin Simon and his wife Bren, of the Simon Property Group, donated $50 million to the Indiana University Cancer Center in Indianapolis to create an endowment to attract researchers, support laboratory research, and support expansion of the patient-care facility.[8]

- Harvard Medical School (MA), Johns Hopkins School of Medicine (MD), MIT (MA), Stanford University School of Medicine (CA), and the University of Chicago Pritzker School of Medicine were among six recipients of a $120 million gift given by the charitable trust of Daniel K. Ludwig to support cancer research.[9]

2006 Pension Protection Act spurs some giving; too early for complete assessment

The National Committee on Planned Giving (NCPG) reported a poll in which it found that at least 157 retirement account gifts of more than $4.3 million were donated as result of the Pension Protection Act by the end of 2006.[10] Through spring 2007, nearly 3,000 IRA gifts had been reported to

the NCPG with a combined value of $56 million.[11] The NCPG poll reaches members of that organization and is not a representative sample of all institutions receiving these types of gifts.

The Pension Protection Act permitted transfers from an Individual Retirement Account to a charity, and the donor would not be subject to income tax (but could not also take a charitable deduction for the gift). Colleges and universities are some of the key beneficiaries of this type of gift, at least in part because these institutions have a development staff and maintain current addresses for alumni as much as possible.

Complete impact of Katrina Emergency Tax Relief Act still unknown

The *Chronicle of Philanthropy* reported mixed results for the impact of the

WHAT THIS MEANS TO YOU

Congressional action in 2005 and 2006 created two special opportunities for donors, the Katrina Emergency Relief Tax Act in 2005 and the Pension Protection Act of 2006, both of which loosened restrictions on charitable deductions. Higher education institutions, in particular, seem to be the beneficiaries of these short-term legislative provisions. This may be in part because very wealthy donors favor education, but it is also the case that educational institutions are highly likely to have staffed development offices that can implement rapid changes in gift processing and solicitation.

Every type of organization should consider how to put a "good news" contingency plan in place to mobilize volunteers and staff when legislative or economic changes create a particularly favorable environment for fundraising.

At least through the end of 2007, and longer if legislation is enacted to make this provision longer-lasting, continue to promote gifts from IRA rollovers from those aged 70½ and older. This is a very efficient giving vehicle for donors who have IRAs and other pension plans and reliable sources for their retirement needs.

Katrina Emergency Tax Relief Act (KETRA),[12] a law passed by the U.S. Congress following the 2005 hurricane disasters. KETRA allowed donors of cash to deduct up to 100 percent of their income if the recipient was a qualified charitable organization (not a private foundation or a supporting organization). Prior to KETRA, there were caps for donations of 50 percent for contributions to charitable organizations and 30 percent for donations to private foundations.

Higher education institutions were reportedly among the recipients of some of the largest gifts, with Cornell University raising as much as $30 million, and Haverford College in Pennsylvania raising more than $3.1 million.

Billion-dollar campaigns now multibillion dollar campaigns

The first billion-dollar campaign in higher education closed in late 2002, when the University of Southern California raised $2.85 billion—after an initial goal of $1 billion launched in 1993.[13] In 2006, at least five billion-dollar campaigns were announced, and four of them had goals of $3 or $4 billion. Table 4 lists the announced campaigns and the amount raised, per tables printed in the *Chronicle of Philanthropy* throughout 2006. Note that CASE campaign standards state that a campaign should be no more than seven years long.[14]

Table 4
Billion-dollar higher education campaigns announced in 2006

Institution	Announced	Planned to close	Goal ($)	Raised ($)	As of
Cornell University & Weill Cornell Medical College (NY)	October 2006	December 2011	$4B	$1.03B	November 9, 2006
Columbia University (NY)	September 2006	December 2011	$4B	$1.62B	October 12, 2006
Liberty University (VA)	May 2006	December 2011	$1B	$5M	September 28, 2006
University of Virginia	September 2006	December 2011	$3B	$1.24B	October 12, 2006
Yale University (CT)	September 2006	December 2011	$3B	$1.3B	October 12, 2006

Data: The campaign report appearing in the *Chronicle of Philanthropy*.
No billion-dollar campaigns were closed in 2006, according to the *Chronicle*'s information.

Reports released about earlier years

Studies about giving to education fall into three types: Studies of donors and their priorities; studies of fundraising vehicles and the success found with them; and academic studies that explore a particular topic with strict methods. In 2006, some of each appeared and are summarized as follows.

Education giving is top priority for high net-worth donors

The *Bank of America Study of High Net-Worth Philanthropy*, conducted by the Center on Philanthropy at Indiana University, found that among households with $200,000 or more in income and/or $1 million or more in net worth, education garnered a large share of the gift, with 21.7 percent of the total just slightly behind religion at 22 percent.[15]

On average, the donors in this survey gave $25,852 to education in 2005. Nearly 8 in 10 high net-worth households (79.6 percent) contributed to educational organizations in 2005. Nearly two-thirds (64.6 percent) of the respondents to this study, which reached more than 1,000 households, said they had given to a capital campaign (not necessarily in education) in 2005. These donors also more frequently reported making stock gifts than cash contributions.

CASE campaign study finds trends toward longer campaigns and an "80:10" Rule

In its campaign study for 2005–2006, the Council for Advancement and Support of Education (CASE) found that 22 percent of institutions reported campaigns of more than 7 years, up from 18 percent in 2004–2005 and 13 percent in 2003–2004.[17]

Among all types of institutions in the study, on average, the top 1 percent of donors accounted for 59 percent of funds raised among the nearly 200 institutions reporting. The top 10 percent of donors accounted for 80 percent of donations. In fundraising, the "conventional wisdom" has been that 80 percent of the funding comes from 20 percent of the donors. The CASE

WHAT THIS MEANS TO YOU

High stock market prices tend to reassure donors about future financial security. Donors who feel financially secure give more.[16]

Most educational institutions during good market years promote stock gifts. Remind the donors that their cost of giving equals only the original purchase price of the stock, and all the market appreciation on top of the stock's purchase price may be deducted.

Stock gifts make sense during weak markets, too. Some donors find it helpful to purge their portfolios of nonperforming stocks, either those with low dividends or where value has fallen. Donors who sell these stocks themselves, then give the proceeds of the sale to your institution, get a tax benefit from a capital loss (if the stock sold below the donor's cost basis) and a charitable deduction for the by-then cash contribution.

data suggest that the top donor group is increasingly important in campaigns at nearly every type of institution.

Figure 3 shows data from the past three campaign surveys, and the percentage of donations that came from the 10 percent of donors giving the most. The values for 2003–2004 are, overall, higher than for following years. This reflects trends in that year for fewer large gifts.[18]

Figure 3
Percentage of total campaign dollars from 10 percent of donors giving largest gifts, 2003–04 to 2005–06

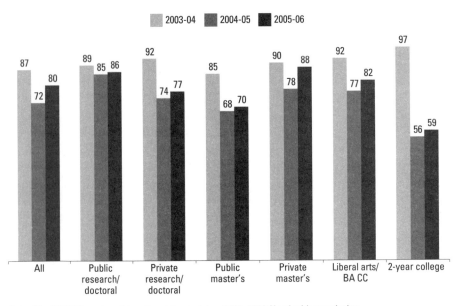

Data: *The CASE Report on Educational Fundraising, 2005–2006.* Used with permission.

Mixed impact of changes on giving from state appropriation declines and tuition hikes

Ying Liu of Vanderbilt University analyzed private giving by alumni, non-alumni, corporations, and foundations at 161 public four-year colleges and universities in the United States.[19] Findings include:

- Institutional type and endowment growth positively affected corporate and foundation giving. Doctoral/ research universities raised the most money from these institutional donors.

- Increases in tuition positively affected alumni giving.

- Increases in tuition negatively affected corporate, foundation, and total private giving. That is, declines in institutional giving exceeded growth in alumni giving, so that the overall impact of a tuition increase was a drop in private giving.

- Increases in state appropriations had a negative impact on alumni giving and a positive impact on corporate giving.

At state or public colleges and universities, when giving by alumni rises with tuition increases, there are several possible reasons that bear further research. These include:

a) Institutions implement fundraising programs when appropriations decline, so alumni are asked more often to give;

b) Tuition hikes are measures of school quality, so giving rises as perceptions of quality increase;

c) Increased tuition limits the number of students who can attend, which heightens the market value of the degree obtained because fewer students matriculate; or

d) Gifts are made for scholarships or other funding to reduce the need for future tuition hikes.

It is not clear from the research to date which (or what else) is driving giving.

Historically Black Colleges and Universities (HBCUs) have opportunity to strengthen their case for support

Rodney Cohen, an independent researcher in Atlanta, Georgia, found in a study of 1,000 alumni of four HBCUs that the communications and materials from the alma mater are not persuading alumni to give.[20] Alumni in this study were likely to be philanthropic toward other institutions (notably their religious congregations) and felt that their alma maters did not need their financial support.

Matching gifts increased giving; 1:1 match effective, higher match ratios had no greater impact

A study conducted by Dean Karlan of Yale University and John List of the University of Chicago found that of more than 50,000 direct mail donors, contributions were 19 percent higher from those who received matching-gift solicitations as opposed to those who were merely asked to make a gift. The study also found that larger matching gift ratios (3:1) had no greater impact on giving than smaller ratios (1:1).[21]

WHAT THIS MEANS TO YOU

Research shows that one way to leverage major gifts is to work with these donors to create challenge or matching campaigns to attract (and later, retain) new annual-fund donors.

Key data from annual studies summarized

Table 5 presents three years of data from several studies appearing annually about giving to education. Web site addresses are provided so readers can access the full reports.

Table 5
Key findings from other studies about giving to educational organizations

$5 million dollar list, gifts from individuals to education Center on Philanthropy at Indiana University, www.philanthropy.iupui.edu (percentages exclude gifts to foundations)			
	2004	2005	2006
Number, higher education	136	196	195
Largest gift, higher education	$300 million from Wisconsin United for Health Foundation, one gift each of that amount to Medical College of Wisconsin and to University of Wisconsin Medical School	$165 million to Oklahoma State University for the athletics program from T. Boone Pickens, announced in early 2006 as made in the last days of 2005	$105 to Stanford University from Phillip H. Knight, for the business school
Dollars to higher education as percentage of all gifts on list	46.8 percent	64.7 percent	56.2 percent
Number, K–12 education	4	11	16
Largest gift, K–12 education	$45 million, a group of anonymous donors to Jewish day schools in Boston	$50 million to public schools in Mississippi from James Barksdale	$25 million to the Peddie School from the estate of Randall Terry
Dollars to K–12 education as a percentage of all gifts on list	1.8 percent	3.7 percent	3.9 percent

Foundation Giving Trends: Update on Funding Priorities Grants to education Foundation Center, www.foundationcenter.org			
	2003	2004	2005
Average grant amount	$142,910	$141,128	$150,748
Median grant amount	$28,000	$30,000	$30,000
Education funding as a percentage of grant dollars	24.5 percent	23.4 percent	24.0 percent

CASE Report of Educational Fundraising Campaigns
Council for Advancement and Support of Education, www.case.org

From all reporting institutions	2003–2004	2004–2005	2005–2006
Percentage of goal received from top 10 percent of donors	87	72	80
Percentage of goal received from top 1 percent of donors	66	54	59
Average percentage of alumni who gave to campaign	29	24	25
Planned (deferred) commitments as percent of total (present value)	10	12	13

National Independent School Facts at a Glance
National Association of Independent Schools
Taken from reports dated 2003–2004; 2004–2005, and 2005–2006, www.nais.org

	2003–2004	2004–2005	2005–2006
Average annual giving per student	$1,348	$1,489	$1,572
Average endowment per student	$29,246	$33,668	$33,639
Giving by alumni			
Average gift	$276	$302	$357
Participation	20.7%	20.9%	16.3%
Giving by current parents			
Average gift	$859	$975	$1,039
Participation	63.2%	64.1%	63.1%
Giving by trustees			
Average gift	$4,334	$4,867	$5,147
Participation	92.3%	93.1%	93.1%

Voluntary Support of Education
Council for Aid to Education*
www.cae.org

	2003–2004	2004–2005	2005–2006
Giving by alumni	$905	$971	$1,195
Average gift			
Participation	12.8%	12.4%	11.9%

*CAE does not measure trustee giving or parent giving in ways that are comparable to the NAIS research.

IRS tax-exempt organizations in education Charities and Other Tax-exempt Organizations, 2001, 2002, and 2003 *Statistics of Income Bulletin*, www.irs.gov			
	2001	2002	2003
Number of organizations	41,153	45,163	47,117
Charitable revenue**	$52.47 billion	$54.73 billion	$59.86 billion

**Includes direct public support (from individuals, foundations, and corporations, as in *Giving USA*) and indirect public support (transfers from other nonprofits, such as United Way, or a membership association or other collective funding source).

1 The education subsector includes colleges and universities, scholarship funds such as the United Negro College Fund and Scholarship America, private schools for grades kindergarten through high school, tutoring programs, private libraries, supporting organizations raising funds for public libraries or public schools, vocational institutes, organizations formed to provide adult continuing education, and educational service organizations, including the foundations formed by fraternities and sororities. Educational organizations are in section B of the National Taxonomy of Exempt Entities. The *Giving USA* estimate includes funds given to public higher education, thanks to the estimates created by the Council for Aid to Education.

2 *Giving USA* sent surveys to 713 educational organizations, including every organization that raised $20 million or more in charitable gifts in 2003, 2004, or 2005, and a random sample of medium-sized and small organizations. Responses came from 112 organizations (a return rate of 15.7 percent). Not all responses were complete, leaving 106 that could be analyzed. Nearly one-third (31.9 percent) of the large organizations responded. Large organizations account for about one-half of all giving to education.

3 Press release, Contributions to colleges and universities up by 9.4 percent to $28 billion: Strong growth driven by personal giving, February 21, 2007, www.cae.org.

4 *Chronicle of Philanthropy*, January 11, 2007, www.philanthropy.com.

5 Ibid.

6 Press release, Contributions to colleges and universities up by 9.4 percent to $28 billion: Strong growth driven by personal giving, February 21, 2007, www.cae.org.

7 Baylor College of Medicine Press Release, viewed at www.bcm.edu/news/packages/cancercenter.cfm.

8 No author, Indiana U. Receives $50-Million for Its Cancer Center; Other Recent Gifts, *Chronicle of Philanthropy*, December 7, 2006.

9 A. Howard, Tycoon's Trust Awards $120-Million to Six Cancer-Research Centers, *Chronicle of Philanthropy*, November 23, 2006, www.philanthropy.com.

10 P. Panepento, Older Americans Flock to Give in Response to Tax Incentives, *Chronicle of Philanthropy*, December 7, 2006.

11 J. Stewart, Gifts from IRAs on the rise, *Baltimore Sun*, March 18, 2007. Viewed at www.lexis-nexis.com.

12 H. Hall, A Special Katrina-Inspired Tax Break Produced Mixed Results for Charities, *Chronicle of Philanthropy*, January 26, 2006, http://philanthropy.com.

13 *Giving USA 2004*, page 113.

14 *CASE Management and Reporting Standards: Standards for Annual Giving and Campaigns in Educational Fund Raising* (3rd edition), 2004, pg. 79, "CASE recommends that no campaign exceed seven years in duration.

15 Center on Philanthropy, *Bank of America*

High Net-Worth Philanthropy Study, October 2006, http://newsroom.bankofamerica.com/index.php?s=press_kit&item=63.

16 This finding is confirmed in a number of studies, including work by Independent Sector and others. For a dramatic result released in 2006 and presented in graphic form, see the Center on Philanthropy at Indiana University, *Bank of America Study of High Net-Worth Philanthropy*, page 17.

17 Council for Advancement and Support of Education, *The CASE Report of Educational Fundraising Campaign, 2005–2006,* released mid-2007, www.case.org.

18 *Chronicle of Philanthropy*, Center on Philanthropy Million Dollar List, and other sources.

19 Y. Liu, Determinants of Private Giving to Public Colleges and Universities, *International Journal of Educational Advancement*, Vol. 6(2), 2006, pages 119–140.

20 R. Cohen, Black college alumni giving; A study of perceptions, attitudes, and giving behaviors of alumni donors at selected Historically Black Colleges and Universities, *International Journal of Educational Advancement*, May 2006.

21 H. Hall, Bigger Matching Gifts Don't Produce More Donors, *Chronicle of Philanthropy*, June 15, 2006, www.philanthropy.com. An article summarizing the study can be viewed at aida.econ.yale.edu/karlan/papers/MatchingGrant.pdf.

13 Giving to foundations

- In, 2006, giving to foundations reached and estimated $49.260 billion—an increase of 7.4 percent (4.1 percent adjusted for inflation) from the revised estimate of $27.46 billion for 2005.

- Giving to foundations represented 10.0 percent of total estimated charitable contributions in the United States in 2006.

- Gifts to foundations in 2006 include major donations of Warren Buffett ($1.9 billion), Herbert and Marion Sandler ($1.3 billion), and Bernard Osher ($0.7 billion) as well as bequests from the estates of Jim Joseph ($500 million) and Mary Joan Palevsky ($212.8 million).

- FoundationSearch America showed 2,146 newly registered foundations established since January 2006, including trusts and scholarship funds. Many new foundations receive contributions that are not included in the gifts received by grantmaking foundations. For 2006, an unknown amount was given to foundations that are not (yet) grantmaking.

- Giving to foundations has grown an average of 13.6 percent a year (9.1 percent adjusted for inflation) since data began in 1978. In the past 10 years, giving to foundations has increased an annual average of 14.6 percent (11.7 percent adjusted for inflation).

Basis for the estimate

For 2006, estimated gifts to foundations includes an estimate of $26 billion to grantmaking independent and community foundations and an estimated $3.5 billion for the fair-market value of product donations to operating foundations that provide patient assistance. The estimate is developed jointly by Giving USA and the research department of the Foundation Center. Donations to corporate foundations are treated as corporate donations and are not counted in the "giving to foundations" amount.

Major gifts to foundations announced in 2006

The largest-ever foundation gift, a plan to give more than $30 billion over 20 years to the Bill & Melinda Gates Foundation, was announced in June 2006 by Warren Buffett. Mr. Buffett selected the Gates Foundation to receive the bulk of his personal fortune and directed additional gifts to foundations established by members of his family.[1]

In addition to Mr. Buffett's gifts, other major donors recognized as among the top 60 philanthropists of 2006 contributed an estimated $4 billion to foundations in 2006.[2] Table 1 summarizes the largest foundation gifts reported as paid in 2006.

Table 1

Major announced contributions to foundations, 2006

Amount paid to foundation ($ millions)	Donor	Recipient
1,700	Herbert and Marion Sandler	Sandler Family Supporting Foundation
1,600	Warren Buffett	Bill & Melinda Gates Foundation
723	Bernard A. Osher	Bernard Osher Foundation
500	Jim Joseph (Estate)	Joseph Foundation
213	Mary Joan Palevsky (Estate)	California Community Foundation
160	T. Boone Pickens	T. Boone Pickens Foundation
151	Warren Buffett	Susan Thompson Buffett Foundation
138	Eli and Edythe L. Broad	Broad Foundation
100	Lorry I. Lokey	Lorry Lokey Supporting Foundation
80	Henry M. and Wendy J. Paulson	Bobolink Foundation
74	Joseph Neubauer	Neubauer Family Foundation
69	Jon L. Stryker	Arcus Foundation
56	Wallace D. Malone	Malone Family Foundation
53	Warren Buffett	Howard G. Buffett Foundation
53	Warren Buffett	NoVo Foundation
53	Warren Buffett	Susan A. Buffett Foundation
$5,723	Total	

Amounts reported as paid to the recipient by the *Chronicle of Philanthropy*, February 22, 2007. The *Chronicle* listed more foundation recipients than appear here. This table stops at $50 million.

Donor-advised funds are not the same as foundations, but fundraising processes are similar

Donor-advised funds organized by for-profit investment firms are categorized in the "public-society benefit" subsector, as they are charitable organizations that receive funds, which are then allocated to numerous other types of nonprofits. They are not considered foundations, nor is giving to them tracked with giving to foundations. The largest donor-advised funds reported contributions exceeding $2 billion in the fiscal year that ended June 30, 2006. This is summarized in the pubic-society benefit chapter of *Giving USA*.

WHAT THIS MEANS TO YOU

Charitable organizations should monitor foundation formation, especially in their own geographic region. The vast majority of foundations give to local causes. Information about foundation formation can be found through search engines, including FoundationSearch America and the Foundation Center.

It appears that an increasing number of donors are using foundations as a vehicle to direct their personal giving in their lifetime.

Studies of giving to foundations

The Foundation Center, the Columbus Foundation, and FoundationSearch America all provide information about giving to foundations. In addition, surveys of households inform our understanding of who gives to foundations. Studies released in 2006 are summarized below.

New foundation formation and new gifts to foundations increase rate of growth in 2005 compared with earlier years of decade

The Foundation Center reported increased rates of growth for new gifts to foundations and new foundation formation in 2005, especially compared with 2001 and 2004.[3] In 2005, the gifts to independent, community, and operating foundations were $27.47 billion. The Foundation Center attributes this to:

- Increases in wealth largely due to corporate profits and a strong stock market;

- Younger donors, who are forming foundations and providing annual funding to them for annual grantmaking, with the intent (perhaps) to endow them later;

- Potentially, efforts through organizations such as New Ventures in Philanthropy and others to increase formation of foundations as one of many possible giving vehicles; and

- A rise in the fair-market value of product donations to operating foundations, reaching $3.2 billion in 2005, from $1.7 billion in 2004.

The Foundation Center reports 71,095 grantmaking foundations in 2005, including 63,059 independent (private) foundations, 707 community foundations, 4,722 operating foundations, and 2,607 corporate foundations. *Giving USA* does not count gifts to corporate foundations because those donations are typically paid out in grants to recipient charities within a year.

The Foundation Center is studying the percentage of new gifts that are granted within a year (pass-through). *Giving USA* will incorporate findings from this study in its future editions.

Giving to funds and foundations by the wealthiest households

The *Bank of America Study of High Net-Worth Philanthropy* conducted by the Center on Philanthropy at Indiana

About 20 percent of high net-worth households in a national study reported that they have established a foundation.

Donors typically take the initiative to establish a foundation or a donor-advised fund as a result of a larger financial planning process that takes into consideration multiple goals beyond tax deductions. For example, 70 percent of the households in the study discuss their philanthropy with their children, suggesting that family considerations play a role, and 35 percent allow children to participate in giving decisions with the family.

WHAT THIS MEANS TO YOU

University[4] found that 33 percent of households with net worth (including a home) of $1 million or more contributed to a foundation OR a donor-advised fund (commercial or housed at a charity, as at a community foundation, university, or other type of organization). On average, the donors reported giving $114,683 to these vehicles, which are typically a method to set aside money for future gifts. These contributions accounted for 17 percent of the total giving to all causes reported by these households.

Key findings from other studies

To permit readers to compare findings over time, *Giving USA* presents some key data points from the Foundation Center and the Community Foundation studies from 2003 through 2005 in Table 2. Web site addresses are provided to help readers quickly access the original reports.

Table 2
Key findings from other studies about giving to foundations

Gifts to foundations* *Foundation Yearbook*, 2005, 2006 editions and *Foundation Growth and Giving Estimates*, 2007 www.foundationcenter.org			
	2003	2004	2005
Independent foundations, new gifts received	$15.85 billion	$13.65 billion	$17.37 billion
Community foundations	$3.48 billion	$3.86 billion	$5.59 billion
Operating foundations	$2.30 billion	$2.81 billion	$4.51 billion
Total for these three foundation types	$21.63 billion	$20.32 billion	$27.46 billion

*Data for 2006 will be available from the Foundation Center in 2008.

Gifts to community foundations, including inactive ones Survey of community foundations Columbus Foundation, www.columbusfoundation.org			
	2003	2004	2005
New gifts received	$3.80 billion	$4.20 billion	$5.70 billion

---

1   *Chronicle of Philanthropy*, February 22, 2007, www.philanthropy.com.
2   Ibid.
3   S. Lawrence et al., *Foundation Growth and Giving Estimates, 2007*, April 4, 2007, www.foundationcenter.org.
4   Center on Philanthropy, *Bank of America High Net-Worth Philanthropy Study*, October 2006. The Bank of America Study is the first scientific study (using a random sample) of high net-worth households and their philanthropy. Prior studies had been based on samples from client lists. This study defined high net-worth households as those with income of $200,000 or more or net worth of $1 million or more. More than 1,400 surveys were returned. The first report, released in October, 2006, included about 1,000 respondents. Later reports appeared in 2007. See http://newsroom.bankofamerica.com/index.php?s=press_kit&item=63 for a copy of the October 2006 report.

14 Giving to human services

- Giving to organizations in the human services subsector is estimated to be $29.56 billion in 2006. This is 10.0 percent of total estimated giving.

- In current dollars, giving to human services declined by an estimated 9.2 percent in 2006. Adjusted for inflation, this is a drop of 12.0 percent.

- The decline estimated for 2006 follows exceptional growth in 2005 related to contributions for disaster relief and to bequests of $1.3 billion reported by one charitable organization.

- After adjusting for disaster relief gifts estimated for 2005 and 2006, giving to human services is $27.94 billion in 2005, which includes bequests, and $28.86 billion for 2006.

- The rate of change without considering disaster relief giving in 2005 or 2006 or the billion-dollar bequest in 2005 is 3.3 percent (0.1 percent adjusted for inflation).

- The 40-year average rate of growth in giving to human services is 5.7 percent (1.5 percent adjusted for inflation). In the past decade (1997–2006), the average growth rate in human services has been 9.4 percent (8.9 percent adjusted for inflation).

Giving USA findings for benchmarking giving to human services organizations, 2006

As with all *Giving USA* estimates, the amount estimated for giving to organizations in the human services subsector includes gifts received of cash, cash equivalents (securities), and in-kind gifts (artwork, patents, real estate, and other items of value). *Giving USA* tries to exclude from its estimates the value of deferred or planned gift commitments and new pledges.

Each year, *Giving USA* surveys organizations to develop an estimate of the distribution of charitable giving by subsector. For human services organizations,[1] Table 1 summarizes the average and median[2] amounts raised by organizations providing data about 2005 and 2006, categorized by organizational size.[3] The average raised at large organizations—excluding outliers—fell from nearly $44 million in 2005 to just over $32 million in 2006. The other sizes of organizations saw an increase, on average, in 2006 compared with 2005.

Giving to human services

Table 1
Charitable revenue received by human services organizations
in 2005 and 2006, by organizational size

Organizational size	Number of completed surveys	2005 average ($)	2005 median ($)	2006 average ($)	2006 median ($)
Large	17	43,696,515	4,387,200	32,387,398	4,620,059
Moderately sized	13	5,872,875	6,500,000	6,383,316	6,972,736
Medium-sized	33	1,902,686	1,444,701	2,027,961	1,251,205
Small	26	229,081	30882	278,363	40,500

Large denotes organizations that receive $20 million or more in charitable revenue; *moderately sized* organizations have charitable revenue between $5 million and $19.99 million; *medium-sized* is used for organizations having charitable revenue between $1 million and $4.99 million, and *small* is for organizations that have charitable revenue of less than $1 million.

Table 2 summarizes the average and median increases or decreases in charitable revenue reported for 2006 by organizational size.

- Nearly 6 in 10 (65 percent) of the large organizations saw an increase, with average growth of $1.5 million. However, the average $34.8 million decline in the 35 percent of organizations that reported a drop vastly overshadowed the increase in the majority.

- Moderately sized organizations responding to the survey were likely to report an increase, with 7 in 10 seeing a result for 2006 that was $1.2 million more, on average, than in 2005.

- Medium-sized organizations were also very likely to report growth in charitable gifts, with 64 percent showing an increase averaging close to $620,000.

- Almost 6 in 10 (58 percent) of small organizations reported an increase, with an average change of about $129,430.

For all sizes considered together, when comparing dollars received in charitable gifts between 2005 and 2006:

62.9 percent saw an increase;

28.1 percent saw charitable giving drop in 2006; and

9.0 percent reported a change that was 1 percent or less.

Table 3 shows bequest receipts by organizational size. The average for 2005 includes one organization that received an exceptionally large bequest. The median rose in 2006 for all but the small organizations.

Table 2
Increases or decreases in charitable revenue of human services organizations, 2006

Organizational size	Number	Percentage of organizations in size group	Average change ($)	Average change (%)	Median change ($)	Median change (%)
Large						
Increase	11	65	1,544,177	17	485,624	13
Decrease	6	35	-34,873,490	-33	-18,485,761	-29
No change	–	–				
Total*	17	100				
All large organizations			-11,309,117	-1	82,952	4
Moderately sized						
Increase	9	69	1,260,585	35	561,417	28
Decrease	4	31	-1,177,384	-12	-1,114,754	-13
No change	–	–				
Total*	13	100				
All moderately sized organizations			319,644	20	160,043	17
Medium-sized						
Increase	21	64	619,423	38	246,464	14
Decrease	8	24	-1,108,304	-38	-1,066,798	-41
No change	4	12				
Total*	33	100				
All medium-sized organizations			125,276	15	15,062	4
Small						
Increase	15	58	129,434	106	10,000	43
Decrease	7	27	-94,384	-32	-25,000	-17
No change	4	15	125	0	0	0
Total*	26	100				
All small organizations			51,235	19	500	6

*Total does not always equal 100 due to rounding.

Table 3
Bequests received by human services organizations in 2005 and 2006
by organizational size

Organizational size	Percentage with bequest revenues	2005 average ($)	2005 median ($)	2006 average ($)	2006 median ($)
Large	63	202,625,631	102,000	35,566,602	159,962
Moderate	57	1,226,337	295,940	1,190,875	485,230
Medium	53	390,875	51,867	494,553	119,416
Small*	11	57,806	23,318	78,550	2,012

*Three small human services organizations provided bequest information. The result is summarized here but it is not sufficient data to use to generalize to all small human services nonprofits.

Million-dollar gifts to human services organizations increase in number and amount in 2006 compared with 2005

The Center on Philanthropy's Million Dollar List recorded 103 gifts in 2006 of $1 million or more from living individuals, estates, foundations, and corporations for human services organizations, almost doubling the recorded million-dollar gifts from 2005. Donations totaled $344 million, more than triple what was recorded in 2005. The three largest gifts announced by individuals or estates in the media and found for the Million Dollar List are as follows:

- The estate of Hector Guy and Doris Di Stefano gave $33 million to the Salvation Army. The Di Stefanos' wealth derived from UPS shares that Mrs. Di Stefano received as an inheritance.[4]

- Stanley Druckenmiller of Pittsburgh gave $25 million to the endowment for Harlem Children's Zone in New York City.[5]

- The Charles E. Lakin family of Omaha, Nebraska, gave two donations totaling $12 million to construct a center that will house five social services charities in Council Bluffs, Iowa.[6]

The Chronicle of Philanthropy's annual list of the largest nonprofit charities in the U.S., the Philanthropy 400, reported that two human services organizations ranked in the top 10 for recipients of philanthropic dollars in the U.S. in 2005.[7] The Salvation Army ranked second, raising $3.6 billion, and the American Red Cross came in fourth with $1.3 billion. United Way, which is the largest organization on the Philanthropy 400, is classified in the public-society benefit subsector, although much funding contributed to United Way is allocated to human services providers.

Conditions for the disadvantaged continue to decline, requiring an increase for human service organizations to meet the needs

During 2006, a number of sources reported growing needs for social services in communities, which occurred simultaneously with decreases in funding. This placed continued strain on human services organizations' capability to deliver social services and to find and develop additional funding.

- A study released by Baruch College found that more than 60 percent of survey respondents—more than 100 human-service agency leaders in New York—believe conditions for the poor declined in 2005, and 40 percent said conditions are also worse for immigrants, at-risk youth, and older adults.[9]

- A survey conducted by Catholic Charities USA found that assistance requests from organizations grew much faster than the funds needed to provide the services.[10] Around three-quarters (76 percent) of the 88 chapters surveyed nationally reported that it is harder to meet the growing needs of the people they serve, and 99 percent say the greatest need is financial contributions. Regarding funding:

  – 37 percent of surveyed Catholic Charities USA agencies reported increases in donations from individuals, while 21 percent reported a decline in 2006;

  – 25 percent reported a decrease in government funding; and

  – 20 percent of agencies reported increases in foundation and corporate support, about 50 percent reported no change, and 10 percent reported a decline.

Studies document level of needs for specific human services

A number of nonprofit and government agencies released studies in 2006 documenting the extent of basic needs in the U.S.

- *Scanning the Horizon: Trends, Developments, and Innovations Impacting the Future of Child and Family Services*, published by the Alliance for Children and Families, showed an increase in American income inequality.[11] In a second income study, Opportunity Agenda and the Tides Center used data from the Economic Policy Institute. The study found that "wages

WHAT THIS MEANS TO YOU

Donors of large sums tend to favor organizations with a strong infrastructure to manage a significant dollar gift. Demonstrating your organization's effectiveness in financial management and its capacity to deliver services can help your charity raise more funds for its work.

Large charities become large just as large companies do, through name recognition, consumer or donor trust, and consistent delivery of services. Despite the fact that human services organizations historically have been comparatively small and many are neighborhood- or community-based, one study shows that there is a trend under way toward consolidation in the human services subsector, with organizations increasing in size.[8] It is not clear whether this is driven by funder concerns, organizational priorities, client needs, other factors, or a combination of many forces.

increased less than one percent in adjusted dollars between 1979 and 2003 for those in the bottom tenth of wage earners, but increased by 27 percent among the top wage-earning tenth during the same period."[12]

- *Hunger in America 2006*, a study of the national charitable response to hunger by America's Second Harvest, found that the need for private hunger-relief agencies' services remains high.[13] Among all client households served by food pantries and other hunger-relief programs, 70 percent are estimated to be food insecure (according to the U.S. government's official food security scale), and 33 percent experience hunger regularly.

- The U.S. Department of Housing and Urban Development (HUD) studied homelessness in 80 cities and estimates that 704,000 people nationally used emergency shelter or transitional housing from February through April 2005.[14] Using counts from 3,800 communities, HUD estimates that more than 750,000 people were in shelters or on the streets on one night in January 2005. The nation has capacity for an estimated 647,000 homeless on one night, either in emergency shelters or transitional housing.[15]

Disaster relief gifts continue to address needs; does not draw much away from other giving

Charitable donations for rebuilding efforts in countries affected by the December 2004 tsunami and for reconstruction in areas devastated in hurricanes Katrina, Rita, and Wilma continued in 2006. A summary of the events in the U.S. Gulf Coast appears in Chapter 6.

WHAT THIS
MEANS TO YOU

Reports issued in 2006 showed pronounced needs for food, shelter, employment, and other social services. Data in these reports can provide a national context as you prepare a case for support for the work your charity performs.

Increasingly, human services organizations are addressing immediate needs, as well as causes and longer-term solutions to these deep issues affecting society. Human services organizations would do well to position themselves as issue solvers, not just as immediate ameliorators of these profound issues.

Fundraising results improve when human services nonprofits become more savvy in fundraising, moving away from government support and seeking more private support. This requires an investment in the development enterprise.

Where appropriate, human services nonprofit organizations can conduct major capital campaigns for funding over more than one year. This helps to expand capacity to serve the poor on many levels. In this endeavor, donors will respond more positively to demonstrated results and transformation of people's lives.

WHAT THIS MEANS TO YOU

In most cases, disaster relief giving does not appear to replace giving to other causes. Exceptions may occur in amounts contributed for local use to national organizations collecting for disaster relief (United Way, American Red Cross, Salvation Army, and others).

Charities not engaged in disaster relief directly may decide to refrain from fundraising for a brief period out of respect for victims of a disaster, but the disaster event itself is not likely to be a reason for reduced receipts in the course of a year.

Donor fatigue has little effect on long-term giving

Many in the nonprofit world suspected that national disaster donations would negatively affect giving to organizations not involved with disaster relief—the concept of "donor fatigue." *Giving USA 2006* reported on the Center on Philanthropy's study, the *Philanthropic Giving Index (PGI)*, which found a striking difference between what fundraising professionals said they experienced (no substantial change in gifts received) compared with their perception of the state of nonprofits as a whole (dramatic falls in giving). One year after the hurricanes, the Center predicted that some organizations could experience a decrease in donations in the short term, but for the majority of nonrelief nonprofits, the impact would not be long term.[16]

Additional studies produced similar findings in 2006. The Conference Board found that about 90 percent of the 5,000 Americans surveyed who gave to causes directly related to 2005 hurricane relief also continued supporting their favorite charities.[17] A survey by the Association of Fundraising Professionals also found that 76 percent of the 506 fundraisers surveyed thought that they had raised as much or more money in 2005 compared with 2004,[18] and even higher percentages reported raising more in 2006 than in 2005.[19] The *Chronicle of Philanthropy*'s annual *Philanthropy 400* survey found that disaster donations did not account for much of the 13 percent growth in donations to America's largest charities in 2005 and that many organizations (human services and other) that are not involved in disaster relief still experienced a healthy rise in giving.[20]

Human services organizations criticized for disaster relief glitches; publicity might impact fundraising results for 2006

Throughout the year, the American Red Cross faced increased Congressional scrutiny and public doubts about its capability to respond to disasters.[21] While under investigation for allegations of fraud related to 2005 disaster relief efforts, the organization sought a new chief executive after the resignation of Marsha J. (Marty) Evans in late 2005.[22] As a result of continued criticism and an extensive review, the American Red Cross announced drastic changes to its governance practices in October 2006. Changes include halving its 50-member board and reducing influence by presidential appointees.[23] In April 2007, Mark Everson, previously commissioner of the Internal Revenue Service, was selected to be the next CEO at the American Red Cross.[24]

Habitat for Humanity was criticized for the speed of its disaster response. Eighteen months after the Gulf Coast hurricanes destroyed more than 250,000 homes, Habitat had rebuilt only 416 homes, with 300 more under construction. Habitat's response in the Gulf was called "halting and piecemeal" in comparison with its efforts following the 2004 tsunami, where it built and repaired 8,500 homes in Indonesia, Thailand, India, and Sri Lanka.[25] The *New York Times* suggests the slow pace of home construction in the U.S. is attributable to:

- The type of houses the organization tends to build in the United States;
- Complicated government regulation and insurance claims;
- Habitat's rigid procedures; and
- Working through independent local affiliates.

Studies of giving for human services

A number of studies that advance the understanding of contributions for human services organizations were released in 2006. Summaries of three appear as follows.

High net-worth households value opportunity to meet critical needs but give low percentage to human services
The *Bank of America Study of High Net-Worth Philanthropy*,[26] completed by the Center on Philanthropy at Indiana

University, found 5.2 percent of the amount given by households that qualified for the study directly supported programs that helped meet people's basic needs.[27] In answering questions about why they give, survey respondents overwhelmingly identified the option, "meet critical needs and support community causes" (86.3 percent identified this as important or very important). The average donation for meeting people's basic needs was $4,550. Three-quarters (75 percent) of high net-worth households contributed to at least one charitable organization that addressed people's needs for food, shelter, clothing, or other necessities.

A lower percentage of households gave to help meet basic needs in 2004 compared with 2002
Every two years, the Center on Philanthropy Panel Study (COPPS) asks families about their giving, reaching the same families in each wave. Data released in March 2007 show that in 2004, about 28 percent of households contributed to organizations that help meet basic needs. The average donation was $482 ($514 adjusted for inflation to 2006 dollars).[28] In the prior wave of COPPS, about giving in 2002, 34 percent gave for human services and the average donation was $459 ($514 in 2006 dollars).[29] In 2000 (COPPS 2001), 27 percent gave an average of $431 ($506 adjusted to 2006 dollars) to help meet basic needs. As of April 2007, researchers had not explored various potential explanations for the changes in the percentage of households giving to help meet basic needs and in the average donation amount.

Human services organizations remain a priority for foundation giving

The Foundation Center reports that human services organizations received 14.8 percent of grant dollars from foundations in 2005, compared with 13.9 percent in 2004.[30] This small increase parallels the slightly positive rate of growth in grant dollars since 1999. Education, 24.0 percent, and health, 20.8 percent, are the only subsectors that captured larger shares of foundation dollars than human services in 2005.

Scholarly research investigates changes in human services subsector

Scholars studying nonprofit organizations often focus on human services providers because of the importance of this subsector to public policy. A number of studies appeared in 2006. This section summarizes two studies that have some relationship to fundraising or donations for human services organizations.

Food pantries replacing government cash; hunger remains chronic

In their study of food assistance, Beth Osborne Daponte of Yale University and Shannon Bade of the Organization of the NorthEast report that the charitable food distribution network developed over 20 years as federal food policies shifted. That network now includes dozens of food banks, most of which are affiliated with America's Second Harvest, a facilitator of corporate food donations. Through the food banks, thousands of food pantries and food service sites (day care centers, senior centers, and so on) receive products to distribute. Food pantries now provide food for about 12 percent of U.S. adults, and one-third of these households have not applied for government food aid. Another third or so receive food stamps, but find that the stamps run out after two or three weeks. Because the distribution network relies on charitable, often volunteer-based organizations, Osborne Daponte and Bade write, "Needy people living in urban areas with a large number of charitable organizations have a much higher chance of being served than equally needy people ... in rural areas (p 681)."[31]

Profits promote organizational strengths, but do not enhance service delivery at human services charities

Baorong Guo at the University of Missouri-St. Louis analyzed data

WHAT THIS MEANS TO YOU

Giving to help meet basic needs is widespread, with 75 percent of high net-worth households and about a quarter to a third of average income households contributing. The challenge for charities in this subsector is to help donors have the right information and connection to the charity to inspire them to contribute more. The average gift amounts trail donation averages for many other secular causes, including education, health, the arts, and international affairs.

Government policies affect growth (or decline) in the number of charities in the human services sector. Networks such as America's Second Harvest for food banks give local charities access to national resources. Forming or joining these networks can be an important way to strengthen capacity and extend impact for a community-based charity.

Diversification of funding is an important step for charitable organizations. One often-considered option is selling services for fees. Increasing reliance on commercial activities can ease operational concerns about cash flow, but it does not necessarily enhance services to clients. The focus on selling or marketing might also conflict with donor relations and with volunteer engagement.

collected about human services non-profits, including revenue sources, mission fulfillment, reported reputation (by agency personnel), financial self-sufficiency, and other elements. A high level of commercial revenues (more than 30 percent of all revenues) was associated with comparatively low donations and low government funding. High commercial revenues were also associated with an organization's self-sufficiency, capability to attract and retain staff, and self-reported

reputation. When controlling for other variables, commercial revenues did not contribute positively to the organization's capability to attract donors and volunteers, fulfill its mission, or provide services.[32]

Key findings from annual studies summarized

Table 4 provides three years of findings from annual studies about giving to human services organizations. Web site addresses are provided so readers can access full reports.

Table 4

Key findings from other studies about giving to human services organizations

$5 million dollar list, gifts from individuals to human services Center on Philanthropy at Indiana University, www.philanthropy.iupui.edu			
	2004	2005	2006
Number of gifts to human services organizations	2	9	8
Largest gift to human services organizations	$1.5 billion to the Salvation Army in a challenge gift, estate of Joan Kroc, widow of the entrepreneur who created McDonald's	$15 million to Hebrew SeniorLife of Boston from Dr. Miriam and Sheldon G. Adelson to support the building of a proposed multi-generational community	$64 million to the Salvation Army in Phoenix from the estate of Ray and Joan Kroc to help expand and renovate the South Mountain Youth Center (asset transfer from previously announced gift)
Human services dollars given as percentage of all individual gifts on list of $5 million+	31.5 percent (the largest gift is unusually large for this subsector)	1.6 percent	2.8 percent

Foundation Giving Trends: Update on Funding Priorities Grants to human services organizations Foundation Center, www.foundationcenter.org			
	2003	2004	2005
Average grant amount	$72,100	$66,464	$71,159
Median grant amount	$25,000	$25,000	$25,000
Human services funding as a percentage of grant dollars (surveyed foundations, including corporate foundations)	15.6 percent	13.9 percent	14.8 percent

IRS tax-exempt organizations in human services Charities and other tax-exempt organizations. Statistics of Income Bulletin, www.irs.gov			
	2001	2002	2003
Number	91,131	94,735	100,835
Charitable revenue*	$59.09 billion	$58.81 billion	$58.76 billion

*Charitable revenue includes gifts and foundation grants (which is comparable to what *Giving USA* tracks) as well as government grants and allocations from other nonprofit agencies such as United Way and United Jewish Communities (which are not included in *Giving USA* estimates for contributions).

1   Giving to human services organizations includes contributions to organizations formed to strengthen public protection services, provide disaster relief or training to avoid disasters, offer social services, supply basic needs for food or shelter, assist with employment or job training, promote healthy development of youth, or offer recreational opportunities. The American Red Cross, the YMCA, food banks, legal clinics, and Olympic sports are all included in human services. In the National Taxonomy of Exempt Entities (NTEE), human services covers organizations in codes I, J, K, L, M, N, O, and P.

2   The median is the midpoint: Half of the organizations responding had higher charitable revenue; the other half had lower charitable revenue.

3   *Giving USA* sent surveys to 645 organizations in the human services subsector. Responses from 95 organizations (15 percent) form the basis for this analysis. Six organizations provided incomplete information or could not be analyzed because the change in their charitable revenues was extreme. The outliers were added at the end of the estimating process. The response rate among large organizations was 31 percent. Just 78 large organizations are estimated to receive approximately 60 percent of all dollars donated to the more than 92,500 human services organizations. The sample was selected based on charitable revenue received circa 2003 (includes some organizations that reported only in 2001 or only in 2002), supplemented with information obtained about human services organizations appearing on the *Chronicle of Philanthropy* list of the 400 charities receiving the most charitable revenue in 2004 and 2005.

4   Record-Breaking Giving, *Chronicle of Philanthropy*, February 22, 2007, www.philanthropy.com.

5   *Chronicle of Philanthropy*, October 26, 2006, http://philanthropy.com.

6   T. Shaw, Donor gives aid groups $12 million: Five service agencies will occupy a Bluffs center named for Omahan Charles Lakin, *Omaha World-Herald*, November 26, 2006, www.lexis-nexis.com.

7   Philanthropy 400, *Chronicle of Philanthropy*, October 2006, http://philanthropy.com.

8   D. Tucker and D. Sommerfeld, The larger they get: The changing size distributions of private human service organizations, *Nonprofit and Voluntary Sector Quarterly*, June 2006, http://nvsq.sagepub.com.

9   M. Souccar, Conditions in NYC worsening for poor: Survey. *Crain's New York Business*, March 27, 2006, www.newyorkbusiness.com.

10 2006 Catholic Charities USA Survey, *Catholic Charities USA*, November 2006, www.catholiccharitiesusa.org.

11 Alliance for Children and Families, *Scanning the Horizon: Trends, Developments, and Innovations Impacting the Future of Child and Family Services, Alliance for Children and Families, 2006,* www.alliance1.org.

12 Opportunity in America, *The Opportunity Agenda*, www.opportunityagenda.org.

13 *Hunger in America 2006*, America's Second Harvest: www.hungerinamerica.org.

14 HUD releases landmark homeless study, GovPro, March 1, 2007, www.govpro.com/News/Article/45629/.

15 Annual Homeless Assessment Report to Congress, *US Department of Housing and Urban Development Office of Community Planning and Development*, 2007, www.huduser.org/Publications/pdf/ahar.pdf.

16 Nonprofit fundraisers divided on whether hurricane relief giving is hurting nonrelief charities, Center on Philanthropy at Indiana University press release, www.philanthropy.iupui.edu.

17 The Conference Board, April 2006, www.conference-board.org.

18 Association of Fundraising Professionals, April 2006, www.afpnet.org.

19 Association of Fundraising Professionals, March 2007, www.afpnet.org.

20 Philanthropy 400, *Chronicle of Philanthropy*, October 2006, http://philanthropy.com.

21 Charity at a Crossroads, *Chronicle of Philanthropy*, January 12, 2006, www.philanthropy.com.

22 Fraud Investigations Raise New Questions for Beleaguered Red Cross, *Chronicle of Philanthropy*, April 6, 2006, www.philanthropy.com/premium/articles/v18/i12/12004601.htm.

23 ABCNews, "Red Cross Faces Post-Katrina Overhaul," October 30, 2006, http://abcnews.go.com/US/HurricaneKatrina/wireStory?id=2615868&CMP=OTC-RSSFeeds0312.

24 S. Hendrix, IRS Commissioner named to lead Red Cross, *Washington Post*, April 19, 2007, www.washingtonpost.com.

25 L. Eaton and S. Strom, Volunteer group lags in replacing Gulf houses, *New York Times*, February 22, 2006, www.nytimes.com.

26 This study, funded by Bank of America, analyzed responses from more than 1,000 American households with incomes over $200,000 and/or net worth of more than $1 million.

27 Center on Philanthropy at Indiana University, *Bank of America Study of High Net-Worth Philanthropy* , October 2006, www.philanthropy.iupui.edu.

28 Center on Philanthropy Panel Study, 2005 wave, questions asked about giving in 2004. Data released March 2007. Preliminary analysis by T. Yoshioka, April 2007.

29 Center on Philanthropy Panel Study, 2003 wave, questions asked about giving in 2002. Data released December 2004. Analysis by T. Yoshioka, May 2006.

30 The Foundation Center, *Foundation Giving Trends*, February 2007, http://foundationcenter.org.

31 B. Osborne Daponte and S. Bade, How the Private Food Assistance Network Evolved: Interactions between Public and Private Responses to Hunger, http://nvsq.sagepub.com.

32 B. Guo, Charity for Profit? Exploring Factors Associated with the Commercialization of Human Service Nonprofits, *Nonprofit and Voluntary Sector Quarterly*, March 2006, http://nvsq.sagepub.com.

15 Giving to health

- In 2006, giving to health organizations reached an estimated $20.22 billion, a decrease of 2.3 percent (-5.4 percent adjusted for inflation) from the revised estimate of $20.70 billion for 2005.

- Giving to health organizations represented 6.9 percent of total estimated charitable contributions in the United States in 2006.

- The Bill & Melinda Gates Foundation continued its commitment to world health and made major grants that far surpassed any other single donor's philanthropic support for the subsector.

- The new 40-year average rate of growth for giving to health is 5.9 percent (1.0 percent adjusted for inflation).

- Health giving rose an average 4.2 percent (1.4 percent adjusted for inflation) from 1997 through 2006.

Giving USA findings for benchmarking giving to health, 2006

Notes located at the end of this chapter explain what types of organizations are included in the health subsector and what gift types are counted in the annual Giving USA survey.[1]

Tables 1 through 3 summarize key findings from the Giving USA survey in 2007.[2] Table 1 summarizes the average and median amounts raised by health-related institutions in 2005 and 2006, based on organizational size. Overall, institutions in this subsector saw little change, or saw a decline, in the average total amount received. Except for medium-sized organizations, the median amount received also fell.

Table 1
Charitable revenue received by health organizations
in 2005 and 2006, by organizational size

Organizational size	Number of completed surveys	2005 average ($)	2005 median ($)	2006 average ($)	2006 median ($)
Large	24	72,353,851	22,220,212	72,997,484	20,835,161
Moderately sized	10	23,501,913	13,746,874	22,240,515	10,435,551
Medium-sized	38	3,436,522	2,018,229	3,521,294	2,607,842
Small	25	99,388	23,480	97,469	16,858

Large denotes organizations that receive $20 million or more in charitable revenue; moderately sized organizations have charitable revenue between $5 million and $19.99 million; medium-sized is used for organizations having charitable revenue between $1 million and $4.99 million, and small is for organizations that have charitable revenue of less than $1 million.

Table 2 summarizes the average and median increases or decreases in charitable revenue reported for 2006 by organizational size.

■ Nearly two-thirds of the large organizations saw an increase, with average growth of $2.6 million.

■ Moderately sized organizations responding to the survey were more likely to report a decline, with 6 in 10 seeing an average drop of nearly $3 million each.

■ Medium-sized organizations were likely to report growth in charitable gifts, with 66 percent showing an increase averaging close to $884,000.

■ Small organizations were evenly divided among growth, decline, and no change.

For all sizes considered together, when comparing dollars received in charitable gifts in 2006 and 2005:

53.6 percent saw an increase;

33.0 percent saw charitable giving drop in 2006; and

13.4 percent reported a change that was 1 percent or less.

Even though more organizations saw growth, the amount of the average drop was larger than the average amount of growth. Thus, the overall impact for health giving was a small decline of 2.2 percent.

Table 3 shows bequest receipts by organizational size. In three of the four organizational size groups, the average and the median amount received through bequest declined in 2006, compared with 2005. In the medium-sized organizations, the average increased from $342,614 to $444,824, but the median fell to $120,000.

Table 2
Increases or decreases in charitable revenue of health organizations, 2006

Organizational size	Number	Percentage of organizations in size group	Average change ($)	Average change (%)	Median change ($)	Median change (%)
Large						
Increase	15	63	2,638,470	67	1,463,460	17
Decrease	5	21	-4,674,036	-6	-3,776,538	-4
No change	4	17	-189,916	0	-150,765	0
Total*	24	100				
All large organizations			643,633	41	17,093	3

Organizational size	Number	Percentage of organizations in size group	Average change ($)	Average change (%)	Median change ($)	Median change (%)
Moderately sized						
Increase	4	40	1,256,378	9	1,316,553	6
Decrease	6	60	-2,939,915	-15	-1,562,120	-10
No change	–	–				
Total*	10	100				
All moderately sized organizations			-1,261,398	-5	-205,039	-5
Medium-sized						
Increase	25	66	883,940	53	35,700	35
Decrease	13	34	-1,452,092	-19	-327,853	-13
No change	–	–				
Total*	38	100				
All medium-sized organizations			84,771	28	173,287	8
Small						
Increase	8	32	45,361	34	11,747	30
Decrease	8	32	-50,109	-35	-28,857	-38
No change	9	34	0	0	0	0
Total*	25	100				
All small organizations			-1,919	-1,079	0	0

*Total does not always equal 100 due to rounding.

Table 3
Bequest receipts by organizational size, 2005 and 2006

Organizational size	Percentage with bequest revenues	2005 average ($)	2005 median ($)	2006 average ($)	2006 median ($)
Large	52	10,724,309	2,373,074	9,987,577	2,635,040
Moderate	59	6,354,934	635,000	5,519,980	446,145
Medium	64	342,614	208,564	444,824	120,000
Small*	14	494,142	63,590	76,573	33,115

*The values are reported here, although the number of responses is too low to use in making statistical inferences about all small health organizations.

Gates Foundation reshapes health giving

The Bill & Melinda Gates Foundation continued its commitment to world health and made major grants that far surpassed any other single donor's philanthropic support for the subsector. Since the inception of the Foundation's grant program, total giving to Global Health Programs has exceeded $7.7 billion. Among the Gates Foundation's grants announced in 2006 were:[3]

- $75 million over five years to Pneumococcal Vaccine Solutions to support several pneumococcal vaccine projects;

- $43.1 million to the World Health Organization to support a variety of programs including those dealing with malaria, HIV/AIDS, TB, reproductive health, vaccine-preventable diseases, and rotavirus vaccine supply and development; and

- $90 million to the Seattle-based Program for Appropriate Technology in Health (PATH) to support the Reproductive Health Supplies Coalition (RHSC); to help developing countries to reduce cervical cancer incidence and deaths; to support a project to establish a regional learning community among five African countries; to develop a set of practices for malaria control; and to support development of a vaccine to reduce malaria infection, morbidity, and mortality in infants and children in Africa.

Warren Buffett pledged more than $30 billion to the Bill & Melinda Gates Foundation.[4] Buffet's gift will help

them to continue focusing "on world health—fighting such diseases as malaria, HIV/AIDS, and tuberculosis—and on improving U.S. libraries and high schools."[5]

Cleveland Clinic announces $65 million gift in $1+ billion campaign

The Cleveland Clinic launched a $1.25 billion capital campaign and received a $65 million pledge from an anonymous donor for construction and renovations at the Heart and Vascular Institute.[6] Jane and Lee Seidman of Cleveland pledged $17 million to endow a chair in functional neurosurgery and for other activities. Mr. Seidman is founder and president of the Motorcars Group.[7]

Gifts to medical centers focus on cancer, diabetes research

Individual donors contributed significant sums to medical centers focused on cancer and diabetes. Among 2006's notable gifts are:

- Six cancer research institutions, five of which are affiliated with higher education institutions, will share in $120 million as part of a trust set up by shipping and mining magnate Daniel K. Ludwig. The Dana-Farber Cancer Institute/Harvard Medical School, the Johns Hopkins University School of Medicine, Massachusetts Institute of Technology, Memorial Sloan-Kettering Cancer Center, Stanford University School of Medicine, and the University of Chicago Pritzker School of Medicine each received $20 million, half of which has already been distributed.[8] The only gift counted strictly in the health subsector is the amount for the Memorial Sloan-Kettering Cancer Center; the others are counted in the education subsector.

- Publisher and real estate developer Mortimer B. Zuckerman pledged $100 million to New York's Memorial Sloan-Kettering Cancer Center for a new cancer research facility.[9]

- Eugenia J. Dodson donated $35.6 million to The Diabetes Research Institute at the University of Miami's medical school to support cancer and diabetes research.[10]

Gifts to universities and colleges are recorded in the education subsector, yet a substantial percentage of these gifts are for health-related purposes, whether for research or patient care. The larger of such gifts in 2006 are reported in the education chapter.

U.S. funders emphasize childhood health

With data showing that more than 9 million children aged 6 to 19 are considered overweight,[11] childhood obesity studies and programs were at the forefront of 2006 healthcare funding. The Robert Wood Johnson Foundation pledged more than $32 million in grants to study and develop programs regarding childhood obesity, including:[12]

- $8 million to the American Heart Association in Dallas to fund the Alliance for a Healthier Generation: Healthy Schools Program;

- $3.4 million to the National Foundation for the Centers for Disease Control and Prevention for early assessment of programs and policies on childhood obesity; and

- $2.3 million to the University of Arkansas for Medical Sciences for defining and classifying diseases and risks linked to childhood obesity.

Other donors contributed to the creation or expansion of institutions that provide health care for children.

- The DeVos family donated $50 million to Helen DeVos Children's Hospital in Grand Rapids, Michigan for construction of a new building;[13] and

- The University of Chicago received a $42 million gift from Gary C. & Frances Comer to establish a pediatric care center. The gift also supports recruitment efforts and programs in pediatric medicine.[14]

New York mayor funds global anti-smoking campaign

New York Mayor Michael R. Bloomberg pledged $125 million to build a global anti-smoking campaign. As the largest single contribution to global tobacco control efforts, the donation will be given to existing organizations over the next two years. The funds can be used for one of several approaches, including "developing and expanding quitting and prevention programs, encouraging the adoption of New York-style tobacco taxes and smoking bans, and/or designing a system to track tobacco use and efforts to stop it worldwide."[15]

High net-worth households and giving to health

The *Bank of America Study of High Net-Worth Philanthropy*, conducted by the Center on Philanthropy at Indiana

University, found that 70 percent of high net-worth households contributed to health organizations.[16] The average gift was $21,257 in 2005. Contributions for health causes are an estimated 6.7 percent of all contributions made by high net-worth households. This study reached households with income of $200,000 or more or a net worth of $1 million or more.

In the Center on Philanthropy Panel Study, a survey of a nationally representative sample of American households of all income levels, 23 percent contribute to health organizations, and the average gift in 2004 was approximately $257.[17]

The Association for Healthcare Philanthropy (AHP) estimates $7 billion given to member institutions in 2005

In the FY2005 Report on Giving for the United States, published in July 2006, the Association for Healthcare Philanthropy (AHP) estimated that $5.1 billion was contributed to member institutions in paid contributions and an additional $2.0 million in pledges. Sixty percent of the funding came from individuals.[18] Figure 1 shows the percentage of funds raised by AHP respondents categorized by type of fundraising activity.

Figure 1
Percentage of health care philanthropy by type of fundraising activity

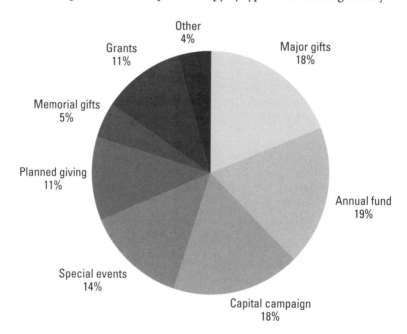

Data: *FY05 Report on Giving,* Association for Healthcare Philanthropy
Adapted from page 4. Excludes percentage shown for amount from endowment interest/income.
Used with permission.

Key findings from annual studies summarized

Table 4 presents three years of findings from studies released annually about giving for health care and health-related causes. Web site addresses are provided so readers may access complete reports.

Table 4
Key findings from other studies about giving to health organizations

$5 million dollar list, gifts from individuals to health (does not include gifts to foundations) Center on Philanthropy at Indiana University, www.philanthropy.iupui.edu			
	2004	2005	2006
Number of health gifts	19	37	35
Largest gift to health	$17.2 million from Earl and Doris Bakken to the Cleveland Clinic	$70 million from Sydell Miller to the Cleveland Clinic	$125 million from Michael Bloomberg to various organizations to support programs to help smokers quit and educate children to prevent them from starting
Health dollars given as percentage of all individual gifts on list of $5 million and above	3.2 percent* *This is unusually low due to an announced gift of $1.5 billion to a human services organizations	9.2 percent	15.4 percent

Foundation Giving Trends: Update on Funding Priorities Grants to health Foundation Center, www.foundationcenter.org			
	2003	2004	2005
Average grant amount	191,596	212,685	199,410
Median grant amount	36,000	35,000	39,720
Health funding as a percentage of grant dollars (surveyed foundations, including corporate foundations)	19.5	22.3	20.8

Report on Giving FY 2003, 2004, and 2005 Association for Healthcare Philanthropy, www.ahp.org			
	2003	2004	2005
Estimated total giving to member organizations; includes pledges	$5.89 billion	$6.1 billion	$7.1 billion
Estimated cash contributions	$4.1 billion	$4.1 billion	$5.1 billion
Median return on $1 spent for fundraising, all institutions	$3.87	$4.22	$3.58

IRS tax-exempt organizations in health category Charities and other tax-exempt organizations, 2001, 2002, 2003 Statistics of Income Bulletin, www.irs.gov			
	2001	2002	2003
Number	32,195	34,138	35,144
Charitable revenue*	$39.62 billion	$40.60 billion	$44.31 billion

*Charitable revenue includes gifts and foundation grants (which is comparable to what *Giving USA* tracks) as well as government grants and allocations from other nonprofit agencies, such as United Way and United Jewish Communities (which are not included in *Giving USA* estimates for contributions).

1   Giving to health-related institutions includes contributions to nonprofit organizations providing health care services; mental health care and crisis intervention; or education, treatment, research, or support for specific disorders and diseases. Gifts to medical schools and to university health training programs appear in education, even when for medical research projects. The health subsector is in NTEE codes E, F, G, and H. As with all *Giving USA* estimates, the amount estimated in giving to health-related organizations includes gifts received of cash, cash equivalents (securities), and in-kind gifts (artwork, patents, real estate, and other items of value). *Giving USA* tries to exclude from its estimates the value of deferred or planned gift commitments and new pledges.

2   *Giving USA* sent surveys to 652 health organizations, including every organization that raised $20 million or more in charitable gifts in 2003, 2004, or 2005; and a random sample of moderate, medium-sized, and small organizations. Useable responses came from 103 organizations (a return rate of 15.8 percent). Not all could be analyzed, as some were outliers. Results are based on 97 responses. 41.7 percent of the large organizations are in the analysis. Large organizations account for 74 percent of all giving to health. The sample was selected based on charitable revenue received circa 2003 (includes some organizations that reported only in 2002 or only in 2001), supplemented with information appearing on the *Chronicle of Philanthropy* list of the 400 charities receiving the most charitable revenue in 2004 or 2005.

3   Bill & Melinda Gates Foundation, Global Health Grants, www.gatesfoundation.org.

4   C. Loomis, A conversation with Warren Buffet, *Fortune Magazine,* http://money.cnn.

com/2006/06/25/magazines/fortune/charity2.fortune/index.htm.

5   C. Loomis, Warren Buffet gives away his fortune, *Fortune Magazine,* http://money.cnn.com/2006/06/25/magazines/fortune/charity1.fortune/index.htm.

6   Cleveland Clinic Catalyst, summer 2006, viewed at www.cms.clevelandclinic.org/giving/workfiles/Catalyst_summer06.pdf.

7   Cleveland Clinic Receives $82 Million; Other Gifts, *Chronicle of Philanthropy,* May 18, 2006, www.philanthropy.com.

8   A. Howard, Tycoon's trust awards $120 million to six cancer-research centers. *Chronicle of Philanthropy,* November 23, 2007, www.philanthropy.com.

9   M. Michaels, $100 million pledged to N.Y. cancer center, *Chronicle of Philanthropy,* May 18, 2006, www.philanthropy.com.

10   Stanford U. receives $90 million in big donations; Other recent gifts, *Chronicle of Philanthropy,* October 26, 2006, www.philanthropy.com.

11   Department of Health and Human Services, Centers for Disease Control and Prevention, Overweight and Obesity, www.cdc.gov/nccdphp/dnpa/obesity/index.htm.

12   Robert Wood Johnson Foundation, Active Grants, Childhood Obesity, www.rwjf.org/portfolios/grantlist.jsp?iaid=138&page=1 (through 6).

13   No author, Gifts & Grants, *Chronicle of Philanthropy,* May 18, 2006.

14   No author, Gifts & Grants, *Chronicle of Philanthropy,* February 9, 2006.

15   D. Cardwell, Bloomberg donating $125 million to anti-smoking efforts, *New York Times,* August 25, 2006.

16   The Center on Philanthropy at Indiana University, *The Bank of America Study of High Net-Worth Philanthropy,* October 2006, http://newsroom.bankofamerica.com.

17   Center on Philanthropy Panel Study, 2005 wave, data released March 2007 and analyzed at the Center on Philanthropy at Indiana University.

18   Association for Healthcare Philanthropy, *FY 2005 Report on Giving, USA,* Association for Healthcare Philanthropy, July 2006.

16 Giving to public-society benefit

- In 2006, giving to public-society benefit organizations reached an estimated $21.41 billion, an increase of 5.7 percent (2.4 percent adjusted for inflation) from the revised estimate of $20.25 billion for 2005.

- Giving to the public-society benefit subsector represented 7.3 percent of total estimated charitable contributions in the United States in 2006.

- Over the past 40 years, the average increase in giving to public-society benefit organizations is 11.4 percent (6.4 percent adjusted for inflation). Since 1996, the average annual rate of change has been 6.6 percent (4.2 percent adjusted for inflation).

- According to the annual Philanthropy 400 rankings, United Way of America raised the most money of any U.S. charity in 2004 and 2005. This includes gifts to more than 1,300 United Way affiliates.

Giving USA findings for benchmarking giving to public-society benefit organizations

As with all *Giving USA* estimates, the estimated amount given to public-society benefit organizations includes gifts received of cash, cash equivalents (securities), and in-kind gifts (artwork, patents, real estate, and other items of value).[1] *Giving USA* tries to exclude the value of planned commitments and new pledges from its estimates.

Tables 1 through 3 summarize *Giving USA* survey findings.[2]

- Table 1 shows the average and median amounts reported in charitable gifts.
- Table 2 shows the direction of change in giving (increase, decrease, or within 1 percent, which is termed "no change").
- Table 3 shows the percentage of organizations that reported bequest receipts and the average and median amount received from bequests for each organizational size.

Table 1
Charitable revenue received by public-society benefit organizations in 2005 and 2006, by organizational size

Organizational size	Number of completed surveys	2005 average ($)	2005 median ($)	2006 average ($)	2006 median ($)
Large	17	38,713,026	28,200,000	40,785,750	32,975,000
Moderately sized	26	7,574,925	6,562,729	7,950,242	8,098,919
Medium-sized	40	2,600,325	2,168,772	2,801,226	2,061,146
Small	27	98,824	13,909	103,890	15,867

Large denotes organizations that receive $20 million or more in charitable revenue; *moderately sized* organizations have charitable revenue between $5 million and $19.99 million; *medium-sized* is used for organizations having charitable revenue between $1 million and $4.99 million, and *small* is for organizations that have charitable revenue of less than $1 million.

Table 2 summarizes average and median increases or decreases in charitable revenue reported for 2006 by organizational size.

- Among large organizations, the shares of organizations with increases and decreases were roughly the same. The average increase, at $8.25 million, exceeded the average decrease of $4.41 million. Among organizations with an increase, the average percentage change was 18 percent.

- More than 60 percent of moderately sized organizations saw an increase, and the average rise was $1.3 million. Among all organizations of this size, the average was growth of $375,318, or 8 percent.

- More than 60 percent of medium-sized organizations reported an increase with an average of $477,695. For all organizations in this size group, the average was an increase of $200,901, or an average of 9 percent.

- Overall, small organizations were almost equally distributed among increases, decreases, and no change.

Among all organizations:

53.6 percent saw an increase in giving in 2006;

30.9 percent saw a decline; and

15.5 percent saw little change (within 1 percent in either direction).

Table 2
Increases or decreases in charitable revenue of
public-society benefit organizations, 2006

Organizational size	Number	Percentage of organizations in size group	Average change ($)	Average change (%)	Median change ($)	Median change (%)
Large						
Increase	8	47	8,256,134	18	4,100,650	14
Decrease	7	41	-4,412,882	-30	-2,455,153	-13
No change	2	12	38,708	0	38,708	0
Total*	17	100				
All large organizations			2,072,724	4	77,416	0
Moderately sized						
Increase	16	62	1,316,726	38	610,886	12
Decrease	9	35	-1,256,594	-14	-454,236	-6
No change	1	4	0	0	0	0
Total*	26	100				
All moderately sized organizations			375,318	18	135,494	3

Giving to public-society benefit

Organizational size	Number	Percentage of organizations in size group	Average change ($)	Average change (%)	Median change ($)	Median change (%)
Medium-sized						
Increase	25	63	477,695	21	218,000	10
Decrease	11	28	-357,138	-16	-282,445	-11
No change	4	10	5,545	0	0	0
Total*	40	100				
All medium-sized organizations			200,901	9	71,393	4
Small						
Increase	10	37	11,848	150,016	5630	11
Decrease	7	26	-2,768	-32	-2,866	-28
No change	10	37	107,800	0	0	0
Total*	27	100				
All small organizations			4,684	1	1	0

*Total does not always equal 100 due to rounding.

Table 3 shows bequest receipts by organizational size. The average and the median fell slightly in large organizations but rose in medium-sized organizations.

Table 3
Bequest receipts by organizational size, 2005 and 2006

Organizational size	Percentage with bequest revenues	2005 average ($)	2005 median ($)	2006 average ($)	2006 median ($)
Large	58	2,374,794	506,280	1,495,252	364,384
Moderate	43	311,037	102,500	411,548	97,771
Medium	24	156,026	5,500	150,154	22,500
Small*	7				

*One small public-society benefit organization reported bequest revenue. The average and median are not shown.

Multimillion-dollar donations for public-society benefit

Corporations, foundations, and individuals announced significant gifts for organizations in the public-society benefit subsector. Charities engaged in economic development or that provide services for veterans received the largest gifts.

- The AT&T Foundation granted $100 million to the One Economy Corporation, Habitat for Humanity affiliates, and other low-income housing providers. The money funds a three-year program called AT&T AccessAll, designed to provide in-home Internet and technology access to benefit low-income families and underserved communities across the country.[3]

- The Hector Guy and Doris Di Stefano estate included $33 million in a bequest gift to the Disabled American Veterans Charitable Service Trust. Most of the money in the estate comes from Mrs. Di Stefano's inheritance of stock from her father, who received shares in UPS when he was a top executive of the company in its earliest days.[4]

- Samuel J. Heyman pledged another $25 million to Partnership for Public Service. Heyman, who founded the Partnership in 2002, serves as chairman of International Specialty Products in New Jersey, owns Heyman Properties in Connecticut, and began his career as an attorney at the U.S. Department of Justice. His pledge continues the Partnership, which seeks to attract talented employees to government jobs.[5]

- The Jewish Funders Network (JFN), on behalf of a number of anonymous donors, contributed $10 million to partner with The Sacta-Rashi Foundation, to provide urgent aid to Israel in response to short- and long-term needs following the summer 2006 war between the militant organization Hezbollah and Israel.[6]

Commercial donor-advised funds report banner year

Donor-advised funds created by financial institutions have become a part of the charitable giving landscape, receiving $2 billion or more in contributions annually. The donations to these funds are considered part of the public-society benefit subsector. Distributions made by these funds are a form of "indirect public support" and are not counted in Giving USA, as they are transfers from one charity (the donor-advised fund) to another (the charitable organization receiving the distribution). Table 4 summarizes four funds that have been the largest—or among the largest—in the past five years. In May 2007, the Chronicle of Philanthropy posted data showing assets of $10 billion in donor-advised funds created independently of another charity. These funds distributed $2.3 billion in 2006.

There are, as of early 2007, no national legal requirements for payout or distribution from donor-advised funds. Each fund manager sets its own rules. Table 4 shows that among the largest funds, in aggregate, distributions exceed the minimum five-percent payout required for private foundations.

Table 4

Four largest commercially sponsored donor-advised funds

Assets, distributions, and new gifts received, circa 2006

($ in millions)

	Assets at end of fiscal year	Charitable distributions during year	Percentage of assets distributed	New gifts received
Fidelity Investments Charitable Gift Fund[1]	$3,532	$934	26.4	$1,150
Vanguard Charitable Endowment[2]	$1,202	$300	25.0	$484
National Philanthropic Trust[3]	$600	$107	17.8	$163
Schwab Fund for Charitable Giving[4]	$1,035	$166	16.0	$698

Data: [1]Fidelity Investments Charitable Gift Fund annual report for fiscal year ended June 2006, and www.charitablegiving.org.

[2]Vanguard Charitable Endowment, annual report for the fiscal year ended June 2006, www.vanguardcharitable.org.

[3]National Philanthropic Trust, financial statements for the fiscal year ended June 2006, at www.npt.org.

[4]Schwab Fund for Charitable Giving, audited financial statements for the fiscal year ended June 2006, at www.schwabcharitable.org.

Percentage of assets distributed: *Giving USA* divided charitable distributions by assets.

National Christian Foundation raised $460 million; granted $230 million in 2006

The National Christian Foundation was incorporated as a public charity in 1982 and classified as a public foundation. This family of funds operates like a community foundation with "community" defined by shared interests rather than by geography.

As a combined-purpose fundraising entity, it is included in the public-society benefit subsector.[7] It raises funds nationally and through 29 affiliates. The organization provides donors with a number of giving options, including a gift fund (a donor-advised fund); and vehicles for planned giving, endowment giving, annuities, and more.[8] In 2006, the National Christian

Foundation reported that it received $464 million in new gifts and made distributions of $230 million.[9] The foundation stated that the amount received in 2006 was more than 30 percent more than the amount received in 2005. The amount raised puts it in the top ranks of charities on the Philanthropy 400 list.

Other notable gifts for organizations in this subsector

The public-society benefit subsector also contains other organizations doing important work and receiving significant donations. Table 5 shows the largest gifts for different types of organizations that are included in the public-society benefit subsector, including foundation grants and corporate contributions.

Table 5
Largest gift on record for types of organizations
also included in public-society benefit

Type of organization	Donor	Gift
Research institutes	Ford Foundation	$8.4 million to the National Academy of Sciences for Diversity Fellows program
Civil rights	Ford Foundation	$10 million to the National Women's Law Center
Community and economic development	Kresge Foundation	$10 million to Detroit Riverfront Conservancy to construct a river walk

WHAT THIS MEANS TO YOU

This subsector is used for many different types of organizations. The entities that are the largest component of the public-society benefit subsector are the federated campaigns and combined fundraising programs, and they tend to get detailed review in surveys and media coverage. Organizations providing other types of community services need to be taken into consideration when considering the philanthropic and fundraising climate in a given area.

Complex subsector plays important role in *Chronicle of Philanthropy* 400

Several public-society benefit organizations are in the top tier of the annual *Chronicle of Philanthropy* listing of the top 400 charities by amount raised. Since 2005, the United Way of America has reported its consolidated results (for all 1,300+ affiliates and the national organization) and has been the largest charity. Numerous other organizations in this subsector are included on the list. *Giving USA* coded organizations using the codes at Guidestar.org and found that of the $10 billion raised in 2005 by public-society benefit organizations on the top 400 listing:

- 40 percent went to United Way;

- 23 percent went to freestanding donor-advised funds (Fidelity Charitable Gift Fund, the National Christian Foundation, Ayco Charitable Trust, and others); and

- 18 percent went to Jewish federations, Jewish community funds, or other organizations that raise funds primarily from Jews.

Figure 1 shows the listings from the *Chronicle of Philanthropy 400* list by type of organization within the public-society benefit subsector.

Research institutes included the Aspen Institute (social sciences), the Heritage Foundation (public policy), and the Scripps Research Institute (sciences), among others. Organizations that facilitate in-kind donations include Kids in Distressed Situations and the National Association for the Exchange of Industrial Resources. Community

Figure 1
2006 list of top 400 charities: public-society benefit organizations by specific service

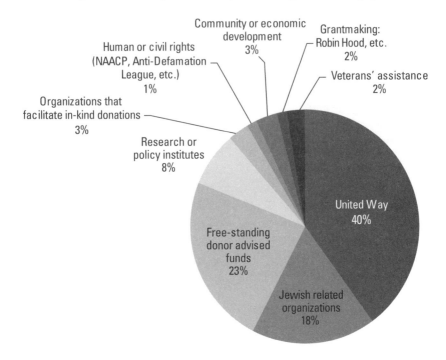

or economic development includes the Local Initiatives Support Corporation, downtown development corporations, and a public housing assistance fund.

Combined Federal Campaign expands its eligibility for nonprofits

According to Bill Huddleston, immediate past president of the CFC Association, the Combined Federal Campaign (CFC) is the largest workplace-giving program in the world, reaching an estimated 1.4 million federal employees.[10] As the federal government's workplace giving program, it is organized regionally with more than 300 CFCs operating where the federal government has offices. The campaign is managed by the

Office of Personnel Management (OPM), and in each site the campaign is conducted by federal staff members who serve as volunteers. Extensive regulations prevent donor coercion.

The CFC raises funds for an estimated 20,000 local charities and more than 1,500 national and international charities. Over the past five years, federal employees around the world (the CFC reaches those stationed overseas) participating in the CFC have donated a cumulative total of more than $1 billion. It raised more than $59 million in the 2006 campaign.[11] If the CFC were a foundation, in terms of giving, it would be the tenth-largest foundation in the United States. Much of the money contributed through the CFC is unrestricted funding for the participating organizations.

The Office of Personnel Management (OPM), Office of CFC Operations, is the federal agency responsible for the CFC. Procedures and regulations were changed dramatically for the 2007 and future campaigns. The changes are designed to streamline and modernize the processes for the CFC. Two of the changes with the potential to have the most impact on nonprofits include:

- Removal of the 25 percent cap on administrative expenses for a nonprofit to receive funds from the CFC; and

- Removal of the rule that previously prohibited nonprofits from receiving more than 80 percent of their funds from government entities from applying for inclusion in the CFC.

The effect of these two changes is to open up the CFC to thousands of nonprofits that previously would not have qualified for the CFC. Recent Government Accounting Office (GAO) reviews of the CFC distributions suggest that charities that apply for admission will be scrutinized to ensure that they comply with laws regulating employers' payment of payroll taxes and nonprofit organization operations.[12]

United Jewish Communities/ The Federations of North America reaching younger constituency through special initiatives

The United Jewish Communities (UJC) network provides coordination and services to 155 Jewish federations and 400 Jewish communities that do have federations in the U.S. The UJC provides a number of centralized fundraising services for its members, including online giving, women's philanthropy, programs to reach more young Jews, support for major gifts and endowment giving, as well as coordinated efforts for response to crises. One outreach program for younger Jews, the National Young Leadership Cabinet, saw personal contributions from participants increase by an average 23 percent.[13]

In other special efforts in 2006, the UJC Israel Emergency Campaign raised $350 million in response to the summer 2006 war between Israel and Lebanon.[14] The UJC also raised a total of $28 million in Hurricane Katrina relief, including gifts made in 2005 and 2006.[15] Through its online giving portal, UJCweb, donors contributed $5 million between January 1, 2006 and September 30, 2006. This is an average gift of more than $240.[16]

WHAT THIS MEANS TO YOU

If you are involved with a charity located near a site of federal employment, find out if your organization might be eligible for inclusion in the CFC. Check the Web site of the Office of Personnel Management for application information: www.opm.gov/cfc/charities/.

United Jewish Communities experienced a period of strategic realignment and thoughtful work to focus its fundraising. Some of the innovative approaches identified in that process—including activities to engage younger donors, creation of a leadership pathway to prepare the next generation, and focused efforts for crises—can be models for other organizations.

Giving by the wealthy

The *Bank of America Study of High Net-Worth Philanthropy* found that 60 percent gave to public society benefit organizations and the average gift was $7,750.[17]

Key findings from other studies summarized

Table 7 presents three years of findings from studies released annually about contributions to public-society benefit organizations. Web site addresses are provided so readers can access the full reports.

Table 7
Key findings from other studies about giving to public-society benefit organizations

$5 million dollar list, gifts from individuals to public-society benefit (does not include gifts to foundations) Center on Philanthropy at Indiana University, www.philanthropy.iupui.edu			
	2004	2005	2006
Number of public-society benefit gifts	7	6	7
Largest gift to public-society benefit	$12 million from the estate of Werner and Ellen Lange to the Jewish Community Foundation of Los Angeles.	$20 million from Albert Willner to the Weizmann Institute of Science	$33 million from the estate of Hector and Doris Di Stefano to the Disabled American Veterans Charitable Service Trust.
Public-society benefit dollars given as percentage of all individual gifts on list of $5 million and above	0.5 percent	1.8 percent	1.5 percent

Giving to public-society benefit

Foundation Giving Trends: Update on Funding Priorities Grants to public-society benefit organizations Foundation Center, www.foundationcenter.org			
	2003	2004	2005
Average grant amount	$116,483	$125,536	$116,166
Median grant amount	$30,000	$30,000	$45,000
Public-society benefit funding as a percentage of grant dollars (surveyed foundations, including corporate foundations)	13 percent	13 percent	11.2 percent

Results of United Way campaigns and other fundraising United Way of America, www.unitedway.org			
	2003–2004	2004–2005	2005–2006
Total raised in campaigns	$3.59 billion	$3.86 billion	$3.63 billion
Gifts to specific initiatives	$77 million	$83 million	$102 million
Realized bequests, endowment gifts, and other realized planned gifts	$58 million	$62 million	$67 million

Combined Federal Campaign Office of Personnel Management, www.opm.gov/cfc			
	2003	2004	2005
Total amount raised	$249.23 million	$256.8 million	$268.5 million
Average gift per donor	$185.00	$198.52	$214.55
Percentage participation	33.9	32.5	32

IRS tax-exempt organizations in public-society benefit subsector Charities and Other Tax-Exempt Organizations, 2001, 2002, and 2003 *Statistics of Income Bulletin*, www.irs.gov			
	2001	2002	2003
Number	21,537	21,433	23,339
Charitable revenue*	$27.36 billion	$25.30 billion	$28.67

*Charitable revenue includes gifts and foundation grants (which is comparable to what *Giving USA* tracks) as well as government grants and allocations from other nonprofit agencies such as United Way and United Jewish Communities (which are not included in *Giving USA* estimates for contributions).

1   The public-society benefit subsector includes organizations collecting funds for distribution to a number of other agencies, such as United Ways; Jewish federations and appeals; commercially sponsored donor-advised funds; and combined funds, such as the Combined Federal Campaign, America's Charities, and others. Foundations, both private and community, are treated in a separate section of *Giving USA*. Estimates for giving to foundations appear there. This subsector also includes many other types of nonprofits, including those that work for civil rights or other social action, those dedicated to community improvement and capacity building, and nonmedical research institutes in the sciences and social sciences. In most years, combined fundraising appeals receive the largest share of charitable revenue in this subsector. In the National Taxonomy of Exempt Entities (NTEE), the public-society benefit sector, as reported by *Giving USA*, includes major category codes R, S, T (except private foundations and community foundations), U, V, and W.

2   *Giving USA* sent surveys to 746 organizations in the public-society benefit subsector in spring 2007. Of the organizations receiving the survey, 110 (14.7 percent) provided a useable response. The useable response rate from large organizations was 16.5 percent. The sample was selected based on charitable revenue received circa 2003 (includes some organizations that reported only in 2001 or only in 2002), supplemented with information obtained about public-society benefit organizations appearing on the *Chronicle of Philanthropy* list of the 400 charities receiving the most charitable revenue in 2004 and 2005.

3   AT&T Announces $100 Million "AT&T AccessAll" Signature Program, IP Links, www.ipphila.com/iplinks/v4/is27/a5.htm.

4   America's Most-Generous Donors: Donations in 2006, *Chronicle of Philanthropy*, www.philanthropy.com.

5   Donors Who Pledged $25-Million or More to Charity, *Chronicle of Philanthropy*,

February 7, 2002, www.philanthropy.com/free/articles/v14/i08/08001001.htm.

6   Jewish Funders Network Provides $10 Million for Northern Recovery Efforts in Israel, Jewish Funders Network, September 28, 2006, www.jfunders.org/newsroom/jewish-funders-network-provides-10-million-for-northern-recovery-efforts-in-israel.

7   Guidestar, consulted March 30, 2007.

8   National Christian Foundation, www.nationalchristian.com. Viewed March 30, 2007.

9   S. Chapman, 29th largest U.S. Charity—the National Christian Foundation—receives record $464 million in contributions in 2006, January 25, 2007, www.nationalchristian.com.

10 B. Huddleston, *A Hidden Treasure for Non-Profits, How to Tap into the CFC, America's Largest Workplace Giving Campaign*, Huddleston Consulting Group, 2007.

11 Final Audited 2006 Campaign Total Announced, *Combined Federal Campaign of the National Capital Area*, www.cfcnca.org/about/message/auditedtotal.php.

12 S. Hoffman, Fund gives charity tax cheat millions: Some 1,280 nonprofits receiving cash from CFC owe government $36 million, *MSNBC*, November 27, 2006, www.msnbc.msn.com/id/15832673/.

13 UJC annual report 2005–2006, www.ujc.org. UJC National Young Leadership Cabinet, page 6.

14 UJC Responds: Israel Emergency Campaign, www.jewishcommunities.org/content_display.html?ArticleID=208106&page=7. Viewed March 30, 2007.

15 UJC Responds: Hurricane Katrina, *United Jewish Communities*, www.ujc.org/content_display.html?ArticleID=176396. Viewed March 30, 2007.

16 UJC Annual report, Inside UJC: UJC Communications.

17 Center on Philanthropy at Indiana University, *Bank of America Study of High Net-Worth Philanthropy*, October 2006, www.philanthropy.iupui.edu.

17 Giving to arts, culture, and humanities

- In 2006, giving to arts, culture, and humanities organizations reached an estimated $12.51 billion, an increase of 9.9 percent (6.5 percent adjusted for inflation) from the revised estimate of $11.38 billion for 2005.

- Giving to the arts, culture, and humanities subsector represented 4.2 percent of total estimated charitable contributions in the United States in 2006.

- The 40-year average increase in gifts to arts, culture, and humanities organizations is 8.5 percent (4.2 percent adjusted for inflation). In the years from 1997 to 2006, the average annual increase is 5.5 percent (4.9 percent adjusted for inflation).

Giving USA findings for benchmarking giving to arts, culture, and humanities organizations

As with all *Giving USA* estimates, the amount estimated in giving to organizations in the arts, culture, and humanities subsector[1] includes gifts received of cash, cash equivalents (securities), and in-kind gifts (artwork, patents, real estate, and other items of value). *Giving USA* tries to exclude from its estimates the value of deferred or planned gift commitments and new pledges.

Tables 1 through 3 summarize the findings from the *Giving USA 2007* survey.[2]

- Table 1 shows the average and median amounts reported in charitable gifts.

- Table 2 shows the direction of change in giving (increase; decrease; or within 1 percent, which is termed "no change").

- Table 3 shows the percentage of organizations that reported bequest receipts and the average and median amount received from bequests for each organizational size.

Table 1 shows that arts, culture, and humanities institutions responding to this survey saw an increase in average amounts received in 2006, when compared with 2005. However, the median gift amount declined slightly in large and moderately sized organizations. The median gift amount rose in the medium-sized and small arts organizations.

Table 1
Charitable revenue received by arts, culture, and humanities organizations
in 2005 and 2006, by organizational size

Organizational size	Number of completed surveys	2005 average ($)	2005 median ($)	2006 average ($)	2006 median ($)
Large	14	38,100,930	24,560,463	40,295,390	24,144,918
Moderately sized	33	6,382,080	5,770,301	7,199,234	5,685,502
Medium-sized	30	1,913,904	1,571,351	2,095,936	1,666,920
Small	31	100,114	24,000	109,409	27,635

Large denotes organizations that receive $20 million or more in charitable revenue; *moderately sized* organizations have charitable revenue between $5 million and $19.99 million; *medium-sized* is used for organizations having charitable revenue between $1 million and $4.99 million, and *small* is for organizations that have charitable revenue of less than $1 million.

Table 2 summarizes the average and median increases or decreases in charitable revenue reported for 2006 by organizational size.

- Nearly 6 in 10 (57 percent) of the large organizations saw an increase, with average growth of more than $8 million.

- Moderately sized organizations responding to the survey were likely to report an increase, with 6 in 10 seeing a result for 2006 that was $1.8 million more, on average, than in 2005.

- Medium-sized organizations were also very likely to report growth in charitable gifts, with 60 percent showing an increase averaging close to $400,000.

- Just over half (54 percent) of small organizations reported an increase, with an average change of about $28,000.

For all sizes considered together, when comparing dollars received in charitable gifts in 2006 and 2005:

58.3 percent saw an increase;

34.2 percent saw charitable giving drop in 2006; and

7.4 percent reported a change that was 1 percent or less.

Table 3 shows bequest receipts by organizational size. The average declined among the reporting large organizations, but increased in the other three size groups.

Table 2
Increases or decreases in charitable revenue of
arts, culture, and humanities organizations, 2006

Organizational size	Number	Percentage of organizations in size group	Average change ($)	Average change (%)	Median change ($)	Median change (%)
Large						
Increase	8	57	8,062,038	21	75,77,671	17
Decrease	6	43	-5,628,976	-35	-4,357,089	-34
No change	–	–				
Total*	14	100				
All large organizations			2,194,460	3	781,162	3
Moderately sized						
Increase	20	61	1,807,619	32	1,296,050	21
Decrease	13	39	-706,638	-11	-541,373	-9
No change	–	–				
Total*	33	100				
All moderately sized organizations			817,154	15	380,574	10
Medium-sized						
Increase	18	60	401,153	25	292,487	17
Decrease	9	30	-197,003	-14	-139,733	-8
No change	3	10	4,413	0	10,139	1
Total*	30	100				
All medium-sized organizations			182,032	11	146,589	9
Small						
Increase	17	54	28,349	46	7,932	30
Decrease	9	29	-21,532	-26	-6,000	-25
No change	5	16	0	0	0	0
Total*	31	100				
All small organizations			9,295	16	500	8

*Total does not always equal 100 due to rounding.

Table 3
Bequest receipts by organizational size, 2005 and 2006

Organizational size	Percentage with bequest revenues	2005 average ($)	2005 median ($)	2006 average ($)	2006 median ($)
Large	66	3,388,642	368,550	1,987,147	785,550
Moderate	74	1,030,262	311,577	1,322,578	302,821
Medium	48	143,674	102,000	247,999	99,000
Small*	15	4,344	0	126,466	75,000

*Five small organizations reported bequests. The results do not represent all small arts organizations.

Million-dollar gifts awarded to arts, culture, and humanities organizations

In the Million Dollar List maintained by the Center on Philanthropy at Indiana University, donations to organizations in the arts, culture, and humanities subsector shows arts gifts as follows:

- The average reported gift made by a family or individual was $7.5 million.[3]

- The largest gift given for an arts purpose in 2006 was $50 million to Florida State University for the John and Mable Ringling Museum of Art from Helga Wall-Apelt.[4] She gave cash and in-kind art to expand the museum's facilities and to build an endowment. Because the museum

is part of Florida State University, and the gift was made to FSU, the gift will be counted in giving to education.

- The largest gift to an arts institution was made by Jeannik Mequet Littlefield, a longtime member of the board at the San Francisco Opera, who gave that organization $35 million.[5]

- The largest gift ever given to an American regional theater was a $35 million gift from Gilbert and Jaylee Mead to the Arena Stage in Washington, D.C. for renovation of its facilities and the creation of a state-of-the-art theater campus.[6]

- The largest in-kind donation, reported to be "priceless," was from Bruce Kovner, a financier ranked 93 on the Forbes 400 list of wealthy

WHAT THIS MEANS TO YOU

In charitable organizations nationally, individuals give three-quarters of the total. Even after adjusting to consider only secular giving, individual donations account for a significant majority of the adjusted total (see Chapter 11, Giving to Religion). Arts organizations that successfully engage individuals as donors have strong annual fundraising programs. This regular fundraising effort helps the organization find the individuals whose interest in the organization's work and history of loyal giving confirms their potential as major gift donors.

Sponsorship is increasing as a form of corporate support for the arts. Between 2000 and 2005, at least, various reports suggest that outright gifts from corporations and corporate foundations are—at best—holding steady or declining.

Corporate funders are entering partnerships with arts organizations with direct business objectives in mind—entertainment for clients, for example, or boosting the company's image within a specific demographic group.

Nonprofit organizations need to evaluate carefully the costs and potential benefits of a corporate partnership. Companies can offer volunteers, expertise from their staff, and ways to reach new audiences. As is true in corporate fundraising for all types of charities, a few carefully selected partnerships may be more beneficial for both partners than a large number of transactions would be.

Americans in 2005, who gave a collection of music manuscripts to the Julliard School.[7]

Educational institutions often receive major gifts for arts programming or for arts facilities. *Giving USA* follows the NTEE in classifying gifts by institutional purpose, not the program supported by the gift. Thus, these contributions are donations to educational institutions, even though text about them appears in this chapter.

Arts organizations adjust to corporate funding decrease

The New York Times reported that arts organizations are adjusting to a funding climate with less corporate support. In one example, the Altria Group (the parent company of Philip Morris USA and Philip Morris International, which has contributed more than $210 million to the arts over the last four decades) announced its plans to phase out its support for arts institutions.[8]

Corporations support the arts in diverse ways, including sponsorships

(which are not treated as gifts because the company receives publicity). IEG, a consulting group that monitors sponsorships, has noted a steady increase in sponsorship support for arts and art events. However, not all these events are for charitable organizations; for-profit arts events also receive corporate sponsorship.

Not all companies have reduced their support for the arts. The Business Committee for the Arts honored 10 firms in 2006 with an award as *The Best Companies Supporting the Arts in America.*[9] Among the criteria for selection: a long-term commitment to the arts, community leadership, and the capability to get employees involved. Among the major national companies cited were:

- Boeing Co.;

- HCA Inc.;

- PNC Financial Services Group, Inc.; and

- Time Warner Inc.

Recipients also included local and regional firms in six urban areas.

After several lean years, government support of the arts appears to be on the rise

State arts agencies, ballot initiatives in states and localities, and federal budget approvals all raised the level of arts funding in 2005 and 2006, following three or more years of declines after the terrorist attacks of 2001 and the recession and slow economic recovery of 2001–2003.

Total legislative appropriations to state arts agencies in 2006 stood at $330.7 million.[10] Between fiscal years 2005 and 2006, state arts agencies gained $24.8 million in state funds. Fiscal year 2006 marks the second consecutive year of gains for the arts, following three years of sharp declines.

The 2006 mid-term elections proved successful for the arts. Americans showed their overwhelming support for the arts by approving local and state ballot measures and by electing pro-arts candidates at the local, state, and federal levels. According to Americans for the Arts Action Fund, 100 percent of the arts ballot measures passed.[11]

The local and state ballot measures will infuse millions of dollars for arts education programs in local schools and will increase funding for both cultural facilities and general operating support for nonprofit arts organizations.

The National Endowment for the Arts (NEA) awarded 1,744 grants in 435 congressional districts in 2006.[12]

- Forty percent of all NEA program funds are re-granted through state arts agencies, ensuring that federal funding reaches local programs.

- On average, each NEA grant leverages at least seven dollars from other state, local, and private sources, thus expanding the federal investment's impact.

- In 2006, a bipartisan group of 43 U.S. Senators signed a "Dear Colleague" letter calling for a funding increase for the NEA and the National Endowment for the Humanities (NEH).

The National Endowment for the Arts reports that total funds have increased from fiscal year 2005 ($121,263,614) to fiscal year 2006 ($124,406,355).[13]

WHAT THIS MEANS TO YOU

Government funding will ebb and flow over time, so it is essential that arts organizations maintain a diversified funding base. Applications for public funding will be more successful if they show clear information about the people using the arts organization. Maintain good records of the numbers and types of people serviced onsite and through outreach.

Public funding is also more likely if an institution can show public support through philanthropic contributions. A strong donor base enhances an application for public funding.

President George W. Bush signed a funding policy for performing arts centers in times of national disaster. The policy directs the Federal Emergency and Management Agency (FEMA) to include performing arts facilities in disaster relief funding. The bill demonstrates that the performing arts are essential to human and economic recovery in times of disaster.[14]

High net-worth households are very likely to give to the arts; average gift nearly $17,000

The *Bank of America Study of High Net-Worth Philanthropy*, conducted by the Center on Philanthropy at Indiana University, found that 70 percent of high net-worth households contributed to arts organizations. The average gift was $16,657 in 2005. Arts contributions are an estimated 10.8 percent of all contributions made by high net-worth households.[15] This study reached households with income of $200,000 or more or a net worth of $1 million or more.

In the Center on Philanthropy Panel Study, a survey of a nationally representative sample of American households at all income levels, 8 percent

contribute to the arts and the average gift in 2004 was approximately $272.[16]

Individual and foundation support for theaters increases, 2005

In its annual study of nonprofit theaters, the Theatre Communications Group (TCG) study[17] found that the funding difficulties experienced in the early years of this decade by nonprofit theaters have been improved. In the TCG analysis:

- Total contributions to nonprofit theaters in 2005 were an estimated $801 million, an increase of 12 percent compared with the prior year;

- Total individual giving was the greatest source of contributed funds;

- Average corporate support for the theaters decreased 2 percent from 2004 to 2005;

- Average foundation support for theaters increased by 18 percent from 2004 to 2005; and

- The average number of foundation gifts remained the same over the past five years—at 19 grants per theater.

WHAT THIS MEANS TO YOU

The general trend in 2005 and into 2006 was for improved funding at arts organizations, including theaters and museums. Individual support and foundation giving was increasing, with theaters seeing a decline in corporate giving but museums reporting no change in corporate giving.

Arts funding, being more reliant on wealthy individuals and foundations than some other subsectors, may be more tied to changes in the stock market and in personal wealth than other charitable organizations.

Survey shows stability in funding for art museums, 2005

The Association of Art Museum Directors (AAMD) annual *State of North America's Art Museums* survey[18] revealed stability across an array of museum activities. The 129 responding museums reported a stable financial picture, with only minor changes in overall revenue, earned income, and endowment income.

- Total revenue either remained constant or increased for 84 percent of art museums.

- Endowment income remained unchanged or increased for 91 percent of those surveyed.

- Individual giving and corporate support also remained steady for 84 percent of museums.

- Foundation support rose, with 50 percent of museums reporting an increase.

- Government funding stabilized, with only 16 percent of art museums reporting declines.

Key data from annual studies summarized

Table 4 presents three years of data from several studies appearing annually about giving to arts, culture and humanities organizations. Web site addresses are provided so readers can access the full reports.

Table 4
Key findings from other studies about giving to arts organizations

$5 million dollar list, gifts from individuals to the arts Center on Philanthropy at Indiana University, www.philanthropy.iupui.edu			
	2004	2005	2006
Number of gifts to arts, culture, and humanities	15	23	31
Largest gift to arts, culture, and humanities: Cash	$205 million for the Overture Center for the Arts in Wisconsin from W. Jerome (Jerry) Frautschi	$100 million pledged to the Museum of Modern Art by David Rockefeller	$35 million to the San Francisco Opera from Jeannik Mequet Littlefield
In-kind	$500 million or more in cash and gifts-in-kind, estate of Caroline Weiss Law to the Houston Museum of Fine Arts	$400 million in artwork from Marguerite and Robert Hoffman, Cindy and Howard Rachofsky, and Debbie and Rusty Rose to the Dallas Museum of Art	Priceless music manuscript collection from Bruce Kovner to the Juilliard School of Music.

$5 million dollar list, gifts from individuals to the arts
Center on Philanthropy at Indiana University, www.philanthropy.iupui.edu

	2004	2005	2006
Arts, culture, and humanities giving as percentage of all individual gifts on list of $5 million and above	12.1 percent	14.7 percent	8.1 percent

Foundation Giving Trends, 2004, 2005, and 2006 editions
Grants for the arts
Foundation Center, www.foundationcenter.org

	2003	2004	2005
Average grant amount	$100,121	$106,910	$109,885
Median grant amount	$25,000	$25,000	$25,000
Arts funding as percentage of grant dollars (surveyed foundations)	13 percent	13 percent	12.5 percent

State of North America's Art Museums Survey
Association of Art Museum Directors, www.aamd.org

Survey conducted about significant change in:	2003 N=128	2004 N=114	2005 N=129
Overall Revenue			
Decline	39%	21%	16%
Increase	41%	49%	47%
No change	20%	30%	37%
Individual Gifts			
Decline	10%	8%	7%
Increase	56%	68%	70%
No change	34%	24%	23%
Foundations			
Decline	26%	14%	12%
Increase	39%	40%	50%
No change	35%	46%	38%
Corporations			
Decline	34%	22%	20%
Increase	32%	38%	34%
No change	34%	40%	46%
Earned income			
Decline	32%	25%	16%
Increase	36%	43%	44%
No change	32%	32%	40%

Giving to arts, culture, and humanities

Theatre Facts — Theatre Communications Group, www.tcg.org			
	2003	2004	2005
Average contributions by "Universe Trend" Theatres (n=100) that responded each year over 5 years	$2.70 million	$3.07 million	$3.36 million
Average percentage of contributions in "Trend" Theatres (n=100) from:			
Individuals	24.5	28.2	26.2
Foundations	18.9	16.9	18.3
Corporations	14.0	13.3	11.9
Government	12.6	11.3	15.9
Other (in-kind, events, arts funds)	5.1	4.2	3.8
Contributions as a percentage of net income in "Trend" Theatres (n=100)	42.3	43.5	44.0

IRS tax-exempt organizations in arts, culture, and humanities — Charities and Other Tax-exempt Organizations, 2001, 2002, and 2003 — Statistics of Income Bulletin, www.irs.gov			
	2001	2002	2003
Number of organizations	26,006	27,129	27,285
Charitable revenue*	$12.93 billion	$12.82 billion	$14.01 billion

*Charitable revenue includes gifts and foundation grants (which is comparable to what *Giving USA* tracks) as well as government grants and allocations from other nonprofit agencies such as United Way and United Jewish Communities (which are not included in *Giving USA* estimates for contributions).

1   Giving to arts, culture, and humanities organizations includes contributions to museums; performing arts; historical societies; and other activities involving arts, culture, and humanities. In the National Taxonomy of Exempt Entities (NTEE), arts, culture, and humanities cover organizations in code A.

2   *Giving USA* sent surveys to 703 arts organizations, including all organizations that raised $20 million or more in 2003 or 2004 and a random sampling of small, medium-sized, and moderate organizations. 108 surveys were returned (a response rate of 15.4 percent). 30.0 percent of the large organizations responded. 16.4 percent of the moderate and medium-sized organizations; and 13.2 percent of small organizations replied. The sample was selected based on charitable revenue received circa 2003 (including some organizations that reported only in 2001 or only in 2002), supplemented with information obtained about arts organizations appearing on the *Chronicle of Philanthropy* list of the 400 charities receiving the most charitable revenue in 2004 or 2005.

3   Million Dollar List 2007, The Center on

Philanthropy at Indiana University.

4   Dr. Helga Wall-Apelt funds Asian art center at Ringling Museum of Art, largest gift in Florida State University's history, press release, January 17, 2006, www.ringling.org.

5   J. Kosman, S.F. opera patron donates $35 million: Largest gift of its kind in U.S.—no strings attached, *San Francisco Chronicle*, October 4, 2006. Viewed at lexis-nexis.com.

6   Arena Stage Press Release, viewed at www.arenastage.org/about/press-room/press-releases/releases/nextstage/next-stage_annoucement-12-06-06.pdf.

7   D. Wakin, Juilliard receives music manuscript collection, *New York Times*, March 1, 2006. Viewed at lexis-nexis.com.

8   R. Pogrebin, As corporate support shifts its focus, arts organizations are adjusting, *New York Times*, February 21, 2007. Viewed at www.lexis-nexis.com.

9   *The Best Companies Supporting the Arts in America*. The Business Committee for the Arts.,www.adlubow.com/bca.htm.

10 *Legislative Appropriations Annual Survey*. National Assembly of State Arts Agencies, January 2007.

11 *100% of Local and State Arts Ballot Measures Pass*. Americans for the Arts Action Fund., www.artsactionfund.org/pdf/arts_ballot_measures_2006.pdf.

12 *NEA: Promoting creativity and public access to the arts*. American Arts Alliance, www.americanartsalliance.org/americanartsalliance/NEA_issue_brief.html.

13 NEA Appropriations History Fiscal Years 1966 to 2007, www.AmericansForTheArts.org.

14 *President Bush enacts law making performing arts centers eligible for FEMA relief*. Association of Performing Arts Presenters. www.artspresenters.org/newsroom/2006releases/pr092906.cfm?

15 Center on Philanthropy, *Bank of America Study of High Net-Worth Philanthropy*, October, 2006, http://newsroom.bankofamerica.com.

16 Center on Philanthropy Panel Study, 2005 wave, data released March 2007 and analyzed at the Center on Philanthropy at Indiana University.

17 Theatre Communications Group, *Theatre Facts 2005*, covering September 2005 through August 2006, www.tcg.org. The 2006 report will be released in the second half of 2007.

18 *State of North America's Art Museums*. Association of Art Museum Directors, www.aamd.org/newsroom/documents/2006SNAAMFINAL.pdf.

18 Giving to international affairs

- In 2006, giving to international affairs organizations reached an estimated $11.34 billion, a decrease of 9.2 percent (-12.0 percent adjusted for inflation) from the revised estimate of $12.49 billion since 2005.

- The amount in 2005 includes giving for relief after the December 2004 tsunami. The decline in 2006 is the first drop in giving for this subsector since 1993.

- Giving to the international affairs subsector represented 3.8 percent of total estimated charitable contributions in the United States in 2006.

- In 1987, *Giving USA* began collecting data on gifts for international affairs, including aid, relief, and development giving, as well as contributions for student exchange programs and organizations working on global peace and security issues. Since 1987, giving for international affairs has increased an average of 16.3 percent annually (12.9 percent adjusted for inflation).

- From 1997 through 2006, giving to this subsector increased at an average annual rate of 12.5 percent (10.0 percent annually, after adjustment for inflation).

- Gifts to international affairs organizations include cash and in-kind contributions. In-kind gifts, often from corporations, include supplies, products, and equipment. U.S. recipient organizations are permitted by law to record those donations at fair-market value, which may exceed the amount allowed in deductions for the donor.

- An increasing amount of corporate cash support for international development is not through U.S. headquarters offices. It is contributed through operating units in other countries and might appear as a charitable deduction under U.S. law.

- At least half of the dollars contributed to large international affairs organizations go to organizations rooted in faith traditions.[1]

Giving USA findings for benchmarking giving to international affairs, 2006

As with all *Giving USA* estimates, the amount estimated in giving to organizations in the international subsector[2] includes gifts received of cash, cash equivalents (securities) and in-kind gifts (artwork, patents, real estate, and other items of value). *Giving USA* tries to exclude from its estimates the value of deferred or planned gift commitments and new pledges.

Table 1 summarizes average and median[3] amounts raised by international affairs organizations in 2005 and 2006 based on organizational size.[4] The survey asked organizations to report disaster giving separately. Therefore, these figures are calculated without disaster relief giving included.

Table 1
Charitable revenue received by international organizations
in 2005 and 2006, by organizational size

Organizational size	Number of completed surveys	2005 average ($)	2005 median ($)	2006 average ($)	2006 median ($)
Large	16	79,700,682	56,943,028	76,259,195	46,551,287
Moderately sized	27	8,185,048	6,194,564	9,392,947	6,785,481
Medium-sized	30	3,122,249	1,406,939	3,558,129	1,496,172
Small	30	186,693	107,500	201,058	97,931

Large denotes organizations that receive $20 million or more in charitable revenue; moderately sized organizations have charitable revenue between $5 million and $19.99 million; medium-sized is used for organizations having charitable revenue between $1 million and $4.99 million, and small is for organizations that have charitable revenue of less than $1 million.

The decline observed in charitable contributions occurred predominantly in large organizations. Moderate, medium and small organizations reported a small increase in average contributions.

Table 2 shows the increases and decreases among the organizations responding to the *Giving USA* survey.

- Large organizations were very likely to see a decline in charitable giving. This drop is found even after removing disaster gifts from both 2005 and 2006 values. Nearly 6 in 10 (56 percent) of large organizations reported a drop, averaging $14.2 million.

- Moderately sized organizations were about evenly divided between increases (52 percent) and decreases (44 percent), with 5 percent reporting a change within 1 percent of last year's amount. The average increase,

at $3.1 million, exceeded the average drop of less than $1 million.

- Medium-sized organizations were very likely to report growth in charitable giving, with more than three-quarters (77 percent) averaging an increase of $716,895.

- Not quite half (47 percent) of small organizations saw an increase, averaging $53,572 more in charitable contributions in 2006 compared with 2005.

Overall, 58 percent of international organizations reported growth in charitable giving; 37 percent reported a drop, and 8 percent reported no change. Because of the size of the decline in the largest organizations and because of the disaster-related gifts that lifted the total in 2005, the entire subsector showed a decline for 2006.

Table 2
Increases or decreases in charitable revenue of
international organizations, 2006

Organizational size	Number	Percentage of organizations in size group	Average change ($)	Average change (%)	Median change ($)	Median change (%)
Large						
Increase	6	38	12,078,092	30	10,558,784	26
Decrease	9	56	-14,239,569	-31	-15,907,025	-22
No Change	1	6	623,771	1	623,771	1
Total*	16	100				
All large organizations			-3,441,487	-6	-1,374,036	-3
Moderately sized						
Increase	14	52	3,134,662	62	3,777,938	31
Decrease	12	44	-939,330	-13	-594,250	-11
No Change	1	5	-47	0	-47	0
Total*	27	100				
All moderately sized organizations			1,207,899	18	139,717	13
Medium-sized						
Increase	23	77	716,895	31	329,452	20
Decrease	7	23	-487,456	-25	-218,644	-24
No Change	0	–	–	–	–	–
Total*	30	100				
All medium-sized organizations			435,880	26	201373	2
Small						
Increase	14	47	53,572	46	45,187	23
Decrease	10	33	-32,105	-32	-17,584	-25
No Change	6	20	333	0	0	0
Total*	30	100				
All small organizations			14,365	11	912	1

*Total does not always equal 100 due to rounding.

Charitable bequests to international affairs organizations rose slightly in 2006 compared with 2005, especially among large organizations. Table 3 shows the percentage of organizations reporting bequest revenue and the average and median amounts received in 2005 and 2006.

Table 3
Bequest receipts by organizational size, 2005 and 2006

Organizational size	Percentage with bequest revenues	2005 average ($)	2005 median ($)	2006 average ($)	2006 median ($)
Large	53	1,615,735	823,000	2,045,145	1,315,000
Moderate	46	401,021	310,992	447,964	273,412
Medium	32	468,072	75,000	423,904	81,144
Small*					

*Just one response, with $58,000 in bequest revenue in 2006.

International funding is not always in the international subsector in *Giving USA*

At least three different types of support for international activities occur but are not reported in *Giving USA* in the international subsector. In one case, the gift is made to another type of organization, which expends the funds elsewhere. In the other two cases, the gift is made to an organization that is not registered with the Internal Revenue Service. For foundation grantmaking, the amount of the donation is known and included in *Giving USA*. For corporations and individuals, the donation is not included in *Giving USA* at all because the amount is not known—it is not a gift eligible for a tax deduction under U.S. tax law and no data about such gifts are available. Each of these cases is explained a bit further below.

Case 1: International activities by other types of organizations. Many organizations in other subsectors conduct international activities, such as universities, health care organizations, arts and cultural institutions, youth development programs, religious entities, and many more. *Giving USA* reports gifts to those organizations in the subsector that reflects the purpose for which the recipient organization was founded. If that recipient expends some funds in another country, that expenditure is not recorded here as an international activity. The Hudson Institute's Index of Global Philanthropy, first released in spring 2006, collects data to track international expenditures of organizations in other subsectors. A new edition was released too late in spring 2007 to be incorporated into *Giving USA 2007*.[5] A summary of the philanthropic components of the 2006 Index of Global Philanthropy appears in *Giving USA 2006*.

Case 2: Foundations. When foundations make grants to organizations in other countries, the foundation's IRS Form 990-PF shows the grant amount and recipient. The Foundation Center tracks those grants by subsector, but if the recipient organization does not file an IRS Form 990, *Giving USA* does not receive data about these international gifts. This type of international support appears as a portion of the "unallocated" *Giving USA* estimate.

The donor's contribution is known by the Foundation Center, but the recipient organization is not required to provide data in the U.S. system about receiving the funds.

Case 3: Donations to non-U.S. charities by corporations or individuals. Corporations make gifts for charitable purposes in other countries, and if the recipient is not a U.S. entity but is operating in the other nation, the donor company cannot claim a deduction for a charitable purpose in the U.S. tax system. The Conference Board, a New York-based membership association of major companies, annually surveys firms about charitable giving. In editions issued since 2000, the *Corporate Contributions Report* has reported increasing corporate support for charitable activity in other countries with 2005 corporate donations of an estimated $2 billion, much of the value calculated from in-kind donations.[6] These contributions are not included in *Giving USA* as a donation nor are they allocated for a recipient type.

Individual or household donors also give to organizations operating in other nations and not registered in the U.S. These transfers are not tracked in the U.S. tax system as charitable gifts. When the donation is from a recent

immigrant to the U.S., it is called a remittance, and may benefit only the immigrant's family or may be intended to support a community project such as a school or clinic. The Hudson Institute counts financial remittances in its global philanthropy index, without distinguishing clearly between transfers for the immigrant's family and those for community projects.

Microfinance gets credit

Dr. Muhammed Yunus, founder of Bangladesh's Grameen Bank, received the Nobel Peace Prize in 2006. His successful application of microcredit, the extension of small loans to entrepreneurs too poor to qualify for traditional bank loans, helped nonprofit microfinance organizations receive significant donations for their work.[7]

One of the largest gifts for microfinance in 2006 was a $50 million pledge to Opportunity International from John and Jacque Weberg. The gift is the largest private donation ever given to a microfinance institution,[8] although Tufts University received $103 million for a microfinance program from alumni Pierre and Pam Omidyar in 2005. Other notable gifts toward microfinance programs in 2006 include:

- Grants from the Bill & Melinda Gates Foundation including some

Donors are aware of microfinance as a mechanism for economic development now, in part because of the coverage of Dr. Yunus' receipt of the Nobel Peace Prize. If your organization works in international development or poverty relief, your case for support should show how your organization's work is distinct from or supportive of microfinance.

to organizations based in other countries that are not included in the estimate for giving to the international subsector in the U.S. Two examples among several of the Gates Foundation grantmaking in this area are:

— $14.97 million to BRAC Foundation Tanzania Chapter (formerly known as the Bangladesh Rural Advancement Committee) to implement integrated microfinance, agriculture, and health programs aimed at the poorest segments of the rural population in Tanzania;[9] and

— $5.8 million to ACCION to develop new partnerships with microfinance institutions and commercial banks in West Africa and India in order to improve access for low-income people to microloans and related financial services.[10]

- Lenovo donated more than $1 million in computers to Opportunity International's microfinance program.[11] Lenovo is a global company that began in China and acquired IBM's personal computing division in 2004. The company has executive headquarters in Raleigh, North Carolina and manufacturing plants in China and India.[12]

High-profile donors make commitments to alleviate poverty

Global poverty alleviation has become a priority of many high-profile business leaders. The UN Millennium Development Goals sought to reduce poverty and improve lives in measurable ways (cut AIDS rates, increase access to clean water, lift the rate of enrollment in primary education, etc.) between 1990 and 2015. The World Bank put the cost of reaching the goals by the target date of 2015 at $40 billion to $60 billion a year.[13] Most of the funding is provided through development aid from governments, but increasingly, private donations seem to be playing a role. By 2006, progress had been made toward the eight goals in many areas, although Sub-Saharan African nations trailed the progress seen in most other developing regions.[14] Many of the donations for international aid in 2006 appeared to be linked directly to the Millennium Development Goals to eliminate poverty.

Bono and Bill and Melinda Gates were named *TIME* magazine's "People of the Year" at the end of 2006, in part because of their efforts to draw attention to global poverty and the health crises in the developing world.[15] Perhaps because of this type of attention, 2006 saw a number of major philanthropic commitments for alleviating poverty.

- David Rockefeller announced his intent to bequeath $225 million to the Rockefeller Brothers Fund (RBF) endowment to create the David Rockefeller Global Development Fund. The proposed fund addresses challenges of poverty, health care, sustainable development, the global economy, international trade, and the multilateral system.[16]

- George Soros donated $50 million to the Millennium Promise Alliance for the Millennium Villages program in African nations, which seeks to lift people out of poverty by addressing many problems at the same time, such as health, food production, education, access to clean water, and essential infrastructure.[17]

- The Global Development program of the Hewlett Foundation awarded 46 grants to 40 organizations for a grand total of more than $23 million. Many of the grants funded organizations that deal with agriculture, economics, or media.[18]

Former president Bill Clinton and the William J. Clinton Foundation held a meeting of the Clinton Global Initiative in September 2006, which raised $2.1 billion in pledges for donations and business initiatives directed at various global needs.[19] Pledges within the category of poverty alleviation made by U.S.-based donors include:

- Opportunity International, a non-profit that raises funds and loans them in microfinance programs, at $500 million;

- Citigroup's $100 million commitment for a microfinance program;

- FINCA International, a microfinance nonprofit based in Washington, DC, at $40 million; and

- Robert L. Johnson, founder of Black Entertainment Television and of The RLJ Companies, at $30 million.

Internationally, contributions for poverty alleviation were pledged by

WISeKey, a world internet security company headquartered in Switzerland, at $1 billion dollars and the U.K.-based Standard Chartered Bank at $500 million. The Clinton Global Initiative also raised funds for public health and for energy and climate, which are not included here.[20]

Bono began a project in early 2006 to seek grassroots support for ambitious goals to control the AIDS epidemic through a cause-related branding campaign called RED, in partnership with manufacturers for various products such as cell phones, shoes, clothing, and more.[21]

The estate of Hector Guy and Doris Di Stefano included $33 million for Direct Relief International. Mr. and Mrs. Di Stefano left contributions of this amount to seven different charitable organizations in several subsectors: environment/animals, human services, public-society benefit (veterans) and health.[22] Mr. Di Stefano died in Washington State in 2006.

Overview of international crises

Wars and refugees dominated international affairs news in 2006. The U.S. was in its fourth year of conflict in Afghanistan and Iraq. In Iraq, violence among Iraqis killed tens of thousands of civilians and exacerbated the

Interest in international aid and development is on the rise among public figures in business and entertainment. It is not clear as of early 2007 how this might affect the giving of the typical U.S. donor. Five percent of U.S. households gave an average of $340 each in 2005 to international affairs.

humanitarian crisis in that nation. Charitable organizations responded with aid for displaced persons in those countries. A brief war in summer 2006 occurred between Israel and fighters based in Lebanon, generating contributions for refugees and for reconstruction work in both nations. The long conflict in Sudan and a parallel fight in the Darfur region of that nation also made the news in 2006, with continuing famine and flight despite many efforts at intervention.

Iraq humanitarian crisis worsens as factional fighting grows to civil war

A new government took office in Iraq in May 2006.[23] Saddam Hussein went on trial for genocide[24] and was found guilty then executed, which led to protests and violence.[25] Increasing attacks spurred by doctrinal differences between Shiites and Sunnis,[26] and by factions within each sub-group[27] led to many tens of thousands of Iraqi deaths in 2006. By year's end, some were calling the ongoing violence a civil war.[28] Throughout the year, there were continuing militia attacks on U.S. military, which struggled to impose security and order. Daily life in Iraq cities, especially Baghdad, became a struggle for survival.[29]

The United Nations High Commission on Refugees estimated that 700,000 Iraqis fled their homes between early 2006 to early 2007.[30] The total Iraq population in July 2006 was estimated to be 26.8 million.[31] The International Rescue Committee (IRC) reported a population of 1.8 million displaced persons within Iraq, and 2 million

Iraqis who had fled to other countries and were living as refugees in Egypt, Jordan, Lebanon, Syria, Turkey, and elsewhere.[32] These figures mean that at least 14 percent of the population were refugees. That is equivalent to 42 million U.S. residents.

Many U.S.-based charities continued to respond to humanitarian needs in Iraq. In just a few examples of the work underway, Relief International reported its involvement in school reconstruction and about assistance it provided for internally displaced persons. Beginning in August 2006, Relief International began a micro-finance program for small businesses.[33] International Relief and Development provided emergency humanitarian aid in northern Iraq; facilitated a process of community stabilization to create employment and revitalize community infrastructure; and fostered self-governance initiatives at the grassroots level (community action groups).[34] International Medical Corps focused on rehabilitating the Iraqi healthcare system infrastructure, including providing support for more than 130 health clinics and more than 40 hospitals.[35] Funding for these and other activities included support from the U.S. Agency for International Development[36] and from charitable donations.

Middle East conflict destroys portions of Lebanon and Israel

A number of agencies raised funds to help people caught in the summer 2006 conflict between Hezbollah, a Lebanon-based militant group, and

One of the hardest things in fundraising is keeping an ongoing crisis at the top of people's minds and hearts without risking boredom, the view that gifts make little difference, or worse, anger at repeated appeals.

Showing progress toward reasonable goals is an important dimension of this type of work. Ending suffering is a lofty ambition but difficult to measure. Structure appeals to focus on specific people or communities who are helped. Report progress about specific projects and tasks that are completed or goals—even local ones—that are attained.

Israel. The International Committee of the Red Cross set a global fundraising goal of $81 million; United Jewish Communities in the U.S. sought $300 million; and Islamic Relief had a worldwide goal of $6.4 million and raised at least $1.4 million in the U.S.[37]

The US-Lebanon Partnership Fund formed to support rebuilding in Lebanon by providing assistance with crisis relief and response, information and communication technology, workforce training, and job creation.[38] The fund will match a pledge of $230 million in US governmental aid to Lebanon. The fund's creators are the heads of Intel Corporation, Cisco Systems Inc, Ghafari Inc, and Occidental Petroleum Corporation.[39]

To benefit people in Israel who suffered from air strikes, the Baltimore-based Harry and Jeanette Weinberg Foundation gave $5 million to United Jewish Communities' Israel Crisis Relief Fund in support of humanitarian and social services for victims of air strikes on Israeli cities.[40] Other organizations raising funds to respond in Israel include the YMCA, Save the Children, Brother's Brother Foundation, the

American Jewish Joint Distribution Committee, and the American Friends Service Committee.[41]

Sudan and its region, Darfur, remain in crisis

The 21-year Sudanese civil war that ended officially in 2005 destroyed food production capacity and displaced more than 600,000 people. Throughout 2006, the people of Sudan continued to face food crises and other urgent needs for health care, clean water, and food. The United Nations World Food Programme maintained efforts in the country but in April 2006 announced it would cut its delivery of food supplies when funding ran out.[42] A few weeks later, Pierre and Pam Omidyar announced a gift of $1 million to the United Nations World Food Programme for Sudan.[43]

Although the Sudanese civil war was officially ended, a separate conflict in the region of Darfur continued into a fourth year. In federal fiscal year 2006, various nongovernmental organizations and US Agency for International Development collectively provided more than $450 million in food, health services, water, and other basic needs.[44] InterAction, the American

Council for Voluntary International Action, shows more than 20 U.S.-based charities working in Darfur as of May 2006.[45] By late December, many organizations limited or ended at least some of their activities in response to attacks on aid workers.[46]

Investing in permanent solutions to famine

Two major foundations made a significant commitment to improve crop growing for small farmers in Africa. The Rockefeller Foundation and the Bill & Melinda Gates Foundation partnered to fund the Alliance for a Green Revolution in Africa (AGRA) with an initial donation of $150 million. The initial donation went to the development of seeds and to ensure their distribution to small farmers. The seeds' specific design allows for higher production of crop yields in Africa's diverse climates.[47]

In a related development, the Conrad N. Hilton Foundation awarded $7.2 million to the Millennium Water Alliance for its work to provide potable water for people in African countries.[48]

Company gives software products and money to improve disaster relief response

Microsoft made a donation of software and cash totaling $41 million. The gift was split between the Interagency Working Group on Emergency Capacity Building (ECB) and to NetHope.[49] Both organizations consist of a consortium of other nonprofit, non-governmental organizations. NetHope members focus on international development and ECB members concentrate on collaboration and capacity in disaster response.

Studies of giving to international affairs

In general, in the U.S. population, approximately 5 percent of households give for this type of cause and the average gift in 2004 was approximately $340, according to a preliminary analysis of data from the Center on Philanthropy Panel Study.[50] The *Bank of America Study of High Net-Worth Giving*,[51] which provided information for other chapters in this edition, included international affairs among a group of "other types of charities," so giving to this subsector by this group cannot be estimated separately.

Table 4
Key findings from other studies about giving to international affairs organizations

$5 million dollar list, gifts from individuals to international affairs (does not include gifts to foundations) Center on Philanthropy at Indiana University, www.philanthropy.iupui.edu			
	2004	2005	2006
Number of international affairs gifts	2	5	4
Largest gift to international affairs	$15 million from Herbert and Marion Sandler to Human Rights Watch	$53 million from Robert Edward (Ted) Turner to the United Nations Foundation	$50 million from Warren E. Buffett to the Nuclear Threat Initiative $50 million from George Soros to help eliminate poverty in African nations $50 million pledge from John and Jacque Weberg to Opportunity International
International affairs dollars given as percentage of all individual gifts on list of $5 million and above	0.2 percent	0.6 percent	3.1 percent

Foundation Giving Trends: Update on Funding Priorities Grants in the major subject category of international affairs, development, and peace Foundation Center, www.foundationcenter.org			
	2003	2004	2005
Average grant amount	$140,828	$150,202	$172366
Average grant amount	$50,000	$50,000	$45,000
International subsector funding as a percentage of grant dollars (surveyed foundations, including corporate foundations)	2.5 percent	2.76 percent	3.6 percent

IRS tax-exempt organizations in international affairs subsector Charities and Other Tax-Exempt Organizations, 2001, 2002, and 2003 *Statistics of Income Bulletin*, www.irs.gov			
	2001	2002	2003
Number filing IRS Form 990	3,360	3,505	3,131
Charitable revenue reported*	$9.33 billion	$11.40 billion	$13.10 billion

*Charitable revenue includes gifts and foundation grants (which is comparable to what *Giving USA* tracks) as well as government grants and allocations from other nonprofit agencies, such as United Way and United Jewish Communities (which are not included in *Giving USA* estimates for contributions).

1 *Giving USA* estimates, based on the Philanthropy 400, that at least 50 percent of the amount received at 58 international organizations is to charities created at least in part as an expression of faith. This analysis includes any international organization listed on the Philanthropy 400 between 2000 and 2005. Contributions data for each year for each organization were obtained from IRS Forms 990 posted at www.guidestar.org. Coding for faith-basis was done by checking the organizations' Web sites and reading for Christian, Jewish, God, faith, holy, and related words.

2 Giving to the international affairs subsector includes contributions to organizations formed for purposes of providing international relief and development aid, promoting international understanding or exchange, engaging in policy issues related to national and international security, or advancing human rights internationally. Organizations in this subsector are classified in the National Taxonomy of Exempt Entities (NTEE) as being in Major Category Q.

3 The median is the mid-point. One-half of the organizations responding had higher charitable revenue; the other half had lower.

4 *Giving USA* sent surveys to 687 organizations in the international affairs subsector. Responses from 103 organizations (15.0 percent) form the basis for this analysis. The response rate from large organizations was 27.0 percent. About 60 large organizations account for

approximately 53 percent of the total charitable revenue in this subsector of an estimated 5,000 organizations (including small organizations that do not file an IRS Form 990). The sample was selected based on charitable revenue received circa 2003 (includes some organizations that reported only in 2001 or only in 2002), supplemented with information obtained about international organizations reporting in 2004 and 2005 and appearing on the *Chronicle of Philanthropy* list of the 400 charities receiving the most charitable revenue in 2004 and 2005.

5 Center for Global Prosperity, *Index of Global Philanthropy*, Hudson Institute, http://gpr.hudson.org.

6 S. Muirhead, *2006 Corporate Contributions Report*, The Conference Board, page 8.

7 "Microfinancing" is the term used for small loans to people with low income. Institutions that provide microfinance services are being started in many areas of both the developing and industrial worlds. These institutions are often started by public or charitable gifts. This summary is taken from Microfinance: Services The Poor Can Bank On, *BusinessWeek*, 2 May 2006, www. businessweek.com.

8 J. Gangemi, $50 Million Microfinance Pledge Is Largest Ever, *BusinessWeek*, 20 September 2006, www.businessweek.com/ smallbiz/content/sep2006/sb20060920_ 378485.htm?chan=top+news_ top+news+index_small+business.

9 Special Initiatives – Grant, *Bill & Melinda Gates Foundation*, 3 Nov 2006, www. gatesfoundation.org.

10 B. MacDonald, Bill & Melinda Gates Foundation Awards $5.8 Million Grant to ACCION for Microfinance Development in Africa and India, *Accion International*, 30 Jan 2006, www.accion.org.

11 S. Scott, Opportunity International Receives $1 Million In-Kind Gift from Lenovo, *Opportunity International*, 23 June 2006, www.opportunity.org.

12 Lenovo web site, www.pc.ibm.com/us/lenovo/locations.html, viewed 4-29-07.

13 World Bank, The cost of attaining the Millennium development goals, http://www.worldbank.org.

14 United Nations, *The Millennium Development Goals Report, 2006*, http://unstats.un.org.

15 N. Gibbs, The Good Samaritans: Melinda Gates, Bono and Bill Gates: three people on a global mission to end poverty, disease— and indifference, *TIME*, 19 December 2006, www.time.com.

16 G. Fuller, David Rockefeller and the Rockefeller Brothers Fund Establish Fund to Address Poverty, Health, and Development, *Rockefeller Brothers Fund*, 20 November 2006, www.rbf.org.

17 Soros Invests $50 Million in Poverty Ending Projects in Africa, *Millennium Promise*, 13 September 2006, www.millenniumpromise.org.

18 Grants – Global Development, *The William and Flora Hewlett Foundation*, 2006, www.hewlett.org.

19 C. Dugger, Clinton Effort Reaps Pledges of $7.3 Billion in Global Aid, *Clinton Global Initiative*, 23 Sept 2006, www.clintonglobalinitiative.org.

20 Browse Commitments, *Clinton Global Initiative*, 2006, www.clintonglobalinitiative.org.

21 CBS News, Bono seeing 'RED' over AIDS: Helps launch 'red' line of products to help fund fight vs. HIV, AIDS, January 26, 2006, http://www.cbsnews.com/stories/2006/01/26/earlyshow/main1241892.shtml.

22 Top 60 donors in 2006, *Chronicle of Philanthropy*, February 22, 2007, www.philanthropy.com.

23 J. Burns, For some, a last, best hope for U.S. efforts in Iraq, *New York Times*, May 21, 2006, www.nytimes.com.

24 E. Wong, Hussein charged with genocide in 50,000 deaths, *New York Times*, April 5,

2006, www.nytimes.com.

25 J. Burns, As attacks go on, Iraqis are riveted by Hussein video, *New York Times*, December 31, 2006, www.nytimes.com..

26 S. Tavernise, A fresh pattern of revenge fuels Baghdad killings, *New York Times*, November 20, 2006, www.nytimes.com.

27 J. Burns, Deeper crisis, less U.S. sway, *New York Times*, November 29, 2006, www.nytimes.com.

28 E. Wong, A matter of definition: what makes a civil war, and who declares it so, *New York Times*, November 26, 2006, www.nytimes.com.

29 S. Tavernise, Iraqis see the little things fade away in war's gloom, *New York Times*, November 29, 2006, vwww.nytimes.com.

30 United Nations High Commission on Refugees, The Iraq Situation, viewed April 26, 2007, www.unhcr.org/cgi-bin/texis/vtx/iraq?page=intro.

31 No author, *CIA World Fact Book*, www.cia.gov.

32 Iraqi refugees: A humanitarian crisis of historic proportions, International Rescue Committee, http://www.theirc.org, viewed May 15, 2007.

33 Self sufficiency through microfinance, Relief International, http://ri.org, viewed May 15, 2007.

34 Where we work: Iraq, International Relief and Development, viewed April 26, 2007. www.ird-dc.org/draft/where/iraq.htm.

35 Program information sheet, International Medical Corps, date of creation August 21, 2006, viewed April 26, 2007, www.imcworldwide.org/pdf/IMC_Programs_082106.pdf.

36 USAID.gov/iraq viewed April 29, 2007.

37 C. Preston, More than $125 million raised for humanitarian aid in the Middle East, *Chronicle of Philanthropy*, August 10, 2006, www.philanthropy.com.

38 About the Fund, *Lebanon Partnership Fund*, 2006, www.lebanonpartnership.org/gs_disaster_relief/about.html.

39 News Release: Four of America's Corporate Leaders Launch Lebanon Rebuilding Effort, *Cisco Systems Inc*, 25 September 2006, http://newsroom.cisco.com.

40 Weinberg Foundation Awards $5 Million to Israel Crisis Relief Fund, *Philanthropy*

News Digest, 22 July 2006, http://
foundationcenter.org.

41 Interaction, Crisis in the Middle East,
www.interaction.org/mideast/, viewed
April 26, 2007.

42 L. Polgreen, UN cuts Darfur food aid as
donations trickle away, *Intl Herald Tribune*,
April 30, 2006.

43 World Food Programme Press release,
5-23-06.

44 US Agency for International Development,
Sudan-Complex Emergency, Situation
Report #8, January 12, 2007.

45 No author, *InterAction Member Activity
Report: Sudan and Chad*, May 2006, www.
interaction.org/files.cgi/5133_Sudan_&_
Chad_May_2006.pdf

46 USAID, Situation Report #8, as in note 44
above.

47 Bill & Melinda Gates, Rockefeller
Foundations Form Alliance to Help Spur

"Green Revolution" in Africa, *Bill &
Melinda Gates Foundation*, 12 September
2006, www.gatesfoundation.org.

48 World Vision Awarded $7.2 Million from
Hilton Foundation to Provide Safe Water
and Improved Sanitation in Ethiopia, *Social
Funds*, 5 July 2006, www.socialfunds.com.

49 Press release, Microsoft gifts $41 million
in software and cash to help groups better
collaborate in times of crisis, Microsoft,
February 22, 2006, www.microsoft.com/
presspass/features/2006/feb06/02-
22NGOCollaborate.mspx.

50 Center on Philanthropy Panel Study, 2005
wave, data released March 2007 and analyzed
at the Center on Philanthropy at Indiana
University.

51 Center on Philanthropy at Indiana
University, *Bank of America Study of High
Net-Worth Philanthropy*, October 2006,
www.philanthropy.iupui.edu.

19 Giving to environment and animals

- In 2006, giving to the environment and animals subsector reached an estimated $6.60 billion, an increase of 1.9 percent from the revised estimate of $6.48 billion for 2005 (-1.3 percent adjusted for inflation).

- Giving to environment and animals organizations represented 2.2 percent of total estimated charitable contributions in the United States in 2006.

- Since 1987, when giving to environment and animals organizations began to be tracked separately, the average annual increase has been 8.1 percent (6.9 percent adjusted for inflation).

- From 1997 to 2006, the average annual increase has been 8.1 percent (7.2 percent adjusted for inflation).

Giving USA findings for benchmarking giving to environment and animals organizations, 2006

As with all *Giving USA* estimates, the estimated amount given to the environment and animal subsector[1] includes gifts received of cash, cash equivalents (securities), and in-kind gifts (artwork, patents, real estate, and other items of value). Gifts to the environment also include allowed values for conservation easements, as reported by the recipient organizations. *Giving USA* tries to exclude from its estimates the value of deferred or planned gift commitments and new pledges.

Tables 1 through 3 summarize the *Giving USA 2007* survey findings.[2] Table 1 illustrates the average and median amounts reported in charitable gifts; Table 2 illustrates the direction of change in giving (increase, decrease, or within 1 percent, which is termed "no change"); and Table 3 shows the percentage of organizations that reported bequest receipts and the average and median amount received from bequests for each organizational size.

Table 2 summarizes the average and median increases or decreases in charitable revenue reported for 2006 by organizational size. In all size groups, a higher percentage of organizations reported growth than reported decline.

- Among the large organizations, 8 in 10 reported an increase averaging $3.2 million. Just 20 percent reported a decline. In total, among large organizations, charitable gifts rose an average of $2.4 million.

- In moderate organizations, 54 percent reported an increase averaging $2.4 million. While a smaller percentage, 35 percent, reported a decline, the average drop was $3.6 million. In sum for the moderate organizations reporting, the change among all of them was a relatively small increase of about $80,000.

- Medium-sized organizations were nearly evenly divided between growth (50 percent) and decline (47 percent). The average growth of $414,949 exceeded the average drop, so the net result was modest growth in this size of environment/animals organizations of $62,596 among those responding to the survey.

- In small organizations, 46 percent reported an increase averaging $53,024. 31 percent reported a decline, averaging $34,800. In total, organizations in this survey that are small environment/animals organizations saw a change averaging $14,041.

Table 1
Charitable revenue received by environment and animals organizations
in 2005 and 2006, by organizational size

Organizational size	Number of completed surveys	2005 average ($)	2005 median ($)	2006 average ($)	2006 median ($)
Large	10	32,952,254	32,143,848	35,028,606	38,656,039
Moderately sized	26	6,823,940	5,124,610	6,905,759	4,001,804
Medium-sized	32	1,888,380	1,583,670	1,950,976	1,536,164
Small	39	115,307	49,743	129,014	39,500

Large denotes organizations that receive $20 million or more in charitable revenue; *moderately sized* organizations have charitable revenue between $5 million and $19.99 million; *medium-sized* is used for organizations having charitable revenue between $1 million and $4.99 million, and *small* is for organizations that have charitable revenue of less than $1 million.

Table 2
Increases or decreases in charitable revenue of
environment and animal organizations, 2005

Organizational size	Number	Percentage of organizations in size group	Average change ($)	Average change (%)	Median change ($)	Median change (%)
Large						
Increase	8	80	3,234,662	26	789,449	4
Decrease	2	20	-2,556,892	-29	-255,892	-29
No change						
Total*	10	100				
All large organizations			2,417,369	18	351,519	2
Moderately sized						
Increase	14	54	2,437,310	41	1,130,529	21
Decrease	9	35	-3,557,944	-34	-2,448,778	-24
No change	3	12	8,822	0	0	0
Total*	26	100				
All moderately sized organizations			81,820	10	85,981	4

Giving to environment and animals

Organizational size	Number	Percentage of organizations in size group	Average change ($)	Average change (%)	Median change ($)	Median change (%)
Medium-sized						
Increase	16	50	414,949	35	299,557	20
Decrease	15	47	-309,073	-15	-161,900	-8
No change	1	3	0	0	0	0
Total*	32	100				
All medium-sized organizations			62,596	11	10,450	2
Small						
Increase	18	46	53,024	5,647	44,707	71
Decrease	12	31	-34,800	-37	-14,487	-28
No change	9	23	-253	0	0	0
Total*	39	100				
All small organizations			14,041	34	0	0

*Total does not always equal 100 due to rounding.

Table 3 shows bequest receipts by organizational size. The average and the median receipts declined in large organizations. In moderate organizations, the average fell but the median increased. The average charitable bequest receipts rose in medium-sized organizations. In small organizations, the average increased and the median remained the same, suggesting a few organizations with higher amounts pulled up the average.

Table 3
Bequest receipts by organizational size, 2005 and 2006

Organizational size	Percentage with bequest revenues	2005 average ($)	2005 median ($)	2006 average ($)	2006 median ($)
Large	78	4,951,371	3,376,841	3,614,713	3,201,362
Moderate	85	1,287,842	299,009	840,691	436,463
Medium	58	194,397	91,637	245,116	40,000
Small*	24	37,773	13,000	188,580	14,000

*For 2006, nine small environment and animals organizations provided bequest information. The values are reported here although the number of responses is too low to use in making statistical inferences about small environment and animals organizations.

Multi-million dollar gifts directed to environment or animal organizations

Most of the largest announced gifts to organizations in this subsector during 2006 went to entities that focus on the environment; not very many gifts went specifically to organizations focusing on domestic or wild animals.[3] The average gift from an individual or family was $11.5 million. Four of the top gifts are discussed in more detail below.

Bobolink Foundation receives $80 million

Henry and Wendy Paulson formed the Bobolink Foundation in 1985 with the purpose of supporting environmental, conservation, and education causes. During 2006, they contributed 510,000 shares of Goldman Sachs stock, worth approximately $80 million, to this foundation. In early 2007, Mr. Paulson, US Treasury Secretary and former head of Goldman Sachs, announced his intent to transfer the bulk of his personal fortune to philanthropy in the coming years.[4] The Paulsons also gave 127,500 shares of Goldman Sachs stock, worth about $20 million, to the Goldman Sachs Philanthropy Fund, a donor-advised fund. The Paulsons declined to disclose how the money would be used.[5]

Enterprise Rent-A-Car's 50-million-tree pledge

Enterprise Rent-A-Car pledged $50 million to plant fifty million trees over fifty years in a gift commemorating The National Arbor Day Foundation's 50th anniversary. Fifty million trees is the equivalent of planting a new Central Park every ten days for the next fifty years. The US Forest Service will plant trees in forests across the nation. Year two of the grant includes planting trees in international locations where Enterprise does business.[6]

Estate gift divided among multiple charities

Eight organizations were named as beneficiaries of the Hector Guy and Doris Di Stefano estate. The gift consists of the entire Di Stefanos' estate, worth $264 million. Each organization received $33 million. The World Wildlife Fund, Greenpeace International, and the American Humane Association are three of the recipients named for the gift. Most of the money in the estate came from the UPS stock that Mrs. Di Stefano inherited from her father.

The gift to Greenpeace International was challenged by another recipient, The Salvation Army. The Salvation Army argued that because the gift was intended for Greenpeace International, the Greenpeace Fund should not receive the gift. The Greenpeace Fund argued that because it absorbed Greenpeace International in 2005, the gift should be honored.[7] In May 2007, the case was settled with Greenpeace Fund receiving $27 million, instead of $33 million.[8]

Charitable remainder trust helps preserve biologically diverse region

Roger and Victoria Sant gifted the World Wildlife Federation (WWF) with a $20 million charitable remainder trust for safeguarding the Amazon

Rainforest in Brazil. It is the largest amount ever given to the WWF. The trust will help permanently protect 125 million acres of the tropical rainforest, an area about the size of California.[9] Mr. Sant cofounded and served as president of international power utility Applied Energy Services Corporation, a Virginia-based power company.[10]

Threat of global warming recognized by US organizations

The US Climate Action Partnership (USCAP) released a report, *A Call to Action*, which argues for legislation that would reduce the production of greenhouse gases that contribute to global warming. The report provides a blueprint for a mandatory economy-wide, market-driven approach to climate protection.[11]

The Intergovernmental Panel on Climate Change stated, with 90 percent certainty, that global warming is caused by human activity.[12] Problems associated with climate change, that are of particular concern for organizations in the environment and animals subsector, include biodiversity loss, increased drought, spread of disease, changes in freshwater supply, and an increase in extreme weather events.[13]

Clinton Global Initiative raises funds to combat global warming

President Bill Clinton and the William J. Clinton Foundation held the Clinton Global Initiative's second annual meeting during September 2006. The Clinton Global Initiative raised pledges from organizations around the world. Highlighted amounts pledged to the Energy and Climate Change category include ABN AMRO Bank at $190 million, Stephen Bing of Shangri-la Entertainment at $40 million, Kleiner Perkins Caufield & Byers at $100 million, Enel S. P. A. at $250 million, and Richard Branson of Virgin Group of Companies at $3 billion.[14] Branson's pledge comes from the Virgin Group of Companies' anticipated profits over the next ten years.[15]

Numerous grants awarded to organizations working in sustainability, climate change, and land conservation

The William and Flora Hewlett Foundation awarded 115 grants in its environmental program, giving 91 organizations totaling more than $45 million. The majority of the grants went to programs involving sustainable energy, clean transportation, air quality, climate change, and the protection of natural areas. The Foundation also awarded 35 additional grants to environmental programs at universities, foundations, and foreign organizations, but these grants were not included in the $45 million figure.[16]

Land donations eased

Despite scrutiny by Congress over the practice of claiming deductions for conservation easements, legislative change in 2006 temporarily removed some of the barriers that had limited tax deductibility for this type of gift. Until it is made permanent, the law only applies to easements donated in 2006 and 2007. The law includes:

- Raising the amount that a donor may deduct from income from 30 percent to 50 percent of adjusted gross income for donating a conservation easement;

- Allowing qualified farmers and ranchers to deduct up to 100 percent of their income; and

- Increasing the number of years over which a donor can allocate deductions from six to sixteen.[17]

Virginia land donated with goal to improve water quality

British Petroleum (BP) America donated 655 acres of undeveloped land to The Nature Conservancy in York County, Virginia. The land was given after BP sold a refinery that it had operated in the area. The tract of land will help protect the York River's water quality. The Virginia Department of Game and Inland Fisheries agreed to include the property in its wildlife management system.[18]

Consortium of small- to medium-sized companies donate 1 percent of sales to environmental organizations

A group named One Percent for the Planet raised $4 million for environmental nonprofit organizations in 2006.[19] Yvon Chouinard of Patagonia and Craig Matthews of Blue Ribbon Flies launched the site which allows businesses to donate to environmental causes. Participating businesses give one percent of their sales to environmental organizations. Businesses choose organizations from a list of member nonprofits.[20] More than $12 million has been raised since the group was launched in 2001.[21]

Target Analysis Group finds drop in giving for animal protection, modest increase for the environment, 2006

Based on 4 major animal-related organizations, Target Analysis Group reported a median decline of 16.3 percent in the amount raised through direct mail (including Web, telemarketing, and event-related revenue) compared with 2005.[22] This decline follows a large increase (median change above 40 percent) in 2005, stimulated at least in part by people's response to the need to rescue animals after the disasters of 2005.

Among 12 major environmental organizations, Target Analysis Group found a median increase of 4.2 percent in direct response revenue.

Study of giving to the environment

In general, in the U.S. population, approximately 9 percent of households give for this type of cause and the average gift in 2004 was approximately $180, according to a preliminary analysis of data from the Center on Philanthropy Panel Study.[23] The *Bank of America Study of High Net-Worth Giving*,[24] which provided information for other chapters in this edition, included environment/animals among a group of "other types of charities," so giving to this subsector by this group cannot be estimated separately.

Table of key studies

Table 4 below summarizes data points from annual studies related to giving for organizations in the environment/animals subsector.

Table 4
Key findings from other studies about giving to environment and animal organizations

$5 million dollar list, gifts from individuals to environment and animals (does not include gifts to foundations) Center on Philanthropy at Indiana University, www.philanthropy.iupui.edu			
	2004	2005	2006
Number of gifts to organizations in the environment and animals subsector	3	8	12
Largest gift to an organization in the environment and animals subsector	$180 million (value) in the form of 146,000 acres of Missouri forest to the L-A-D Foundation, an operating foundation, from Leo and Kay Drey	$93 million from Dave and Cheryl Duffield to Maddie's Fund, to support humane, no-kill treatment of stray and abandoned animals	$80 million from Henry M. and Wendy J. Paulson to the Bobolink Foundation in grants to education, environmental, and conservation groups.
Environment and animals dollars given as percentage of all individual gifts on list of $5 million and above	3.4 percent	2.7 percent	4.4 percent

Foundation Giving Trends: Update on Funding Priorities Grants to environment and animals Foundation Center, www.fdncenter.org			
	2003	2004	2005
Average grant amount	$120,698	$110,296	$126,925
Median grant amount	$30,000	$30,000	$30,000
Environment and animals funding as a percentage of grant dollars (surveyed foundations, including corporate foundations)	6.2 percent	5.3 percent	6.3 percent

IRS tax-exempt organizations in environment and animals category Charities and other tax-exempt organizations, 2001, 2002, 2003 *Statistics of Income Bulletin*, www.irs.gov			
	2001	2002	2003
Number	8697	9413	10,454
Charitable revenue*	$5.38 billion	$5.98 billion	$5.94 billion

*Charitable revenue includes gifts and foundation grants (which is comparable to what *Giving USA* tracks) as well as government grants and allocations from other nonprofit agencies, such as United Way and United Jewish Communities (which are not included in *Giving USA* estimates for contributions).

1   The environment and animals subsector includes organizations working for land conservation, pollution abatement or control, species preservation, animal rescue, environmental education, and outdoor survival, and other activities involving animals or the environment. In the National Taxonomy of Exempt Entities (NTEE), environment and animals covers organizations in codes C and D.

2   *Giving USA* sent surveys to 619 organizations in the environment and animals subsector. Responses from 107 organizations (17.3 percent) form the basis for this analysis. The response rate among large organizations was 41 percent. Just 27 large organizations are estimated to receive approximately 20 percent of all dollars donated to the more than 10,450 environment and animals organizations. The sample was selected based on charitable revenue received circa 2003 (includes some organizations that reported only in 2001 or only in 2002), supplemented with information obtained about environment and animals organizations reporting in 2004 and appearing on the *Chronicle of Philanthropy* list of the 400 charities receiving the most charitable revenue in 2004 or 2005.

3   Million Dollar List 2006, *The Center on Philanthropy at Indiana University*. www.philanthropy.iupui.edu/Research/giving_fundraising_research.aspx

4   Henry Paulson joins ranks of big charity donors, *Charity Blog Network*, January 17, 2007, http://charity2.0television.com/blog/?p=592.

5   The 2006 Slate: The 60 largest American charitable contributions of the year, *Slate*, www.slate.com/id/2159776/pagenum/2.

6   Enterprise Rent-A-Car Makes 50-Year Commitment To Plant 50 Million Trees in National Forests, *Business Wire*, October 12, 2006, http://web.lexis-nexis.com/universe/.

7   America's Most-Generous Donors, *Chronicle of Philanthropy,* 2006, February 22, 2007, www.philanthropy.com.

8   T. Tizon, Salvation Army, Greenpeace call off fight over bequest, *Los Angeles Times*, May 14, 2007, www.latimes.com.

9   D. Cohn, $20 Million Pledged to Protect Amazon, *Washington Post*, May 27, 2006, www.washingtonpost.com/wp-dyn/content/article/2006/05/26/AR2006052601924_pf.html.

10 Entry for Roger W. Sant, *NNDB*, www.nndb.com/people/903/000094621/.

11 *A Call to Action*. United States Climate Action Partnership. www.us-cap.org/.

12 R Black, Humans blamed for climate change, *BBC News*, February 2, 2007, http://news.bbc.co.uk/2/hi/science/nature/6321351.stm.

13 Discover>Global Forces>Climate Change>Basic Information, *World Wildlife Fund*, 2007, http://worldwildlife.org/climate/basic.cfm.

14 *Clinton Global Initiative*, www.clintonglobal-initiative.org.

15 Press Release: 2nd Annual Meeting of Clinton Global Initiative— 3 Days, 215

Commitments, $7.3 Billion, William J. Clinton Foundation, 22 September 2006, www.clintonfoundation.org/.

16   Grants, The William and Flora Hewlett Foundation, 2006, www.hewlett.org/Grants/.

17   News and Updates on the Conservation Tax Incentive, Land Trust Alliance, November 11, 2006, www.lta.org/publicpolicy/tax_incentives_updates.htm.

18   BP, The Nature Conservancy Gift of 655 Acres Benefits State, York County, *The Nature Conservancy*, November 1, 2006, http://www.nature.org.

19   Web site of One Percent for the Planet, www.onepercentfortheplanet.org/

20   *1% for the Planet*, January 2007, http://www.onepercentfortheplanet.org/za/en_us?PAGE=HOME.

21   J Gangemi, Giving Goes Green, *Business Week*, November 27, 2006, http://www.businessweek.com/magazine/content/06_48/b4011091.htm?chan=search.

22   H. Flannery and R. Harris, *Quarterly Index of National Fundraising Performance*, Q 4 2006, Target Analysis Group, www.targetanalysis.com.

23   Center on Philanthropy Panel Study, 2005 wave, data released March 2007 and analyzed at the Center on Philanthropy at Indiana University.

24   Center on Philanthropy at Indiana University, *Bank of America Study of High Net-Worth Philanthropy*, October 2006, www.philanthropy.iupui.edu.

20 Legal and legislative issues

Summary of legal and legislative issues

For those in the nonprofit sector concerned with legislative initiatives and regulation, 2006 was a busy year. Federal elections in November focused attention on economic and international policy issues, resulting in the transfer of control in the House and the Senate to the Democratic Party. Before the election, and before the seating of the 110th Congress in January 2007, Congress passed legislation that includes numerous giving incentives and reforms intended to curb abuse of tax-exempt status and gift deductions. Federal agencies altered the rules for participation in the Combined Federal Campaign, adopted rules concerning the use of unsolicited facsimiles (faxes) by nonprofits, and issued guidance for compliance with new regulations. Courts rendered decisions concerning the free speech rights of nonprofit organizations. State legislatures kept pace with their federal counterparts, passing a variety of bills that increased state oversight of charitable institutions and addressed topics including solicitation, registration of professional fundraisers, and the proper handling of information about donors.

Federal committees query nonprofit activities

Prior to the 2006 mid-term election, several members of Congress demonstrated skepticism about nonprofit operations and governance. Representative Bill Thomas (R-California) chaired the powerful House Ways and Means Committee and challenged several large nonprofit organizations to defend their entitlement to tax-exempt status. In October 2006, Thomas required the National Collegiate Athletic Association, the body governing college sports, to submit documentation supporting the continuation of its nonprofit designation.[1] That review was not complete by early 2007.

WHAT THIS MEANS TO YOU

The section highlights federal and state government actions taken during 2006 that might affect fundraising activities. Federal actions are considered first, followed by state activity, and then recommendations from the Panel on the Nonprofit Sector, organized by INDEPENDENT SECTOR.

This chapter is intended as an overview and does not substitute for professional legal advice. Before taking any actions to change existing policies or procedures at a nonprofit organization, please consult a legal advisor with expertise in law regarding nonprofit organizations.

Many of the items discussed in this section are also critical to other aspects of nonprofit management and legal compliance. Those responsible for the legal compliance of organizations are advised to consult additional resources for a complete discussion of the legislative and regulatory matters discussed here.

On the Senate side, Senator Charles Grassley (R-Iowa), chair of the Finance Committee in 2006, expressed strong concern over issues of governance, transparency, and accountability in nonprofit institutions and instituted aggressive investigations. In one case, Grassley sent a letter to the American Hospital Association expressing "serious concern" over issues related to the operation of nonprofit hospitals, including questioning how these hospitals calculate community benefit.[2] Grassley's pressure ultimately led to the creation of a series of voluntary reforms proposed by Independent Sector. His inquiries also contributed to the inclusion of a number of reform measures in the Pension Protection Act of 2006.[3]

2006 election shifts committee leadership in 2007 in House and Senate

In 2006, voters altered the balance of power in the United States House of Representatives and the Senate. With a different party in the majority, the chairmanship of committees shifted in early 2007, including changes to the leadership of the Senate Committee on Finance and the House Ways and Means Committee. It is too early (as of April 2007) to know how the change in leadership might affect legislation and committee review of the nonprofit sector. Congressional observers have noted some areas in which the new committee chairs may have special interest in issues affecting the nonprofit sector.

Representative Charles Rangel (D-New York), chair of the House Ways and Means Committee beginning in 2007, has stated his opposition to the repeal of the federal estate tax.[4] Rangel has also demonstrated an interest in the amount of charity care provided by nonprofit hospitals.[5]

Senator Max Baucus (D-Montana) assumed the role of chair of the Senate Finance Committee in January 2007. Baucus worked closely with his predecessor, Senator Grassley, and generally supported Grassley's efforts for stronger oversight and controls in the nonprofit sector. The use of tax-exempt status for inappropriate activities is a pressing concern for Senator Baucus. In October 2006, he led Democrats on the Finance Committee to issue a minority staff report about former lobbyist Jack Abramoff's use of tax-exempt organizations in his efforts to manipulate legislation. Abramoff used several nonprofit entities as fronts for his lobbying and bribery.[6]

Pension Protection Act of 2006 includes IRA roll-over provisions, other rules affecting charities

The most significant legislation in 2006 related to nonprofit organizations was the Pension Protection Act of 2006.[7] Though devoted primarily to issues related to pensions, Congress used the Act as a vehicle to deliver a number of reforms that affect nonprofit organizations and charitable giving. President Bush signed the Act on August 17, 2006.

For fundraisers, the most significant provision of the Act gives donors older than 70.5 years of age the opportunity to transfer up to $100,000 per tax year

WHAT THIS MEANS TO YOU

The Pension Protection Act did not benefit all charities equally. One interpretation of the difference is that those most likely to receive additional gifts were those able to communicate quickly with their donors through newsletters, e-mails, and other means. With Congress and state legislatures taking action to regulate charities on one hand and to stimulate more giving on the other, nonprofit organizations in all subsectors and of all sizes will be better able to benefit from changes when staff members can initiate fundraising changes quickly and when donor records are current, permitting rapid communication with constituents.

from traditional or Roth Individual Retirement Accounts to charitable organizations.[8] This provision comes with a time limit. Gifts made under this section must be completed before December 31, 2007. Analysts suggest that this provision alone could generate as much as $1 billion in donations by the expiration date.[9] Nonprofit organizations, especially those with fundraising staff such as institutions of higher education and health care,[10] were quick to get the word out to potential donors and financial planners in the hopes of securing immediate gains.

The Pension Act limits distributions by private foundations and donor-advised funds to certain types of supporting organizations.[11] Generally, the Pension Act recognizes three types of supporting organizations, which are grouped based on the type of relationship between the supporting organization and its supported public charity. Entities making distributions to supporting organizations must pay careful attention to the complicated rules governing these transactions. These rules are outside the scope of the article. One

resource for learning more can be found at the Council on Foundations' Web site.[12]

The Pension Act also prohibits distributions from donor-advised funds to individuals. This created complications for funds that were committed to provide specific individual students with scholarships prior to the Act's August 17, 2006, effective date.[13] To address this problem, the Internal Revenue Service allows a sponsoring organization to make payments from a donor-advised fund to fulfill a pre-existing commitment as long as 1) the grant was awarded on an objective and a nondiscriminatory basis; 2) it is in a reasonable amount; and, 3) it was not awarded to a donor, a donor advisor, or a person related to the donor or advisor.[14] The terms of the award must remain the same as they were prior to the effective date of the Act. This special rule for past scholarship awards is in addition to an exception that permits scholarship awards to be made after August 17, 2006, if the award follows specific selection procedures set forth in the Internal Revenue Code.

The Pension Protection Act imposes a variety of other requirements related to common forms of giving. These rules are effective for all contributions after the August 17, 2006 enactment date of the Act.

- Records for Monetary Gifts.[15] Donors must retain written records of all donations, regardless of the size of the contribution. The Act reduced the type of records that will be considered sufficient to bank records and written correspondence from the recipient. A written receipt from the donee must contain the name of the recipient organization, and the date and amount of the contribution. Most organizations already provide this type of notice.

- Clothing and Household Items.[16] The possible deduction for items that have depreciated since purchase, as is typically the case with clothing and household items, is limited to the fair market value of the item at the time the gift is made. No deduction is available unless the property is "in good used condition or better." Items likely to appreciate in value, including works of art, jewelry, and antiques, are not included on the list of "household items." The deduction for these items is calculated differently.

- Contributions of Food and Book Inventory.[17] A corporation may claim a charitable deduction for gifts of inventory. The amount of the deduction is subject to a variety of rules depending on circumstances and the nature of the gift. The Act extends a provision from the Katrina Emergency Tax Relief Act of 2005 to allow certain businesses to donate food for distribution to those in need and receive a deduction. Again, the amount of the deduction is determined by rules specified in the Act. These provisions will expire on December 31, 2007.

- Donations of Art and Other Museum Display Items.[18] Prior to the Act, a donor could give artwork to a museum, keep the item in her possession until her death, and write off a percentage of the work's value throughout her lifetime. Under these rules, donors whose work appreciated over this period obtained the benefit of an increased deduction. The new rules limit the deduction to the value of the work at the time of the donation and require the donor to deduct the full value within ten years.

WHAT THIS MEANS TO YOU

To claim a tax deduction for a gift, donors must have a written record of a gift—either bank records or correspondence from the organization that received the gift. Every organization should quickly and accurately thank donors in a communication that provides the specific dollar amount contributed (for a cash donation). Most organizations already send acknowledgment letters or e-mail confirmation for online gifts, and some provide year-end statements summarizing all gifts received from a donor.

Federal agencies implement new regulations

Several federal agencies implemented rule changes relevant to charitable giving. Two key regulatory actions are summarized in the following sections.

Combined federal campaign agency rules loosened

The Office of Personal Management issued final rules concerning the Combined Federal Campaign.[19] This workplace giving campaign for federal employees was changed in several important ways.

- The requirement that an organization certify that it has received no more than 90 percent of its total support in revenue from governmental sources was removed;

- Both national organizations and local affiliates may be listed in the campaign if both meet all of the eligibility requirements; and,

- Organizations with administrative and fundraising expenses that exceed 25 percent of their total support in revenue are allowed to participate in the campaign as long as they submit a plan to reduce their expenses.

Junk fax regulations finalized; organization must have existing relationship and provide fax recipient an opportunity to "opt-out"

The Federal Communications Commission adopted a final rule concerning unsolicited faxed advertisements.[20] The rule allows unsolicited faxes between parties with an "established business relationship." (An established business relationship is defined as a prior or existing relationship formed by a voluntary two-way communication on the basis of an inquiry, application, purchase, or transaction regarding products or services.) The May 3, 2006 final rule applies to the Junk Fax Prevention Act enacted in 2005. The existence of a business relationship relieves fax senders from the obligation to obtain permission from a recipient before sending an unsolicited fax advertisement. The sender must, however, provide the opportunity for the recipient to opt out of receiving unsolicited faxes. This means that nonprofits will not have to obtain a member's permission before sending faxes promoting conferences, publications, or membership solicitation as long as a prior relationship exists between the sender and recipient and as long as the fax recipient is provided information about how to get off the list for future faxes.

Federal courts consider limits of First Amendment in fundraising

Federal courts rendered many decisions involving nonprofit organizations as parties. Among these are three decisions related to the ability of nonprofit organizations to solicit contributions. In the case of *American Civil Liberties Union of Nevada v. City of Las Vegas*, the Ninth Circuit of the United States Court of Appeals considered a Las Vegas city ordinance designed to restrict panhandling in certain trendy areas of the city.[21] The rule prohibited solicitation for donations of charity, whether through the distribution of message-bearing leaflets or oral requests. Led by the ACLU, plaintiffs challenged the ordinance as a violation of their First and Fourteenth Amendment rights to free speech. The court held that the ordinance did violate the First Amendment, stating that solicitation is a form of expression entitled to the same constitutional protections as traditional speech.

In two other cases, courts upheld limits on certain modes of communication. In *National Coalition of Prayer, Inc. v. Carter*, the Seventh Circuit of the United States Court of Appeals upheld an Indiana statute that prevented charities from using professional fundraising organizations to raise funds through telephone campaigns.[22] The state's do-not-call list provided an exemption that allowed charities to place solicitation calls to individuals, including calling those who placed their names on a state do-not-call list. The exemption applied only if the person making the call was a volunteer or an employee of the charitable institution. Charities were prevented from hiring professional call centers to place solicitation calls. Several charities sued, claiming a violation of their First Amendment rights. The court rejected the charities' claim and upheld the statute.

Meanwhile, in California, a federal trial court struck down a California law that sought to bar both inter- and intrastate faxes without prior consent.[23] Because the California rule had stricter requirements than the federal Junk Fax Law, and because it did not include an established business relationship exception, the rule was deemed unconstitutional.

In the case of *Glass v. Commission of Internal Revenue,* taxpayers appealed a decision from the IRS denying a deduction for contributions of conservation easements that were made to a qualified conservation organization.[24] The U.S. Court of Appeals upheld the lower court's determination that conservation easements were qualified contributions under the relevant portions of the Internal Revenue Code.

State legislation emphasizes donor privacy and organizational transparency in solicitation practices

In 2006, state legislatures considered and passed rules related to charitable solicitation, the use and security of potentially sensitive donor information, and accountability and financial oversight of charitable organizations. The majority of new laws focus on solicitation practices, particularly those of paid solicitors.[25]

Be aware of your state's laws about protection of personal information and implement safeguards throughout your organization to protect your donors the same way that you would want your own privacy protected.

WHAT THIS
MEANS TO YOU

States act to protect donors' personal information

The increase in crimes associated with the theft of personal information has led many states to adopt new requirements for the handling, storage, and deletion of information such as that often kept by organizations about their donors. Twenty-one jurisdictions require groups that collect and hold personal information about others to notify individuals in cases in which a data breach results in a third party obtaining unauthorized access to the data.[26] This notification must be provided regardless of the nature of the breach.

States enact regulations for charitable solicitation

The following list summarizes some of the key legislative actions taken by states in 2006:

- Hawaii's legislature passed new regulations concerning charitable solicitation that require professional solicitors to identify themselves to potential donors by name, address, and phone number.

- Illinois amended its Solicitation for Charity Act to require the registration of contribution collection agents. These agents are anyone who, for compensation or other consideration, collects contributions in the form of property (such as automobiles, motorcycles, and boats) on behalf of a charitable organization.

- Maine revised its charitable solicitations act to require registration and financial reporting of charitable organizations, professional solicitors, professional fundraising councils, and commercial co-venturers.

- Maryland amended its charitable solicitations act to require that any charitable organization be in total compliance with the requirements of the act prior to soliciting the public.

- Mississippi enacted legislation to require telephone solicitors to purchase the state's no-call database prior to making calls soliciting customers in the state. The rule applies only to solicitors compensated for their efforts and does not apply to those who receive no compensation for their activities.

States implemented and changed registration requirements for fundraising activity. For a complete listing of charitable registration and solicitation regulations by state, see the summary printed in the annual *Giving USA* newsletter issue number 1.

WHAT THIS
MEANS TO YOU

- New Jersey also implemented changes to its charitable registration and investigation act. These amendments increased the disclosure requirements for charities and independent paid fundraisers. The rule also includes new prohibitions against activities potentially misleading to prospective donors.

Nonprofit advocacy organization recommends specific federal legislation and regulation

Organizations that advocate for nonprofits remained busy and visible throughout the year. Much of this activity focused on responding to legislative concerns about ethics and accountability in nonprofit organizations. In June 2006, the Panel on the Nonprofit Sector issued a supplemental report to Congress that addressed a number of topics.[27] Key topics and summary conclusions include:

- International grantmaking: Concludes that U.S. charitable contributions are not likely to be diverted to terrorist organizations, thus Congressional regulation in this area is unwarranted.

- Charitable solicitation: Recommends that states continue to serve as principal regulators of solicitation activity, but encourages the creation of a national electronic filing system to track charitable solicitation and registration.

- Compensation of charitable trustees: Requests new regulations to aid in assessing the reasonableness of compensation to trustees of charitable trusts.

- Prudent investor standards: Opposes the creation of investment standards to be applied to the investment decisions of public charities.

- Nonprofit conversion transactions: Opposes legislation requiring federal approval of conversions of nonprofits to for-profits.

- Taxation on sale of donated property: Concludes that Congress should not respond to problems created by taxpayers who exaggerate the value of their donations by imposing a rule treating gain from the sale of such property as unrelated business income. Instead, the rules concerning qualified appraisals should be strengthened.

1   Rep. Thomas Seeks Answers from NCAA, *The Hill*, October 5, 2006.
2   B. Hopkins, Senator Grassley and Exempt Hospital Reforms, *The Law of Tax-Exempt Organizations Monthly*, May 2006.
3   E. Schwinn, Congress's New Outlook, *Chronicle of Philanthropy*, November 23, 2006, www.philanthropy.org.
4   Ibid.
5   L. Lenkowsky, What the Election Results Mean for Nonprofit Groups, *Chronicle of Philanthropy*, January 23, 2006, www.philanthropy.org.
6   E. Schwinn, Congress's New Outlook, *Chronicle of Philanthropy*, November 23, 2006, www.philanthropy.org.
7   Pension Protection Act of 2006 (H.R. 4, Public Law 109-208).
8   Analysis of Charitable Reforms & Incentives in the "Pension Protection Act of 2006" (Pub. Law 109-208), October 16, 2006, www.independentsector.org.
9   P. Panepento, Older Americans Flock to Give in Response to Tax Incentives, *Chronicle of Philanthropy*, December 7, 2006, www.philanthropy.org.

10 Philanthropic Giving Index, December 2006,
    The Center on Philanthropy at Indiana
    University, www.philanthropy.iupui.edu.

11 Analysis of Charitable Reforms & Incentives
    in the "Pension Protection Act of 2006"
    (Pub. Law 109-208), October 16, 2006,
    www.independentsector.org.

12 www.cof.org/action/content.cfm?itemnumber=
    5275&navItemNumber=5276

13 Internal Revenue Service Notice 2006-109.

14 Ibid.

15 Analysis of Charitable Reforms & Incentives
    in the "Pension Protection Act of 2006"
    (Pub. Law 109-208), October 16, 2006,
    www.independentsector.org.

16 Ibid.

17 Ibid.

18 Ibid.

19 H. Lipman and G. Williams, Limits on
    Charities' Overhead Expenses Dropped
    in Federal Fundraising Drive, *Chronicle
    of Philanthropy*, December 7, 2006,
    www.philanthropy.org.

20 www.FCC.gov/cgb/consumerfacts/
    unwantedfaxes.

21 *American Civil Liberties Union of Nevada
    v. City of Las Vegas*, 466 F.3d 784 (9th Cir.
    2006).

22 *National Coalition of Prayer, Inc. v. Carter*,
    455 F. 3d 783 (7th Cir. 2006).

23 *Chamber of Commerce of the U.S.A. v.
    Lockyear*, 2006 WL 462482 (E.D. Calif.
    2006).

24 *Glass v. Commission of Internal Revenue*,
    472 F.3d 698 (Fed App. 2006).

25 All references to state legislation taken
    from: Independent Sector, 2005-2006
    Charitable Reform—State Legislation
    Tracker, available at http://www.
    independentsector.org/members_only/
    Policy/2005-2006_State_Legislation_
    Tracker.pdf.

26 Indiana Public Law 125.

27 B. Hopkins, Nonprofit Sector Panel Issues
    Sup. Report, *The Law of Tax-Exempt
    Organizations Monthly*, June 2006.

21 Gifts of $5 million or more in 2006

The Center on Philanthropy at Indiana University issues a quarterly list of announced gifts of $1 million or more. From this list, *Giving USA* has compiled gifts or pledges of $5 million or more made by individuals (not corporations or foundations) and announced in 2006. The amounts reported here are those that appear in newspapers or other media outlets; they have not been verified with the recipient institution.

This is not a complete listing of all gifts in the United States of $5 million or more because many such gifts are not reported in the press. It also does not represent actual transfers made to institutions in 2006. Many of the gifts are pledges or estate gifts that will be paid over time. Gifts in kind are reported at values announced in the media.

Gifts are organized in descending order by size and then alphabetically by donor's last name. The size categories are $1 billion and above; $500 million to $999.9 million; $250 million to $499.99 million, $100 million to $249.99 million, $50 million to $99.99 million, $25 million to $49.99 million, $10 million to $24.99 million, and $5 million to $9.99 million.

$1 billion and above

Donor	Amount	Recipient
Warren E. Buffett	$30,000,000,000	Bill and Melinda Gates Foundation
Warren E. Buffett	$3,000,000,000	Susan Thompson Buffett Foundation
Herbert and Marion Sandler	$1,300,000,000	Sandler Family Supporting Foundation
Warren E. Buffett	$1,000,000,000	Howard G. Buffett Foundation
Warren E. Buffett	$1,000,000,000	NoVo Foundation
Warren E. Buffett	$1,000,000,000	Susan A. Buffett Foundation

$500 million to $999.99 million

Bernard A. Osher	$723,200,000	Bernard Osher Foundation
Jim Joseph (estate)	$500,000,000	Jim Joseph Foundation

$250 million to $499.99 million
No gifts found

$100 million to $249.99 million

David Rockefeller (pledge)	$225,000,000	Rockefeller Brothers Fund
Joan Palevsky (estate)	$200,000,000	California Community Foundation
Stanley W. Anderson (pledge)	$150,000,000	Presbyterian Church of the USA
Eli and Edyth L. Broad	$137,600,000	Broad Foundations
T. Boone Pickens	$135,000,000	T. Boone Pickens Foundation
Michael Bloomberg	$125,000,000	Various Organizations
Philip H. Knight	$105,000,000	Stanford University Graduate School of Business
Peter B. Lewis	$101,000,000	Princeton University
Anonymous	$100,000,000	Johns Hopkins University
John Arrillaga	$100,000,000	Stanford University
Dan L. Duncan and Family	$100,000,000	Baylor College of Medicine

$100 million to $249.99 million (cont'd)

Donor	Amount	Recipient
Lawrence J. Ellison	$100,000,000	Ellison Medical Foundation
Ira and Mary Lou Fulton	$100,000,000	Arizona State University Foundation
Lorry I. Lokey	$100,000,000	Lorry I. Lokey Supporting Foundation
Ronald P. Stanton	$100,000,000	Yeshiva University
Mortimer B. Zuckerman	$100,000,000	Memorial Sloan-Kettering Cancer Center

$50 million to $99.99 million

Donor	Amount	Recipient
Henry M. and Wendy J. Paulson	$80,000,000	Bobolink Foundation
Anonymous	$75,000,000	Westmont College
Joseph Neubauer	$74,400,000	Neubauer Family Foundation
T. Denny Sanford	$70,000,000	South Dakota Science and Technology Authority
Anonymous	$65,000,000	Cleveland Clinic
Ray and Joan Kroc (estate)	$64,000,000	Salvation Army, Phoenix
Ed Bass	$60,000,000	Yale University
Ernest Rady (estate)	$60,000,000	San Diego Children's Hospital
Hiroshi Yamauchi	$60,000,000	Kyoto University Hospital
Wallace D. Malone, Jr.	$55,900,000	Malone Family Foundation
Anonymous	$50,000,000	University of Tennessee
Peter and Helen Bing	$50,000,000	Stanford University
Warren E. Buffett	$50,000,000	Nuclear Threat Initiative
William Polk Carey	$50,000,000	Johns Hopkins University
Richard DeVos and Family	$50,000,000	Helen DeVos Children's Hospital
Josephine Ford (estate)	$50,000,000	College of Creative Studies
Tim and Bernadette Marquez	$50,000,000	Denver Scholarship Foundation
John and Tashia Morgridge	$50,000,000	University of Wisconsin—Madison
Melvin and Bren Simon	$50,000,000	Indiana University Cancer Center
George Soros	$50,000,000	Millennium Promise
Larry and Judy Tanenbaum	$50,000,000	Jewish Foundation of Greater Toronto
Helga Wall-Apelt	$50,000,000	John & Mable Ringling Museum of Art
John and Jacquest Weberg	$50,000,000	Opportunity International

$25 million to $49.99 million

Donor	Amount	Recipient
H.F. (Gerry) Lenfest	$48,000,000	Columbia University
Geoffrey Beene (estate)	$44,000,000	Memorial Sloan-Kettering Cancer Center
Mary Jarvis (estate)	$43,000,000	Kansas State University Foundation
Gary and Frances Comer	$42,000,000	University of Chicago
Arthur Zankel (estate)	$42,000,000	Skidmore College
Jack and Marie Lord (estate)	$40,000,000	Hawaii Community Foundation
Jonathan Tisch	$40,000,000	Tufts University
Ming Hsieh	$35,000,000	University of Southern California
Jeannik Mequet Littlefield	$35,000,000	San Francisco Opera
Gilbert and Jaylee Mead	$35,000,000	Arena Stage
Arthur Zankel (estate)	$34,000,000	Zankel Fund
Hector Guy and Doris Di Stefano (estate)	$33,000,000	World Wildlife Fund
Hector Guy and Doris Di Stefano (estate)	$33,000,000	Visiting Nurse and Hospice Care of Santa Barbara
Hector Guy and Doris Di Stefano (estate)	$33,000,000	Santa Barbara Hospice Foundation
Hector Guy and Doris Di Stefano (estate)	$33,000,000	The Salvation Army
Hector Guy and Doris Di Stefano (estate)	$33,000,000	Greenpeace International, Inc.
Hector Guy and Doris Di Stefano (estate)	$33,000,000	Disabled American Veterans Charitable Service Trust
Hector Guy and Doris Di Stefano (estate)	$33,000,000	Direct Relief International
Hector Guy and Doris Di Stefano (estate)	$33,000,000	American Humane Association

$25 million to $49.99 million (cont'd)

Donor	Amount	Recipient
Lorry I. Lokey	$33,000,000	Stanford University
Burt and Deedee McMurtry	$32,000,000	Rice University
Anonymous	$31,500,000	Trinity College
Monte Ahuja	$30,000,000	University Hospitals
Anonymous	$30,000,000	Catholic Diocese of Memphis
Edward A. Doisy and Family	$30,000,000	St. Louis University
Robert E. Fischell and Family	$30,000,000	University of Maryland—College Park
Irwin M. and Joan Jacobs	$30,000,000	American Technion Society
William E. Macaulay	$30,000,000	City University of New York
Jay A. Precourt	$30,000,000	Stanford University
Ward W. and Priscilla B. Woods	$30,000,000	Stanford University
Richard P. Simmons and Family	$29,500,000	Pittsburgh Symphony
Frederic N. and Eleanor Schwartz (estate)	$26,500,000	Syracuse University
Frederic N. and Eleanor Schwartz (estate)	$26,500,000	Brown University
Sheldon B. and Miriam Adelson	$25,000,000	Yad Vashem
Anonymous	$25,000,000	Marquette University
Sid R. and Mercedes Bass	$25,000,000	Metropolitan Opera
Eli and Edyth L. Broad	$25,000,000	University of Southern California
Tristram and Ruth Colket, Jr.	$25,000,000	Philadelphia Children's Hospital
Miles C. and Parker Collier	$25,000,000	Eckerd College
Stanley Druckenmiller	$25,000,000	Harlem Children's Zone
Melvin and Ellen Gordon	$25,000,000	University of Chicago
Dorrance H. Dodo Hamilton	$25,000,000	University of the Arts
John Q. Hammons	$25,000,000	Missouri State University
Peter Karmanos, Jr.	$25,000,000	Barbara Ann Karmanos Cancer Institute
Jules and Gwenn Knapp	$25,000,000	University of Chicago
Lorry I. Lokey	$25,000,000	American Technion Society
Arthur J. Samberg	$25,000,000	Columbia University
William and Joan Schreyer	$25,000,000	Pennsylvania State University— University Park
Carl and Ruth Shapiro	$25,000,000	Brandeis University
Jay H. Shidler	$25,000,000	University of Hawaii
Randall B. Terry, Jr. (estate)	$25,000,000	Woodberry Forest

$10 million to $24.99 million

Donor	Amount	Recipient
Eugenia J. Dodson (estate)	$23,700,000	Diabetes Research Institute Foundation
William Allyn (estate)	$23,000,000	The Allyn Foundation
Edward P. and Gayle G. Roski	$23,000,000	University of Southern California
Joe and Linda Chlapaty	$22,000,000	University of Dubuque
Jim and Natalie Haslam	$22,000,000	University of Tennessee—Knoxville
Mayer and Arlene Mitchell and Abraham Mitchell	$22,000,000	University of South Alabama
Arthur Zankel (estate)	$22,000,000	Carnegie Hall
Anonymous	$20,000,000	Peddie School
Anonymous	$20,000,000	Johns Hopkins University
Anonymous	$20,000,000	Middlebury College
Marvin J. Herb Family	$20,000,000	Rush University Medical Center
Samuel J. Heyman	$20,000,000	Partnership for Public Service
David H. Koch	$20,000,000	Johns Hopkins University
David H. Koch	$20,000,000	American Museum of Natural History
Bruce Kovner	$20,000,000	Lincoln Center for the Performing Arts
William H. Neukom	$20,000,000	Stanford University
Henry M. and Wendy J. Paulson	$20,000,000	Goldman Sachs Philanthropy Fund

Gifts of $5 million or more in 2006

$10 million to $24.99 million (cont'd)

Donor	Amount	Recipient
Ronald O. Perelman	$20,000,000	Carnegie Hall
George R. Roberts and Family	$20,000,000	Claremont McKenna College
Roger and Victoria Sant	$20,000,000	World Wildlife Fund
Donald and Darlene Shiley	$20,000,000	Old Globe Theater
H. Milton and Carolyn Stewart	$20,000,000	Georgia Institute of Technology
Norman C. and Carmelita Teeter	$20,000,000	Western Illinois University
Helen R. Walton	$20,000,000	University of the Ozarks
John Parke and Marie Smith Young (estate)	$20,000,000	Occidental College
Kenneth and Anne Dias Griffin	$19,000,000	The Art Institute of Chicago
Henry William Edwards, Jr. (estate)	$18,000,000	Grace Cathedral
Lee and Jane Seidman	$17,000,000	Cleveland Clinic
Ray and Dagmar Dolby	$16,000,000	University of California—San Francisco
Carl and Edyth Lindner	$16,000,000	Cincinnati Hills Christian Academy
William and Toby Austin and Bart and Barbara Singletary	$15,500,000	University of California—Riverside
Anonymous	$15,000,000	Darlington School
Anonymous	$15,000,000	City of Hope
Anonymous	$15,000,000	Florida West Coast Symphony
Anonymous	$15,000,000	Lawrence University
Jerry Baker	$15,000,000	Western Kentucky University
Richard C. Blum	$15,000,000	University of California—Berkeley
Josephine Clay Ford (estate)	$15,000,000	Detroit Institute of Arts
Judson C. and Joyce Green, Jr.	$15,000,000	DePauw University
Marvin and Judith Herb and Family	$15,000,000	University of Toledo
Roger Holden	$15,000,000	Pitzer College
Kent and Vicki Logan	$15,000,000	Denver Art Museum
J. Peter and Florine Ministrelli	$15,000,000	Beaumont Hospital
David and Patricia Nierenberg	$15,000,000	Southwest Washington Medical Center
Leland and Mary Pillsbury	$15,000,000	Cornell University, School of Hotel Administration
Grace M. Pollock (estate)	$15,000,000	Camp Hill School District
Grace M. Pollock (estate)	$15,000,000	University of Washington
Katherine Hackstaff Schlegel (estate)	$15,000,000	Harvey Mudd College
Wun Tsun Tam (estate)	$15,000,000	Columbia University
Robert Yik-Fong (estate)	$14,200,000	Columbia University
Anonymous	$14,000,000	The Nature Conservancy
Pierre Lassonde	$13,250,000	University of Utah
E. Philip Saunders	$13,000,000	Rochester Institute of Technology
Larry I. Lokey	$12,500,000	University of Oregon
Philip J. Purcell III	$12,500,000	University of Notre Dame
Bob and Cheri VanderWeide	$12,500,000	Spectrum Health
Frances M. Craig	$12,000,000	Iowa State University
Margaret F. Galbraith (estate)	$12,000,000	Inland Northwest Community Foundation
David and Lyn Silfen	$12,000,000	University of Pennsylvania
Eugenia J. Dodson (estate)	$11,900,000	University of Miami Sylvester Comprehensive Cancer Center
Lewis Cullman	$11,000,000	New York Botanical Garden
Russell Fischer (estate)	$11,000,000	Ventura County Community Foundation
Roger and Joyce Howe	$10,500,000	Miami University
William C. Powers	$10,500,000	Princeton University
Madlyn and Leonard Abramson	$10,000,000	Temple University, School of Dentistry
Anonymous	$10,000,000	University of Minnesota, Institute of Technology

$10 million to $24.99 million (cont'd)

Donor	Amount	Recipient
Anonymous	$10,000,000	Jewish Funders Network
Anonymous	$10,000,000	Colgate University
Judy Avery	$10,000,000	Stanford University
Geoffrey Beene (estate)	$10,000,000	Animal Medical Center
George and Margo Behrakis	$10,000,000	Museum of Fine Art (MFA)
Michael Bloomberg	$10,000,000	World Trade Center Memorial Foundation
David F. Bolger	$10,000,000	Northfield Mount Hermon School
Russell L. Carson	$10,000,000	Columbia University
William P. Clements, Jr.	$10,000,000	University of Texas Southwestern Medical Center
Lloyd Cotsen	$10,000,000	University of California—Los Angeles
Harlan and Kathy Crow	$10,000,000	St. Mark's School of Texas
Mike Curb	$10,000,000	California State University
Roy and Elnora Danley (estate)	$10,000,000	University of North Dakota
Douglas C. Floren and Family	$10,000,000	Dartmouth College
John and Ginger Giovale	$10,000,000	Westminster College
John W. and Barbara Glynn	$10,000,000	University of Notre Dame
Robert B. Goergen	$10,000,000	University of Rochester
Sue J. and Willliam H. Gross	$10,000,000	University of California—Irvine
Nancy B. Hamon	$10,000,000	Presbyterian Healthcare System
Walter Blair Hobbs (estate)	$10,000,000	Knox College
Bill Kaplan	$10,000,000	State University of New York—Orange
Giles and Barbara Kemp	$10,000,000	Swarthmore College
Lois Klawon (estate)	$10,000,000	Miami University
Henry R. Kravis	$10,000,000	Columbia University
Charles E. Lakin and Family	$10,000,000	Iowa West Foundation
H.F. (Gerry) Lenfest	$10,000,000	Mercersburg Academy
Kent and Vicki Logan	$10,000,000	Denver Art Museum
Lorry I. Lokey	$10,000,000	University of Oregon
Sheldon B. Lubar	$10,000,000	University of Wisconsin—Milwaukee
Donald and Sally Lucas	$10,000,000	San Jose State University
Tim and Bernadette Marquez	$10,000,000	Colorado School of Mines
MaryAnn and Clayton Mathile	$10,000,000	Ohio Northern University
Jim and Jan Moran and JM Family Enterprises	$10,000,000	Holy Cross Hospital
John and Tashia Morgridge	$10,000,000	Lesley University
Frank and Carol Morsani	$10,000,000	University of South Florida
William S. and Jane Rossetti Mosakowski	$10,000,000	Clark University
Timothy and Linda O'Neill	$10,000,000	Georgetown University
Conrad T. Prebys	$10,000,000	Scripps Health
J. Crayton Pruitt	$10,000,000	University of Florida—Gainesville
Helen Walker Raleigh (estate)	$10,000,000	Rhode Island Institute
Arthur and Toni Rembe Rock	$10,000,000	Stanford University
Ali and Gita Saberioon	$10,000,000	University of Texas
Henry and Elizabeth Segerstrom	$10,000,000	Orange County Performing Arts Center
Bobby and Judy Shackouls	$10,000,000	Mississippi State University
Frederick and Diane Smith	$10,000,000	Memphis Zoo
Robert and Jane Toll	$10,000,000	University of Pennsylvania
Virginia Toulmin	$10,000,000	Florida West Coast Symphony
Sharon and Timothy Ubben	$10,000,000	Posse Foundation
John L. and Barbara Vogelstein	$10,000,000	Vassar College
Robert D. and Margaret M. Walter	$10,000,000	Columbus Museum of Art
Arthur Zankel (estate)	$10,000,000	Teachers College at Columbia University

$5 million to $9.99 million

Donor	Amount	Recipient
Anonymous	$9,600,000	College of William and Mary
Joseph Morton and Jack Mandel	$8,550,000	Jewish Federation Foundation of Palm Beach County
Carol A. Ammon	$8,500,000	Adelphi University
Anonymous	$8,000,000	Willamette University
Preston Green (estate)	$8,000,000	Washington University
Gerald and Margaret Waters Jordan (estate)	$8,000,000	University of Missouri—Columbia
David and Carol Lackland	$8,000,000	Centenary College
David Markin	$8,000,000	Bradley University
T. Boone Pickens	$8,000,000	Texas Scottish Rite Hospital for Children
Lonnie Bo Pilgrim	$8,000,000	Dallas Baptist University
Ruth Rusch Sheppe (estate)	$8,000,000	Connecticut College
Robert Wegman	$8,000,000	St. John Fisher College
Arthur Zankel (estate)	$8,000,000	UJA-Federation of New York
Anonymous	$7,500,000	Valparaiso Family YMCA
Lucille A. Carver and Family	$7,500,000	University of Iowa Foundation
Henry Pease (estate)	$7,300,000	St. George's School
Howard and Abby Milstein	$7,250,000	Weill Medical College of Cornell University
Allen Cook	$7,000,000	University of Pittsburgh
Brian Greenspun and Family	$7,000,000	Newseum
Paul and Carol Schapp	$7,000,000	Hope College
Carl and Ruth Shapiro	$7,000,000	Beth Israel Deaconess Medical Center
Steve G. Stevanovich	$7,000,000	University of Chicago, Center for Financial Mathematics
William Mayhall	$6,700,000	Miami University
Sidney Cox (estate)	$6,500,000	Cornell University
Mary Mildred Whalen (estate)	$6,300,000	Santa Rosa Children's Hospital Foundation
Michael Amini	$6,000,000	City of Hope Cancer Center
Anonymous	$6,000,000	Woodland Park Zoo
Anonymous	$6,000,000	University of the South
Victor Atkins	$6,000,000	Middlesex School
Rick and Tina Caruso	$6,000,000	University of Southern California
Joseph (Joe) Craft, III	$6,000,000	University of Kentucky
Jacqueline Glass	$6,000,000	Chapman University
Robert and Sharon McCord	$6,000,000	Arizona State University
Wayne McElrath	$6,000,000	Auburn University
John D. Miller	$6,000,000	Hofstra University
Jack and Laura Milton	$6,000,000	Syracuse University
T. Boone Pickens	$6,000,000	Johns Hopkins University
J. Gary Shansby	$6,000,000	University of Washington Business School
Mortimer Y. Sutherland, Jr. (estate)	$6,000,000	University of Virginia
William and Virginia Williams (estate)	$6,000,000	The James A. Michener Art Museum
E. Vernon and Eloise Smith	$5,950,000	University of Kentucky
Eileen Mitchell Gibbs (estate)	$5,900,000	Mills College
Bruce V. Green (estate)	$5,900,000	Illinois State University
Larry and Sally Zlotnick Sears	$5,900,000	Case Western Reserve University
Norman Levan	$5,700,000	Bakersfield College
Benjamin and Marian Schuster	$5,500,000	Kettering Medical Center
Park B. Smith	$5,300,000	College of the Holy Cross
Lucy Tull (estate)	$5,300,000	Salisbury University
Anonymous	$5,200,000	University of Oregon
Philip J. Whitcome (estate)	$5,200,000	Providence College
Helen Ginsberg Forman (estate)	$5,100,000	Rhode Island College

$5 million to $9.99 million (cont'd)

Donor	Amount	Recipient
Carl and Carol Ann Montante	$5,100,000	Canisius College
Leonard and Jayne Abess	$5,000,000	University of Miami
Sheldon G. and Miriam Adelson	$5,000,000	Birthright Israel Foundation
Ernest and Elizabeth Althouse (estate)	$5,000,000	Lehigh University
Anonymous	$5,000,000	Trinity College
Anonymous	$5,000,000	Cranbrook Kingswood Girls' Middle School
Anonymous	$5,000,000	Augustana College
George Argyros	$5,000,000	Horatio Alger Association of Distinguished Americans
Arabelle Laws Arrington	$5,000,000	University of Mary Washington
Bernard J. Beazley	$5,000,000	Loyola University Chicago
Charles Becker	$5,000,000	Karmanos Cancer Institute
Victor and Gussie Bert	$5,000,000	Miriam Hospital
Douglas and Diana Berthiaume	$5,000,000	University of Massachusetts—Amherst
Jerry Bisgrove	$5,000,000	Niagara University
Mary and David Boies	$5,000,000	Northern Westchester Hospital
Evelyn V. Butterworth (estate)	$5,000,000	Lasell College
Lucille A. Carver	$5,000,000	University of Iowa Foundation
Max Carrol Chapman, Jr.	$5,000,000	University of North Carolina—Chapel Hill
Steven and Alexandra Cohen	$5,000,000	Stamford Hospital
Donald and Karen Cohn	$5,000,000	Old Globe Theater
John R. Cook and Waverly M. Cole	$5,000,000	Longwood University
Marion Buckelew Cullen (estate)	$5,000,000	Westminster Choir College of Rider University
Mike Curb	$5,000,000	Rhodes College
Bernard J. DelGiorno	$5,000,000	University of Chicago
Theodore P. (Jr.) and Linda Desloge	$5,000,000	St. Luke's Hospital
Kenneth and Frances Eisenberg	$5,000,000	University of Michigan
Miguel B. Fernandez	$5,000,000	Xavier High School
Pauline Foster	$5,000,000	University of California—San Diego
Coleman Fung	$5,000,000	University of California—Berkeley
Robert C. Greenheck	$5,000,000	Marquette University
J.R. (Pitt) and Barbara Hyde	$5,000,000	University of North Carolina—Chapel Hill
Bruce and Gloria Ingram	$5,000,000	Texas State University—San Marcos
Sheila C. Johnson	$5,000,000	University of Virginia, Curry School of Education
Scott and Kathleen Kapnick	$5,000,000	Naples Botanical Garden
Mark Kingdon	$5,000,000	Harlem Children's Zone
Samuel and Michelle Labow	$5,000,000	University of Vermont College of Medicine
William and Elizabeth Latham	$5,000,000	Virginia Tech
John R. Lawson II	$5,000,000	Virginia Tech
Robert M. and Diane Levy	$5,000,000	University of Pennsylvania, Wharton School of Business
James McWethy	$5,000,000	Cornell College
A. Ross Meyers	$5,000,000	Virginia Tech
Leonard and Carolyn Miller	$5,000,000	University of Vermont
David G. Mugar	$5,000,000	Cape Cod Hospital
Daniel S. Och	$5,000,000	University of Pennsylvania
Arthur Ochs-Sulzberger and Family	$5,000,000	Newseum
Evert and Norma Person	$5,000,000	St. Joseph Health System Sonoma County
John M. and Gertrude E. Petersen	$5,000,000	University of Pittsburgh
T. Boone Pickens	$5,000,000	Texas Women's University
E. Pulliam Family	$5,000,000	Newseum

$5 million to $9.99 million (cont'd)

Donor	Amount	Recipient
William B. Quarton	$5,000,000	Cedar Rapids Museum of Art
Jerry and Phyllis Rappaport and the Jerome Lyle Rappaport Charitable Foundation	$5,000,000	Suffolk University Law School
William R. Rhodes	$5,000,000	Northfield Mount Hermon School
David Rockefeller	$5,000,000	Colonial Williamsburg Foundation
Sam Rose	$5,000,000	Dickinson College
Stephen M. and Kara Ross	$5,000,000	Lincoln Center for the Performing Arts
John W. Rowe	$5,000,000	Marine Biological Laboratory
David M. Rubenstein	$5,000,000	Lincoln Center for the Performing Arts
Donald Saltz	$5,000,000	Adas Israel Congregation
Frank and Athena Sarris	$5,000,000	University of Pittsburgh
Dwight C. Schar	$5,000,000	Ashland University
Thomas Schmidheiny	$5,000,000	Tufts University
Weldon and Joan Schumacher	$5,000,000	La Sierra University
Richard Seaver	$5,000,000	California Institute of the Arts
Harold C. Simmons	$5,000,000	University of Texas—Austin
Edward A. St. John	$5,000,000	Severn School
Flora L. Thornton	$5,000,000	University of Southern California
Walter and Sheila Umphrey	$5,000,000	Lamar University
George and Susan Vojta	$5,000,000	Yale Center for Corporate Governance and Performance
Cyril and Lissa Wagner, Jr.	$5,000,000	University of Oklahoma
William & Virginia Williams (estate)	$5,000,000	Union College
Adam Williams Family	$5,000,000	Mission Hospital
Warren P. Williamson, Jr. and Family	$5,000,000	Youngstown State University

For more information about these and other gifts, see The Center on Philanthropy at Indiana University Web site, www.philanthropy.iupui.edu.

Sources used for the Million Dollar List maintained by the Center on Philanthropy include *Chronicle of Philanthropy*, *Chronicle of Higher Education*, *Philanthropy News Digest*, and newspaper articles, tracked for the Center.

Data tables for charts in *Giving USA*: The Numbers

Giving by source, 1966–2006
(in billions of current dollars)

	Total	Percent change	Corpora-tions	Percent change	Founda-tions	Percent change	Bequests	Percent change	Individuals	Percent change
1966	15.79	7.3	0.79	6.8	1.25	10.6	1.31	28.4	12.44	5.2
1967	17.03	7.9	0.82	3.8	1.40	12.0	1.40	6.9	13.41	7.8
1968	18.85	10.7	0.90	9.8	1.60	14.3	1.60	14.3	14.75	10.0
1969	20.66	9.6	0.93	3.3	1.80	12.5	2.00	25.0	15.93	8.0
1970	21.04	1.8	0.82	-11.8	1.90	5.6	2.13	6.5	16.19	1.6
1971	23.44	11.4	0.85	4.2	1.95	2.6	3.00	40.8	17.64	9.0
1972	24.44	4.3	0.97	14.1	2.00	2.6	2.10	-30.0	19.37	9.8
1973	25.59	4.7	1.06	9.3	2.00	0.0	2.00	-4.8	20.53	6.0
1974	26.88	5.0	1.10	3.8	2.11	5.5	2.07	3.5	21.60	5.2
1975	28.56	6.3	1.15	4.5	1.65	-21.8	2.23	7.7	23.53	8.9
1976	31.85	11.5	1.33	15.7	1.90	15.2	2.30	3.1	26.32	11.9
1977	35.21	10.5	1.54	15.8	2.00	5.3	2.12	-7.8	29.55	12.3
1978	38.57	9.5	1.70	10.4	2.17	8.5	2.60	22.6	32.10	8.6
1979	43.11	11.8	2.05	20.6	2.24	3.2	2.23	-14.2	36.59	14.0
1980	48.63	12.8	2.25	9.8	2.81	25.4	2.86	28.3	40.71	11.3
1981	55.28	13.7	2.64	17.3	3.07	9.3	3.58	25.2	45.99	13.0
1982	59.11	6.9	3.11	17.8	3.16	2.9	5.21	45.5	47.63	3.6
1983	63.21	6.9	3.67	18.0	3.60	13.9	3.88	-25.5	52.06	9.3
1984	68.58	8.5	4.13	12.5	3.95	9.7	4.04	4.1	56.46	8.5
1985	71.69	4.5	4.63	12.1	4.90	24.1	4.77	18.1	57.39	1.6
1986	83.25	16.1	5.03	8.6	5.43	10.8	5.70	19.5	67.09	16.9
1987	82.20	-1.3	5.21	3.6	5.88	8.3	6.58	15.4	64.53	-3.8
1988	88.04	7.1	5.34	2.5	6.15	4.6	6.57	-0.2	69.98	8.4
1989	98.30	11.7	5.46	2.2	6.55	6.5	6.84	4.1	79.45	13.5
1990	100.52	2.3	5.46	0.0	7.23	10.4	6.79	-0.7	81.04	2.0
1991	104.92	4.4	5.25	-3.8	7.72	6.8	7.68	13.1	84.27	4.0
1992	111.79	6.5	5.91	12.6	8.64	11.9	9.54	24.2	87.70	4.1
1993	116.86	4.5	6.47	9.5	9.53	10.3	8.86	-7.1	92.00	4.9
1994	120.29	2.9	6.98	7.9	9.66	1.4	11.13	25.6	92.52	0.6
1995	123.68	2.8	7.35	5.3	10.56	9.3	10.41	-6.5	95.36	3.1
1996	139.10	12.5	7.51	2.2	12.00	13.6	12.03	15.6	107.56	12.8
1997	162.99	17.2	8.62	14.8	13.92	16.0	16.25	35.1	124.20	15.5
1998	176.80	8.5	8.46	-1.9	17.01	22.2	12.98	-20.1	138.35	11.4
1999	202.74	14.7	10.23	20.9	20.51	20.6	17.37	33.8	154.63	11.8
2000	229.71	13.3	10.74	5.0	24.58	19.8	19.88	14.5	174.51	12.9
2001	231.08	0.6	11.66	8.6	27.22	10.7	19.80	-0.4	172.40	-1.2
2002	231.54	0.2	10.79	-7.5	26.98	-0.9	20.90	5.6	172.87	0.3
2003	236.28	2.0	11.06	2.5	26.84	-0.5	18.19	-13.0	180.19	4.2
2004	259.02	9.6	11.36	2.7	28.41	5.8	18.46	1.5	200.79	11.4
2005	283.05	9.3	13.77	21.2	32.41	14.1	23.40	26.8	213.47	6.3
2006	295.02	4.2	12.72	-7.6	36.50	12.6	22.91	-2.1	222.89	4.4

Source for foundation giving: The Foundation Center
Note: All figures are rounded. *Giving USA* changed its rounding procedure from the 2003 edition forward. All estimates are rounded to two places then operations performed.

Giving by source, 1966–2006
(in billions of inflation-adjusted dollars)

	Total	Percent change	Corpora-tions	Percent change	Founda-tions	Percent change	Bequests	Percent change	Individuals	Percent change
1966	98.26	4.3	4.92	3.8	7.78	7.6	8.15	24.8	77.41	2.3
1967	102.78	4.6	4.95	0.6	8.45	8.6	8.45	3.7	80.93	4.6
1968	109.21	6.3	5.21	5.3	9.27	9.7	9.27	9.7	85.46	5.6
1969	113.52	3.9	5.11	-1.9	9.89	6.7	10.99	18.6	87.53	2.4
1970	109.29	-3.7	4.26	-16.6	9.87	-0.2	11.06	0.6	84.10	-3.9
1971	116.67	6.8	4.23	-0.7	9.71	-1.6	14.93	35.0	87.80	4.4
1972	117.90	1.1	4.68	10.6	9.65	-0.6	10.13	-32.2	93.44	6.4
1973	116.20	-1.4	4.81	2.8	9.08	-5.9	9.08	-10.4	93.23	-0.2
1974	109.94	-5.4	4.50	-6.4	8.63	-5.0	8.47	-6.7	88.34	-5.2
1975	107.01	-2.7	4.31	-4.2	6.18	-28.4	8.36	-1.3	88.16	-0.2
1976	112.86	5.5	4.71	9.3	6.73	8.9	8.15	-2.5	93.27	5.8
1977	117.12	3.8	5.12	8.7	6.65	-1.2	7.05	-13.5	98.30	5.4
1978	119.27	1.8	5.26	2.7	6.71	0.9	8.04	14.0	99.26	1.0
1979	119.71	0.4	5.69	8.2	6.22	-7.3	6.19	-23.0	101.61	2.4
1980	119.00	-0.6	5.51	-3.2	6.88	10.6	7.00	13.1	99.61	-2.0
1981	122.60	3.0	5.85	6.2	6.81	-1.0	7.94	13.4	102.00	2.4
1982	123.48	0.7	6.50	11.1	6.60	-3.1	10.88	37.0	99.50	-2.5
1983	127.95	3.6	7.43	14.3	7.29	10.5	7.85	-27.8	105.38	5.9
1984	133.06	4.0	8.01	7.8	7.66	5.1	7.84	-0.1	109.55	4.0
1985	134.33	1.0	8.68	8.4	9.18	19.8	8.94	14.0	107.53	-1.8
1986	153.12	14.0	9.25	6.6	9.99	8.8	10.48	17.2	123.40	14.8
1987	145.88	-4.7	9.25	0.0	10.43	4.4	11.68	11.5	114.52	-7.2
1988	150.04	2.9	9.10	-1.6	10.48	0.5	11.20	-4.1	119.26	4.1
1989	159.82	6.5	8.88	-2.4	10.65	1.6	11.12	-0.7	129.17	8.3
1990	155.04	-3.0	8.42	-5.2	11.15	4.7	10.47	-5.8	125.00	-3.2
1991	155.30	0.2	7.77	-7.7	11.43	2.5	11.37	8.6	124.73	-0.2
1992	160.64	3.4	8.49	9.3	12.42	8.7	13.71	20.6	126.02	1.0
1993	163.04	1.5	9.03	6.4	13.30	7.1	12.36	-9.8	128.35	1.8
1994	163.64	0.4	9.50	5.2	13.14	-1.2	15.14	22.5	125.86	-1.9
1995	163.60	0.0	9.72	2.3	13.97	6.3	13.77	-9.0	126.14	0.2
1996	178.73	9.2	9.65	-0.7	15.42	10.4	15.46	12.3	138.20	9.6
1997	204.74	14.6	10.83	12.2	17.49	13.4	20.41	32.0	156.01	12.9
1998	218.67	6.8	10.46	-3.4	21.04	20.3	16.05	-21.4	171.12	9.7
1999	245.33	12.2	12.38	18.4	24.82	18.0	21.02	31.0	187.11	9.3
2000	268.92	9.6	12.57	1.5	28.78	16.0	23.27	10.7	204.30	9.2
2001	263.03	-2.2	13.27	5.6	30.98	7.6	22.54	-3.1	196.24	-3.9
2002	259.45	-1.4	12.09	-8.9	30.23	-2.4	23.42	3.9	193.71	-1.3
2003	258.89	-0.2	12.12	0.2	29.41	-2.7	19.93	-14.9	197.43	1.9
2004	276.43	6.8	12.12	0.0	30.32	3.1	19.70	-1.2	214.29	8.5
2005	292.15	5.7	14.21	17.2	33.45	10.3	24.15	22.6	220.34	2.8
2006	295.02	1.0	12.72	-10.5	36.50	9.1	22.91	-5.1	222.89	1.2

Source for foundation giving: The Foundation Center
Note: All figures are rounded. *Giving USA* changed its rounding procedure from the 2003 edition forward. All estimates are rounded to two places then operations performed. Inflation adjustment uses the Consumer Price Index calculator available at www.bls.gov. 2006 = 100.

Contributions by type of recipient organization, 1966–2006
(in billions of current dollars)

	Total	Percent change	Religion	Percent change	Edu-cation	Percent change	Health	Percent change	Human services	Percent change
1966	15.79	7.3	7.22	7.4	2.06	2.5	2.61	8.8	3.01	3.1
1967	17.03	7.9	7.58	5.0	2.13	3.4	2.80	7.3	3.16	5.0
1968	18.85	10.7	8.42	11.1	2.38	11.7	3.10	10.7	3.07	-2.8
1969	20.66	9.6	9.02	7.1	2.54	6.7	3.37	8.7	3.02	-1.6
1970	21.04	1.8	9.34	3.5	2.60	2.4	3.61	7.1	2.94	-2.6
1971	23.44	11.4	10.07	7.8	2.75	5.8	3.92	8.6	3.02	2.7
1972	24.44	4.3	10.10	0.3	2.98	8.4	4.09	4.3	3.57	18.2
1973	25.59	4.7	10.53	4.3	3.33	11.7	4.52	10.5	3.87	8.4
1974	26.88	5.0	11.84	12.4	3.38	1.5	5.05	11.7	4.98	28.7
1975	28.56	6.3	12.81	8.2	3.19	-5.6	5.13	1.6	5.05	1.4
1976	31.85	11.5	14.18	10.7	3.59	12.5	5.19	1.2	5.13	1.6
1977	35.21	10.5	16.98	19.7	3.89	8.4	5.27	1.5	5.22	1.8
1978	38.57	9.5	18.35	8.1	4.32	11.1	5.30	0.6	5.30	1.5
1979	43.11	11.8	20.17	9.9	4.70	8.8	5.44	2.6	5.36	1.1
1980	48.63	12.8	22.23	10.2	5.07	7.9	5.56	2.2	5.42	1.1
1981	55.28	13.7	25.05	12.7	5.93	17.0	5.69	2.3	5.50	1.5
1982	59.11	6.9	28.06	12.0	6.14	3.5	5.75	1.1	5.56	1.1
1983	63.21	6.9	31.84	13.5	6.71	9.3	5.80	0.9	5.65	1.6
1984	68.58	8.5	35.55	11.7	7.27	8.3	5.80	0.0	5.69	0.7
1985	71.69	4.5	38.21	7.5	8.05	10.7	5.77	-0.5	5.61	-1.4
1986	83.25	16.1	41.68	9.1	9.38	16.5	5.86	1.6	5.67	1.1
1987	82.20	-1.3	43.51	4.4	9.78	4.3	5.96	1.7	5.75	1.4
1988	88.04	7.1	45.15	3.8	10.12	3.5	6.08	2.0	5.68	-1.2
1989	98.30	11.7	47.77	5.8	11.13	10.0	6.51	7.1	6.26	10.2
1990	100.52	2.3	49.79	4.2	11.68	4.9	7.35	12.9	6.46	3.2
1991	104.92	4.4	50.00	0.4	12.36	5.8	7.75	5.4	7.46	15.5
1992	111.79	6.5	50.95	1.9	13.00	5.2	8.46	9.2	8.44	13.1
1993	116.86	4.5	52.89	3.8	14.23	9.5	8.71	3.0	8.74	3.6
1994	120.29	2.9	56.43	6.7	14.08	-1.1	9.17	5.3	8.93	2.2
1995	123.68	2.8	58.07	2.9	15.63	11.0	13.93	51.9	9.74	9.1
1996	139.10	12.5	61.90	6.6	18.46	18.1	14.15	10.4	10.42	4.0
1997	162.99	17.2	64.69	4.5	20.35	10.2	12.76	1.0	12.62	4.1
1998	176.80	8.5	68.25	5.5	23.84	17.1	13.24	3.8	15.55	23.2
1999	202.74	14.7	71.25	4.4	27.22	8.5	15.22	6.3	17.86	14.9
2000	229.71	13.3	76.95	8.0	29.65	8.9	16.43	8.0	20.02	12.1
2001	231.08	0.6	79.87	3.8	32.73	10.4	18.25	11.1	21.76	8.7
2002	231.54	0.2	82.91	3.8	29.96	-8.5	17.76	-2.7	24.40	12.1
2003	236.28	2.0	84.57	2.0	29.77	-0.6	20.54	15.7	23.47	-3.8
2004	259.02	9.6	87.95	4.0	33.75	13.4	20.15	-1.9	24.42	4.0
2005	283.05	9.3	92.69	4.9	37.31	10.5	20.70	2.7	32.55	33.3
2006	295.02	4.2	96.82	4.5	40.98	9.8	20.22	-2.3	29.56	-9.2

Note: All figures are rounded. *Giving USA* changed its rounding procedure in the 2003 edition. All estimates are rounded to two places then operations performed.

	Arts, culture, humanities	Percent change	Public-society benefit	Percent change	Environ-ment/ animals	Percent change	Inter-national affairs	Percent change	Giving to foun-dations	Percent change	Unallo-cated
1966	0.54	22.7	0.39	2.6							-0.04
1967	0.56	3.7	0.41	5.1							0.39
1968	0.60	7.1	0.43	4.9							0.85
1969	0.72	20.0	0.56	30.2							1.43
1970	0.66	-8.3	0.46	-17.9							1.43
1971	1.01	53.0	0.68	47.8							1.99
1972	1.10	8.9	0.82	20.6							1.78
1973	1.26	14.5	0.62	-24.4							1.46
1974	1.46	15.9	0.89	43.5							-0.72
1975	1.49	2.1	1.22	37.1							-0.33
1976	1.54	3.4	1.48	21.3							0.74
1977	1.84	19.5	1.29	-12.8							0.72
1978	1.87	1.6	1.50	16.3					1.61		0.32
1979	1.98	5.9	1.82	21.3					2.21	37.3	1.43
1980	2.12	7.1	2.28	25.3					1.98	-10.4	3.97
1981	2.28	7.5	2.13	-6.6					2.39	20.7	6.31
1982	2.71	18.9	2.42	13.6					4.00	67.4	4.47
1983	2.46	-9.2	2.48	2.5					2.71	-32.3	5.56
1984	2.56	4.1	2.88	16.1					3.36	24.0	5.47
1985	2.75	7.4	3.20	11.1					4.73	40.8	3.37
1986	3.00	9.1	3.78	18.1					4.96	4.9	8.92
1987	3.15	5.0	4.26	12.7	1.08		0.81		5.16	4.0	2.74
1988	3.31	5.1	5.14	20.7	1.14	11.4	0.89	9.9	3.93	-23.8	6.60
1989	3.74	13.0	6.94	35.0	1.40	-14.0	1.71	92.1	4.41	12.2	8.43
1990	3.98	6.4	7.36	6.1	1.55	30.9	2.24	31.0	3.83	-13.2	6.28
1991	4.29	7.8	8.31	12.9	1.70	10.7	2.12	-5.4	4.46	16.4	6.47
1992	4.52	5.4	8.51	2.4	1.72	6.5	2.38	12.3	5.01	12.3	8.80
1993	4.86	7.5	8.68	2.0	1.96	2.2	2.23	-6.3	6.26	25.0	8.30
1994	4.75	-2.3	9.96	14.7	2.04	11.0	2.71	21.5	6.33	1.1	5.89
1995	5.67	19.4	11.25	13.0	2.29	12.5	3.01	11.1	8.46	33.6	-4.37
1996	6.38	12.5	11.33	6.6	2.62	1.6	3.57	18.6	12.63	49.3	-2.36
1997	7.34	-2.8	12.94	10.8	3.09	7.4	4.21	17.9	13.96	10.5	11.03
1998	9.87	34.5	13.95	7.8	3.51	13.6	5.08	20.7	19.92	42.7	3.59
1999	9.24	-6.4	13.02	-6.7	4.24	20.8	6.58	29.5	28.76	44.4	9.35
2000	10.48	13.4	15.36	18.0	4.75	12.0	7.20	9.4	24.71	-14.1	24.16
2001	11.41	5.6	16.52	7.6	5.29	4.0	8.31	13.0	25.67	3.9	11.27
2002	10.83	-5.1	17.97	8.8	5.29	0.0	8.70	4.7	19.16	-25.4	14.56
2003	10.83	0.0	16.42	-8.6	5.44	2.8	9.84	13.1	21.62	12.8	13.78
2004	11.78	8.8	18.82	14.6	5.50	1.1	11.55	17.4	20.32	-6.0	24.78
2005	11.38	-3.4	20.25	7.6	6.48	17.8	12.49	8.1	27.46	35.1	21.74
2006	12.51	9.9	21.41	5.7	6.60	1.9	11.34	-9.2	29.50	7.4	26.08

Note: Giving to foundations from 1992-2005 represents total gifts reported to the Foundation Center, minus gifts to corporate foundations. The Foundation Center also provided data on the assets transferred to health care foundations for the years 1992-1999. These are not charitable gifts, but transfers resulting from conversions of hospitals and other health care institutions from non-profit to for-profit status. These were subtracted from the Foundation Center's report of gifts to foundations. Gifts to foundations for 2006 are estimated here jointly by *Giving USA* and the Foundation Center. The figure will be released in early 2008. Funds given to nonprofits not reported by an organization in a subsector are included in "Unallocated." See the pie chart in Chapter 5, The Numbers, for a definition of Unallocated.

Contributions by type of recipient organization, 1966–2006
(in billions of inflation-adjusted dollars)

	Total	Percent change	Religion	Percent change	Edu- cation	Percent change	Health	Percent change	Human services	Percent change
1966	98.26	4.3	44.93	4.4	12.82	-0.4	16.24	5.7	18.73	0.2
1967	102.78	4.6	45.75	1.8	12.85	0.2	16.90	4.1	19.07	1.8
1968	109.21	6.3	48.78	6.6	13.79	7.3	17.96	6.3	17.79	-6.7
1969	113.52	3.9	49.56	1.6	13.96	1.2	18.52	3.1	16.59	-6.7
1970	109.31	-3.7	48.52	-2.1	13.51	-3.2	18.75	1.2	15.27	-8.0
1971	116.67	6.7	50.12	3.3	13.69	1.3	19.51	4.1	15.03	-1.6
1972	117.90	1.1	48.72	-2.8	14.38	5.0	19.73	1.1	17.22	14.6
1973	116.21	-1.4	47.82	-1.8	15.12	5.1	20.53	4.1	17.57	2.0
1974	109.94	-5.4	48.43	1.3	13.82	-8.6	20.65	0.6	20.37	15.9
1975	107.01	-2.7	48.00	-0.9	11.95	-13.5	19.22	-6.9	18.92	-7.1
1976	112.86	5.5	50.25	4.7	12.72	6.4	18.39	-4.3	18.18	-3.9
1977	117.13	3.8	56.49	12.4	12.94	1.7	17.53	-4.7	17.37	-4.5
1978	119.26	1.8	56.74	0.4	13.36	3.2	16.39	-6.5	16.39	-5.6
1979	119.72	0.4	56.01	-1.3	13.05	-2.3	15.11	-7.8	14.88	-9.2
1980	118.99	-0.6	54.39	-2.9	12.41	-4.9	13.60	-10.0	13.26	-10.9
1981	122.60	3.0	55.56	2.2	13.15	6.0	12.62	-7.2	12.20	-8.0
1982	123.48	0.7	58.62	5.5	12.83	-2.4	12.01	-4.8	11.61	-4.8
1983	127.96	3.6	64.45	9.9	13.58	5.8	11.74	-2.2	11.44	-1.5
1984	133.06	4.0	68.98	7.0	14.11	3.9	11.25	-4.2	11.04	-3.5
1985	134.33	1.0	71.59	3.8	15.08	6.9	10.81	-3.9	10.51	-4.8
1986	153.12	14.0	76.66	7.1	17.25	14.4	10.78	-0.3	10.43	-0.8
1987	145.87	-4.7	77.21	0.7	17.36	0.6	10.58	-1.9	10.20	-2.2
1988	150.03	2.9	76.94	-0.3	17.25	-0.6	10.36	-2.1	9.68	-5.1
1989	159.81	6.5	77.66	0.9	18.09	4.9	10.58	2.1	10.18	5.2
1990	155.05	-3.0	76.80	-1.1	18.02	-0.4	11.34	7.2	9.96	-2.2
1991	155.30	0.2	74.01	-3.6	18.29	1.5	11.47	1.1	11.04	10.8
1992	160.64	3.4	73.21	-1.1	18.68	2.1	12.16	6.0	12.13	9.9
1993	163.03	1.5	73.79	0.8	19.85	6.3	12.15	-0.1	12.19	0.5
1994	163.64	0.4	76.77	4.0	19.15	-3.5	12.47	2.6	12.15	-0.3
1995	163.60	0.0	76.81	0.1	20.67	7.9	18.43	47.8	12.88	6.0
1996	178.72	9.2	79.53	3.5	23.72	14.8	18.18	-1.4	13.39	4.0
1997	204.74	14.6	81.26	2.2	25.56	7.8	16.03	-11.8	15.85	18.4
1998	218.68	6.8	84.42	3.9	29.49	15.4	16.38	2.2	19.23	21.3
1999	245.33	12.2	86.22	2.1	32.94	11.7	18.42	12.5	21.61	12.4
2000	268.92	9.6	90.08	4.5	34.71	5.4	19.23	4.4	23.44	8.5
2001	263.04	-2.2	90.92	0.9	37.26	7.3	20.77	8.0	24.77	5.7
2002	259.46	-1.4	92.91	2.2	33.57	-9.9	19.90	-4.2	27.34	10.4
2003	258.88	-0.2	92.66	-0.3	32.62	-2.8	22.50	13.1	25.71	-6.0
2004	276.44	6.8	93.86	1.3	36.02	10.4	21.50	-4.4	26.06	1.4
2005	292.17	5.7	95.68	1.9	38.51	6.9	21.37	-0.6	33.60	28.9
2006	295.02	1.0	96.82	1.2	40.98	6.4	20.22	-5.4	29.56	-12.0

All estimates are rounded to two places. *Giving USA* changed its rounding procedure in the 2003 edition. All estimates are rounded to two places then operations performed. Inflation adjustment uses the Consumer Price Index calculator available at www.bls.gov. 2006=100.

	Arts, culture, humanities	Percent change	Public-society benefit	Percent change	Environ-ment/ animals	Percent change	Inter-national affairs	Percent change	Giving to foun-dations	Percent change	Unallo-cated
1966	3.36	19.1	2.43	0.0							-0.25
1967	3.38	0.6	2.47	1.6							2.35
1968	3.48	3.0	2.49	0.8							4.92
1969	3.96	13.8	3.08	23.7							7.86
1970	3.43	-13.4	2.39	-22.4							7.43
1971	5.03	46.6	3.38	41.4							9.91
1972	5.31	5.6	3.96	17.2							8.59
1973	5.72	7.7	2.82	-28.8							6.63
1974	5.97	4.4	3.64	29.1							-2.94
1975	5.58	-6.5	4.57	25.5							-1.24
1976	5.46	-2.2	5.24	14.7							2.62
1977	6.12	12.1	4.29	-18.1							2.40
1978	5.78	-5.6	4.64	8.2					4.98		0.99
1979	5.50	-4.8	5.05	8.8					6.14	23.3	3.97
1980	5.19	-5.6	5.58	10.5					4.84	-21.2	9.71
1981	5.06	-2.5	4.72	-15.4					5.30	9.5	13.99
1982	5.66	11.9	5.06	7.2					8.36	57.7	9.34
1983	4.98	-12.0	5.02	-0.8					5.49	-34.3	11.26
1984	4.97	-0.2	5.59	11.4					6.52	18.8	10.61
1985	5.15	3.6	6.00	7.3					8.86	35.9	6.31
1986	5.52	7.2	6.95	15.8					9.12	2.9	16.41
1987	5.59	1.3	7.56	8.8	1.92		1.44		9.16	0.4	4.86
1988	5.64	0.9	8.76	15.9	1.94	1.0	1.52	5.6	6.70	-26.9	11.25
1989	6.08	7.8	11.28	28.8	2.28	17.5	2.78	82.9	7.17	7.0	13.71
1990	6.14	1.0	11.35	0.6	2.39	4.8	3.46	24.5	5.91	-17.6	9.69
1991	6.35	3.4	12.30	8.4	2.52	5.4	3.14	-9.2	6.60	11.7	9.58
1992	6.50	2.4	12.23	-0.6	2.47	-2.0	3.42	8.9	7.20	9.1	12.65
1993	6.78	4.3	12.11	-1.0	2.73	10.5	3.11	-9.1	8.73	21.3	11.58
1994	6.46	-4.7	13.55	11.9	2.78	1.8	3.69	18.6	8.61	-1.4	8.01
1995	7.50	16.1	14.88	9.8	3.03	9.0	3.98	7.9	11.19	30.0	-5.78
1996	8.20	9.3	14.56	-2.2	3.37	11.2	4.59	15.3	16.23	45.0	-3.03
1997	9.22	12.4	16.25	11.6	3.88	15.1	5.29	15.3	17.54	8.1	13.86
1998	12.21	32.4	17.25	6.2	4.34	11.9	6.28	18.7	24.64	40.5	4.44
1999	11.18	-8.4	15.76	-8.6	5.13	18.2	7.96	26.8	34.80	41.2	11.31
2000	12.27	9.7	17.98	14.1	5.56	8.4	8.43	5.9	28.93	-16.9	28.28
2001	12.99	5.9	18.80	4.6	6.02	8.3	9.46	12.2	29.22	1.0	12.83
2002	12.14	-6.5	20.14	7.1	5.93	-1.5	9.75	3.1	21.47	-26.5	16.32
2003	11.87	-2.2	17.99	-10.7	5.96	0.5	10.78	10.6	23.69	10.3	15.10
2004	12.57	5.9	20.09	11.7	5.87	-1.5	12.33	14.4	21.69	-8.4	26.45
2005	11.75	-6.5	20.90	4.0	6.69	14.0	12.89	4.5	28.34	30.7	22.44
2006	12.51	6.5	21.41	2.4	6.60	-1.3	11.34	-12.0	29.50	4.1	26.08

Note: Giving to foundations from 1992–2005 represents total gifts reported to the Foundation Center, minus gifts to corporate foundations. The Foundation Center also provided data on the assets transferred to health care foundations for the years 1992–1999. These are not charitable gifts, but transfers resulting from conversions of hospitals and other health care institutions from non-profit to for-profit status. These were subtracted from the Foundation Center's report of gifts to foundations. Gifts to foundations for 2006 are estimated here jointly by *Giving USA* and the Foundation Center. The figure will be released in early 2008. Funds given to nonprofits not reported by an organization in a subsector are included in "Unallocated." See the pie chart in Chapter 5, The Numbers, for a definition of Unallocated.

Giving as a percentage of gross domestic product (GDP), 1966–2006
(in billions of inflation-adjusted dollars)

	Total giving	GDP	Giving as a percentage of GDP
1966	98.26	4,902.30	2.0
1967	102.78	5,024.74	2.0
1968	109.21	5,272.31	2.1
1969	113.52	5,409.89	2.1
1970	109.30	5,394.81	2.0
1971	116.67	5,610.25	2.1
1972	117.90	5,973.47	2.0
1973	116.21	6,279.29	1.9
1974	109.94	6,134.97	1.8
1975	107.01	6,138.25	1.7
1976	112.86	6,468.11	1.7
1977	117.13	6,756.15	1.7
1978	119.26	7,095.55	1.7
1979	119.72	7,118.30	1.7
1980	118.99	6,825.30	1.7
1981	122.60	6,938.12	1.8
1982	123.48	6,799.67	1.8
1983	127.96	7,159.31	1.8
1984	133.06	7,631.35	1.7
1985	134.33	7,907.63	1.7
1986	153.12	8,208.20	1.9
1987	145.87	8,410.83	1.7
1988	150.03	8,697.68	1.7
1989	159.81	8,916.27	1.8
1990	155.05	8,951.26	1.7
1991	155.30	8,874.93	1.7
1992	160.64	9,107.20	1.8
1993	163.03	9,287.67	1.8
1994	163.64	9,620.73	1.7
1995	163.60	9,785.32	1.7
1996	178.72	10,043.56	1.8
1997	204.74	10,431.23	2.0
1998	218.68	10,818.80	2.0
1999	245.33	11,215.39	2.2
2000	268.92	11,492.62	2.3
2001	263.04	11,528.74	2.3
2002	259.46	11,731.96	2.2
2003	258.88	12,009.20	2.2
2004	276.44	12,500.00	2.2
2005	292.17	12,856.94	2.3
2006	294.85	13,244.60	2.2

Note: Percentages include computer rounding. *Giving USA 2007* uses the data for Gross Domestic Product available from the Bureau of Economic Analysis, release of March 29, 2007. Inflation adjustment uses the Consumer Price Index calculator available at www.bls.gov. 2006=$100.

Individual giving as a percentage of personal income
and disposable personal income, 1966–2006
(in billions of inflation-adjusted dollars)

Year	Personal income	Disposable personal income	Individual giving	Giving as a percentage of personal income	Giving as a percentage of disposable personal income
1966	3,757.93	3,344.74	77.41	2.1	2.3
1967	3,912.49	3,471.94	80.93	2.1	2.3
1968	4,125.14	3,621.09	85.46	2.1	2.4
1969	4,277.47	3,703.30	87.53	2.0	2.4
1970	4,357.40	3,821.82	84.10	1.9	2.2
1971	4,497.26	3,991.04	87.80	2.0	2.2
1972	4,788.71	4,192.47	93.44	2.0	2.2
1973	5,044.05	4,442.78	93.23	1.8	2.1
1974	5,000.41	4,382.82	88.34	1.8	2.0
1975	5,001.87	4,448.86	88.16	1.8	2.0
1976	5,226.08	4,615.52	93.27	1.8	2.0
1977	5,433.13	4,776.11	98.30	1.8	2.1
1978	5,682.44	4,973.10	99.26	1.7	2.0
1979	5,726.74	4,980.56	101.61	1.8	2.0
1980	5,646.93	4,915.59	99.61	1.8	2.0
1981	5,746.95	4,981.37	102.00	1.8	2.0
1982	5,797.58	5,057.87	99.50	1.7	2.0
1983	5,993.32	5,280.16	105.38	1.8	2.0
1984	6,382.42	5,649.98	109.55	1.7	1.9
1985	6,608.02	5,825.93	107.53	1.6	1.8
1986	6,846.42	6,042.12	123.40	1.8	2.0
1987	7,005.15	6,137.18	114.52	1.6	1.9
1988	7,248.98	6,388.38	119.26	1.6	1.9
1989	7,458.62	6,538.29	129.17	1.7	2.0
1990	7,525.22	6,610.83	125.00	1.7	1.9
1991	7,476.32	6,607.90	124.73	1.7	1.9
1992	7,705.13	6,827.71	126.02	1.6	1.8
1993	7,754.60	6,852.54	128.35	1.7	1.9
1994	7,947.90	7,008.30	125.86	1.6	1.8
1995	8,137.96	7,153.70	126.14	1.6	1.8
1996	8,378.00	7,308.88	138.20	1.6	1.9
1997	8,686.22	7,522.67	156.01	1.8	2.1
1998	9,181.20	7,910.82	171.12	1.9	2.2
1999	9,441.43	8,101.40	187.11	2.0	2.3
2000	9,868.53	8,421.92	204.30	2.1	2.4
2001	9,930.68	8,522.25	196.24	2.0	2.3
2002	9,952.82	8,774.20	193.71	1.9	2.2
2003	10,040.10	8,943.25	197.43	2.0	2.2
2004	10,385.70	9,265.31	214.29	2.1	2.3
2005	10,568.95	9,327.11	220.34	2.1	2.4
2006	10,884.00	9,523.10	222.89	2.0	2.3

Note: Percentages include computer rounding. *Giving USA 2007* uses the data for personal income and disposable personal income from the Bureau of Economic Analysis, National Income and Product Accounts, Table 2.1, lines 1 and 26, March 29, 2007. Inflation adjustment uses the Consumer Price Index calculator available at www.bls.gov. 2006 = $100.

Corporate giving as a percentage of pretax corporate profits, 1966–2006
(in billions of inflation-adjusted dollars)

Year	Corporate giving	Corporate pretax profits	Giving as a percentage of pretax profits
1966	4.92	539.51	0.9
1967	4.95	504.21	1.0
1968	5.21	535.57	1.0
1969	5.11	502.04	1.0
1970	4.26	420.74	1.0
1971	4.23	462.23	0.9
1972	4.68	520.07	0.9
1973	4.81	612.39	0.8
1974	4.50	604.33	0.7
1975	4.31	545.31	0.8
1976	4.71	636.79	0.7
1977	5.12	699.98	0.7
1978	5.26	761.09	0.7
1979	5.69	755.13	0.8
1980	5.51	620.25	0.9
1981	5.85	540.57	1.1
1982	6.50	414.75	1.6
1983	7.43	473.48	1.6
1984	8.01	521.16	1.5
1985	8.68	482.36	1.8
1986	9.25	452.38	2.0
1987	9.25	563.63	1.6
1988	9.10	657.93	1.4
1989	8.88	623.88	1.4
1990	8.42	631.69	1.3
1991	7.77	626.10	1.2
1992	8.49	662.56	1.3
1993	9.03	721.40	1.3
1994	9.50	785.01	1.2
1995	9.72	891.93	1.1
1996	9.65	941.84	1.0
1997	10.83	1,002.58	1.1
1998	10.46	888.40	1.2
1999	12.38	938.86	1.3
2000	12.57	905.41	1.4
2001	13.27	805.82	1.6
2002	12.09	861.08	1.4
2003	12.12	994.94	1.2
2004	12.12	1,221.21	1.0
2005	14.21	1,567.59	0.9
2006	12.72	1,810.90	0.7

Note: Percentages include computer rounding. *Giving USA 2007* uses the data for corporate pretax profits from the Bureau of Economic Analysis, National Income and Product Accounts, Table 6.17, line 1, March 29, 2007 for values 1966 to 2005. For 2006, the value is from the BEA press release dated March 29, 2007. Inflation adjustment uses the Consumer Price Index calculator available at www.bls.gov. 2006 = $100.

23 Brief summary of methods used

Overview of methodology for 2006 estimates

Giving USA presents estimates for the four primary sources of giving and for nine principal types of recipients of contributions. These are preliminary estimates for 2006, which use the best information available in March and April 2007. They will be revised in 2007 and in 2008 as more data are available. Revisions of *Giving USA's* estimates for 2005 and earlier are reflected in the data tables in this volume.

The *Giving USA* estimates apply methods developed by scholars of giving and are reviewed and approved by the members of the *Giving USA* Advisory Council on Methodology. Members of that group include research directors from a number of other organizations involved in studying the nonprofit sector and are listed in this volume.

The rest of this chapter provides an overview of the methods used to develop the estimates for 2006, organized to present the sources of giving first, followed by the types of recipients. An expanded discussion of methodologies used for the 2006 estimates and a thorough review of revisions made to earlier years' estimates are in the *Giving USA* methodology papers available at www.givinginstitute.org and at www. philanthropy.iupui.edu. Separate methodology papers are available for estimating giving by individuals, corporations, and bequest; and for

estimating giving to religion. Another methodology paper discusses the *Giving USA* survey that is used to estimate amounts received by the types of recipient organizations.

Estimate of giving by individuals

For giving in 2006, we used the final IRS data about itemized deductions for charitable contributions claimed on individual income tax returns for 2004. To this total are added estimated changes in itemized charitable contributions for 2005 and 2006, plus estimates of giving by households that do not itemize. The nonitemizer household estimate is based on the Center on Philanthropy Panel Study (COPPS), which asks more than 7,800 households about their charitable giving. The Center on Philanthropy at Indiana University did the analysis of 2004 COPPS data to develop an estimate of giving by nonitemizing households. The Center on Philanthropy used survey results from the *Giving USA* survey and information collected from personal contact with major disaster relief organizations that reported significant contributions in 2005 for disaster relief. In addition, information on mega-gifts, those that were at least 0.25 percent of the estimated total giving, was collected to add to the total estimate of individual giving.

Table 1 shows the components of the estimates of individual giving for 2004, 2005, and 2006.

The mega-gift supplement covers the total reported as paid contributions

Table 1
Estimate of individual giving, 2004 through 2006
($ in billions)

2004

Itemized deductions for charitable contributions, IRS	165.564
Estimated giving by nonitemizers, COP using COPPS	35.225
Total estimated individual giving	200.789

2005

2004 itemized deductions for charitable contributions, IRS	165.564
Estimated change in giving by itemizers, 2004, *GUSA*	4.680
Estimated giving by nonitemizers, COP using COPPS	37.392
Disaster relief giving by individuals in 2005, COP	5.830
Total estimated individual giving	213.466

2006

2004 itemized deductions for charitable contributions, IRS	165.564
Estimated change in giving, 2005 itemizers, *GUSA*	4.680
Estimated change in giving, 2006 itemizers, *GUSA*	8.460
Estimated giving by nonitemizers, COP using COPPS	39.350
Total estimated individual giving before disaster relief aid	218.054
Disaster relief giving by individuals in 2005, COP	0.940
Total 2006 before mega-gifts	$218.994
Mega-gift supplement, 2005, COP	$ 3.900
	$222.894

Data sources: IRS=Internal Revenue Service; GUSA=*Giving USA*; COPPS = Center on Philanthropy Panel Study; COP = Center on Philanthropy, using data from COPPS for tsunami giving and from the Conference Board for giving after hurricanes Katrina, Rita, and Wilma.

(not pledges) of Warren Buffett ($1.9 billion), Herbert and Marion Sandler ($1.3 billion), and Bernard Osher ($0.7 billion).

The estimated change in individual giving before the inclusion of disaster relief giving is developed using government data about changes in personal income and tax rates, and the change in the Standard & Poor's 500 Index. The amount of estimated change is based on the long-term historical relationship between these economic variables and changes in itemized deductions for charitable contributions. This method was developed and tested by economists Partha Deb, Mark Wilhelm, and Patrick Rooney.[1] Among many methods studied, this estimating procedure was found to be the most accurate over time for predicting changes in individual itemized charitable deductions.

Estimate of giving by bequest

The method of estimating contributions by bequest follows procedures introduced in *Giving USA 2005*. The procedure uses data collected by the Council for Aid to Education about bequests received.

For charitable bequests in 2006, the estimate of giving by bequest relies on total bequest gifts received at institutions of higher education surveyed by the Council for Aid to Education (CAE). To estimate bequest giving for 2006, *Giving USA* took the CAE result for 2005–2006 and divided it by 15.1 percent (the 15-year average from 1987 through 2002).

Giving USA also estimates giving by estates below the federal estate tax filing threshold. This estimate considers the number of deaths of adults aged 55 and above; the average net worth of adults in that age group; and, based on estate tax returns, the average percentage of net estate value left to charity by adults in that age group.

Finally, the bequest estimate is supplemented by including the amount left to charity by large estates, and announced two years prior to 2006 (or in 2004), in the *Chronicle of Philanthropy*'s list of the largest gifts. The values from the largest of these estates are shown in Table 2. For estimating purposes, *Giving USA* treated these estates as likely to be in the 2006 estate tax returns.

Table 3 shows the several components of the bequest estimate for 2006.

Table 2

Bequests announced in 2004 and included in *Giving USA* estimate for 2006

Decedent	Billion $
Susan T. Buffett	2.60
Caroline Wiess Law	0.45
George D. Cornell	0.20
Burton D. Morgan	0.11
Sally Reahard	0.09
Robert C. Atkins	0.04
Ida Belle Young	0.02
Louise Wheelock Willson	0.02
Total	4.44

Table 3
Bequest estimate, 2006
($ in billions)

Council for Aid to Education (CAE) findings, bequest receipts, higher educational institutions, 2005–2006	2.185
CAE result divided by 0.151 to yield estimate of all giving by estates that file estate tax returns, *GUSA*	14.470
Estimate, giving by estates below $1.5 million, 2006, GUSA	3.999
Supplemental mega-bequests, *GUSA*, 2004 amounts likely to be 2006 estate tax returns	4.440
Total estimated giving by bequest	22.910

Data sources: CAE = Council for Aid to Education; *GUSA* = *Giving USA*.

A more detailed explanation of both elements of the bequest estimate—the relationship between the CAE survey and overall itemized charitable gifts from estates and the estimate of giving by estates below the federal estate tax filing threshold—appears in a methodology paper about estimating giving by bequest at www.givinginstitute.org, at www.philanthropy.iupui.edu, and at www.bc.edu/~cwp.

Estimate of giving by foundations

The estimate of giving by foundations uses the figures released by the Foundation Center for giving by independent, community, and operating foundations in 2006.[2] The Foundation Center also estimates giving by corporate foundations. That component is moved from the Foundation Center's estimate of giving by all types of foundations and put in the *Giving USA* estimate of giving by corporations.

Estimate of giving by corporations

The estimate of giving by corporations is based on the most recent final data available for itemized contributions claimed on federal tax returns, which is modified to

1) Add changes in corporate giving found in an estimating procedure used by *Giving USA*;

2) Deduct corporate contributions to corporate foundations, as estimated by *Giving USA* for the most recent year based on findings about the prior year released by the Foundation Center;

3) Add the Foundation Center's estimate of giving by corporate foundations; and

4) For 2005 and 2006, add a supplement for disaster relief giving based on published reports. Studies have shown that disaster relief contributions are usually made beyond typical corporate giving budgets and do not replace other giving.

For giving in 2006, the final IRS data about contributions itemized by corporations are available for 2004. Table 4 illustrates components of the estimate of corporate giving for 2004, 2005, and 2006.

Table 4
Corporate giving estimate, 2004–2006
($ in billions)

2004

Corporate itemized deductions for contributions, IRS	11.600
Minus corporate contributions to corporate foundations, FC	− 3.667
Subtotal: Corporate giving net of gifts to corporate foundations	7.933
Plus corporate foundation giving, FC	+ 3.430
Total corporate giving	11.363

2005

2004 corporate itemized contributions, IRS	11.600
Plus estimated change in corporate giving, 2005, *GUSA*	+ 0.794
Subtotal: estimated itemized contributions	12.394
Minus corporate giving to corporate foundations, FC	− 4.000
Subtotal: estimated itemized deductions net of gifts to corporate foundations	8.394
Plus corporate foundation giving, FC	+ 3.996
Total estimated corporate giving before disaster relief	12.390
Plus reported corporate donations for disaster relief, COP	+ 1.380
Total estimated corporate giving with disaster relief	13.770

2006

2004 corporate itemized contributions, IRS	11.600
Plus estimated change in corporate giving, 2005, *GUSA*	+ 0.794
Plus estimated change in corporate giving 2006, *GUSA*	− 0.060
Subtotal: estimated itemized contributions	12.334
Less estimated giving to corporate foundations, FC	− 4.000
Subtotal: estimated itemized deductions net of gifts to corporate foundations	8.334
Estimated corporate foundation grantmaking, FC	+ 4.240
Total estimated corporate giving before disaster relief gifts	12.574
Disaster relief giving in 2006, COP	+ .150
	12.724

Data sources: IRS=Internal Revenue Service; *GUSA=Giving USA*; FC=Foundation Center; COP=Center on Philanthropy.

A more technical explanation of the *Giving USA* estimating procedure for corporate giving appears in a paper written in 2004 by W. Chin, M. Brown, and P. Rooney that is available at www.philanthropy.iupui.edu.

Estimates of giving to types of recipient organizations

Giving USA relies on data provided by other research organizations for some components of the estimates of giving by type of recipient. *Giving USA* also conducts a survey of some subsectors to gather data about changes in charitable gifts. The following sections describe briefly the data sources and methods used in developing estimates for each subsector.

Estimate of giving to religion

The estimate of giving to religion relies on data from three sources:

- A baseline estimate from 1986 of $50 billion in giving to religion that was developed separately by three different organizations.[3]

- A percentage change in giving to religion developed when summing contributions data released by the National Council of Churches of Christ of the USA, as compiled by Joseph Claude Harris for the Roman Catholic Church,[4] and as reported by selected members of the Evangelical Council for Financial Accountability.

- For 2005 and 2006, reported contributions received by major religious organizations, either from the *Giving USA* survey or in media reports.

Because the denominational contributions data are typically released a year or more after *Giving USA* releases its initial estimates for giving by subsector, the current year's estimate of giving to religion is a *Giving USA* estimate based on the past 3 years of changes. *Giving USA* averaged the inflation-adjusted percentage changes found in giving to religion from 2003 through 2005.[5] Adjusted for inflation, the multiple-year average is 1.0 percent. Converted to remove the inflation adjustment, that is an estimated 3.2 percent change in giving to religion in 2005, before adding amounts given to religious organizations for disaster relief. Table 5 delineates the steps used in estimating giving to religion.

Table 5
Components of the estimate of giving to religion, 2006
($ in billions)

Inflation-adjusted estimate for 2005, to equivalent of 2006 dollars GUSA + change from NCCC, ECFA, JCH		95.68
Estimated percentage change, 2005, *GUSA**	1.0%	
Dollar change, 2005 using rate of previous change (inflation-adjusted dollars)		.96
Subtotal, 2006 in 2006 dollars		96.64
Disaster relief receipts reported by denominations		+ 0.18
Total, 2006 estimate		96.82

*Inflation-adjusted rate, averaged 2003–2005 was 1.0 percent change. With inflation in 2005 at 3.2 percent, this equates to a 4.3 percent change in current dollars (without inflation adjustment).

Data sources: NCCC = National Council of Churches of Christ; ECFA = Evangelical Council for Financial Accountability; JCH = Joseph Claude Harris, who studies giving to the Roman Catholic Church; *GUSA* = *Giving USA.*

Estimate of giving to education

The estimate of giving to educational organizations relies on data from four sources:

1) An estimate of giving to higher education for the prior fiscal year (July 1, 2005 through June 30, 2006) based on a survey by the Council for Aid to Education.

2) A survey conducted by *Giving USA* from which is estimated:
   a) a rate of change in giving to higher education for the balance of the calendar year (July 1, 2006 through December 31, 2006). The survey yielded 8.0 percent change.
   b) estimated giving to other educational organizations.

3) Data collected by the Center on Philanthropy in its Million Dollar List for major contributions to public schools, gifts made in the latter half of 2006 to organizations in the CAE survey (which covered the fiscal year).

4) Reported disaster relief and recovery contributions made to educational organizations. For 2006, many of the donations were multi-year pledges from corporations. Those were estimated to cover each year equally (a three-year pledge resulted in one-third of the amount being counted for 2006).

Table 6 summarizes the components of the estimate of giving to education for 2006.

Table 6
Estimate of giving to education, 2006
($ in billions)

One-half of CAE 2004–2005 estimate of giving to higher education to yield estimate of giving for first half of year.		14.000
Rate of change found in *Giving USA* survey.	8.0%	
Applied to CAE estimate to get estimate for 2006–2007 to yield estimate of giving to higher education in second half of 2006.		15.120
Change in survey respondents that were outliers for large educational organizations and thus not included in the rate of change calculation.		.030
Subtotal estimated giving to higher education.		29.150
Estimate of giving to other educational organizations not in CAE estimate and surveyed by *Giving USA*.		11.148
Announced gifts of $100 million or more made to major universities in the third and fourth quarters of 2006. Source of gift information: Million Dollar List.		0.350
Announced grants and gifts to public schools, all of $1 million or more. Public schools are not included in the *Giving USA* survey, but are receiving an increasing amount of funding from foundations and private donors.		0.280
Disaster relief gifts		0.050
Estimated total giving to education.		40.978

Estimate of giving to foundations

The Foundation Center and *Giving USA* estimate contributions to foundations of $29.5 billion for 2006. Approximately 30 percent of giving to foundations in any one year is from estates that file income tax returns, based on *Giving USA*'s comparison of estate tax return information about charitable bequests and the Foundation Center's reports of giving to foundations. Typically, major estate gifts to foundations arrive at the foundations over time as the estate is settled.

The estimate for 2006 includes amounts reported as paid by Warren Buffett ($1.9 billion), Mary Joan Palevsky ($200 million), Jack Lord ($40 million), and others. These were listed in the *Chronicle of Philanthropy* table of the top 60 donors in 2006.[6]

Giving USA 2007 *major revision for estimating giving to other subsectors*

This year's edition of *Giving USA* marks the first major revision since 1989 to the estimation procedure used to calculate giving to recipient organizations. The last major revision occurred when data from Independent Sector's survey of household giving made possible the separation of environment/animal and international affairs as separate and distinct types of recipients.[6] For the revision in this edition, data prepared by National Center for Charitable Statistics (NCCS) using IRS Forms 990 presented, for the first time, a consistent series covering 1989 through 2004. NCCS is a program of the Center on Nonprofits and Philanthropy at the Urban Institute.

Selected data from these Forms 990s historically have been available to researchers for analysis within one or two years after the 990s were filed. With the lag time in availability, *Giving USA* researchers have not previously been able to use these data in their annual tabulations. With the exception of religious congregations, which are not required to file a Form 990, the NCCS databases capture all but a small percentage of the revenues and contributions received by more than 300,000 filing public charities, 71,000 private foundations and 120,000 other types of nonprofit organizations. *Giving USA* does not consider revenues or donations to nonprofits that are not granted tax-exempt status under section 501(c)(3) of the Internal Revenue Code.[8]

For many subsectors, the previous *Giving USA* estimates for giving to a subsector were grounded in work done in 1973 and 1974 by the Commission on Private Philanthropy and Public Needs (Filer Commission). In the years following that study, the Council for Aid to Education surveyed higher educational organizations, and those data were incorporated into *Giving USA*. For many years, the data collected by the Association of Healthcare Philanthropy also was used in the *Giving USA* estimates. However, for other subsectors (arts, environment, human services, international, and public-society benefit), the little research that was available was sporadic and covered on some types of charities (e.g., only theaters, not all arts organizations) or covered only some time period but not annually. Thus, *Giving*

USA continued conducting an annual random-sample survey to use when developing estimated changes in giving for each year.

The newly available data from NCCS have allowed *Giving USA* to make adjustments to the estimation of giving to recipient organizations. Adjustments have been made back to 1987 for most giving to the arts, education, environment, health, human services, international, and public-society benefit. An additional adjustment to each of the subsector estimates was made to account for organizations that do not file an IRS Form 990. By fall 2007, *Giving USA* researchers will post a technical paper that will assist researchers and others seeking more information about the changes that were implemented. The paper will also compare the old series (as in *Giving USA 2006*) with the revised estimates based on the NCCS data. That paper will be available at www.givingusa.org and at www.philanthropy.iupui.edu.

Giving USA 2007 *survey for estimating giving to surveyed subsectors*

The estimate for giving to education is summarized above. The estimates of giving to health, human services, arts, public-society benefit, environment, and international affairs rely on data from three sources:

■ An earlier estimate of giving to the subsector, as adjusted this year with the data for 1987 through 2004 now available from NCCS.

■ A rate of change developed from the *Giving USA* survey of organizations

in the subsector. The rate of change is multiplied by the prior year's estimate to generate a dollar amount of change. That dollar change is added to the prior year's estimate to yield this year's estimate.

■ Information about contributions for disaster relief, including survey replies, announced gifts from the Million Dollar List of the Center on Philanthropy, responses to special inquiries made to several of the largest disaster relief recipient organizations.

The *Giving USA 2007* survey was sent to a sample of 4,765 unduplicated organizations. A total of 807 returned the survey, for an overall response rate of 18.1 percent. Not all surveys are completed, and some have such unusual results that they are outliers (exceptionally large rates of change, either up or down). Usable surveys numbered 764, a 16.0 percent response rate.

The sample includes every large organization that can be identified as having received charitable contributions of $20 million or more in a year for any year between 2003 and 2005 and random samples of medium-sized and small organizations. Medium-sized organizations are those that raised between $1 million and $20 million in charitable contributions. Small organizations raised less than $1 million. For this year, the medium-sized sample was divided in the chapters where results are reported into two other groups: moderately sized organizations (raising between $5 million and $19.99 million) and medium-sized organizations (raising between $1 million and $4.99 million). The survey, however, grouped all of these organizations into one category.

The survey included nonprofit organizations in the following subsectors:

Arts

Education

Environment

Health

Human services

International affairs

Public-society benefit (including selected community foundations)

Religion (selected religious organizations on the *Chronicle of Philanthropy*'s list of the 400 nonprofits that raised the most money in 2003, 2004 or 2005).

The survey asked organizations to report total charitable revenue for 2005 and total charitable revenue for 2006. For each subsector, all the usable responses for organizations were tallied to estimate total giving to that subsector for 2005 and total giving for that subsector in 2006. Then, the difference between the two years was calculated to get the percentage rate of change. The percentage rate of change is applied to the estimated total published in *Giving USA 2007* for the prior year.

The total giving estimate uses weighting techniques to take into account how many nonprofits in that size group

are in the subsector and how many were in the sample. For information about how many organizations of each size group were in the study for each subsector, and for an explanation of the method for estimating total charitable revenue in a given year using survey results, please see the longer methodology papers at www.philanthropy.iupui.edu. The example is from an earlier year but the methods remain consistent for removing outliers, using weights, and applying the percentage change to the estimate for the preceding year.

Results of survey of giving for 2006

Giving USA calculates giving to other subsectors by first developing weighted estimates of the rates of change in giving for 2006 that are based on survey responses. This rate of change is then applied to the 2005 revised estimate of giving. Reported giving that was considered an outlier or was for disaster relief when calculating the weighted estimates of the rates of change is then added back into the estimate. Table 7 shows the estimates before and after inclusion of disaster giving and outliers as reported by recipient organizations. This table does not include the columns that show 2005 estimates before adding the disaster relief gifts for that year. The rate of change shown here cannot be applied to the column for 2005, as that rate was applied to the pre-disaster estimated. The full table appears at www.philanthropy.iupui.edu.

Table 7
Estimated giving before and after adding disaster relief
($ in billions)

Surveyed subsectors	2005 revised estimate including disaster giving	Rate of change used for 2005 value before disaster giving that year	2006 estimate before disaster relief	Outlier(s)	Disaster relief	Total 2006 estimate with disaster relief
Education*	37.31	8.0%	40.90	0.03	0.05	40.98
Health	20.70	-2.3%	20.22	-0.01	0.01	20.22
Human services	32.55	7.8%	30.12	-1.26	0.70	29.56
Arts	11.38	10.0%	12.48	0.02	0.01	12.51
Public-society benefit	20.25	5.2%	21.03	0.22	0.16	21.41
Environment and animals	6.48	2.4%	6.61	-0.02	0.01	6.60
International affairs	12.49	4.7%	11.89	-0.57	0.02	11.34
Not in survey, estimated in other ways						
Religion	92.69				.18	96.82
Foundations	20.32				0.03	29.50
Total estimated disaster giving					1.17	

*Education estimate uses Council for Aid to Education values supplemented with survey results. The survey percentage change is reported here but is not a major factor in the result. Table 6 earlier in this section shows the education estimate.

What is excluded in *Giving USA* estimates

Giving USA researchers develop estimates of the amount of philanthropic giving to charitable organizations in the United States, including gifts to houses of worship and their national headquarters. *Giving USA* does not estimate all forms of revenue to nonprofit organizations. Among the types of revenue not included in *Giving USA* are allocations from other charitable organizations, such as United Way or a communal fund; fees for services; payments that are not tax-deductible as gifts because the donor receives services of value in exchange; gross proceeds from special events; and membership dues.

Giving USA estimates giving by type of recipient organization, using eight major subsectors. To develop these estimates, *Giving USA* conducts a survey of nonprofit organizations each spring.

Why can't all giving be allocated to a recipient?

Each year, a portion of total charitable receipts reported by *Giving USA* is labeled as unallocated, meaning that *Giving USA* cannot attribute all giving to a subsector. Unallocated giving occurs for various reasons, which include:

- **All *Giving USA* figures are estimates.** Tax data are used to estimate the sources of giving. A random survey is used for estimating contributions by types of recipient. Surveys have a margin of error, with *Giving USA's* being 9 percent for this edition.

- **Estimates done in different ways should NOT match.** It is not expected that the estimate of sources of giving will exactly match the estimate of uses of these gifts. Government agencies, such as those that release Gross Domestic Product figures, also acknowledge differences between estimates developed using one method and those developed using a different method.[9]

- **Nonprofits formed since 2003 are not included in the survey.** *Giving USA* surveys a sample of nonprofit organizations. That sample is based on IRS Forms 990. In order to have a random sample complete with addresses that represents the nonprofit sector, a year is selected for which most of the required IRS Forms 990 are already received. The population of nonprofits (the count) by subsector does include more recently formed organizations.

- **Gifts made to government agencies are charitable contributions but are not tracked in *Giving USA's* survey of charitable organizations.** *Giving USA* does not track charitable gifts received at government agencies, such as school districts, parks and recreation departments, civic improvement programs, state institutions of higher education, and public libraries. There is no single national list of the public organizations that receive gifts. They cannot be identified and surveyed. The amount donated in recent years to school districts, especially by foundations, has grown significantly. *Giving USA* uses publicly reported large gifts ($1 million or more) to public schools to supplement the estimate of giving to public schools. Other donations, likely to be very frequent in households with children in school, are not included however.

- **A gift in the calendar year may not appear in a fiscal year report by a charity responding to *Giving USA's* survey.** For example, gifts in December 2006 to higher education institutions might not appear in the survey responses provided by those institutions, which typically operate on a fiscal year basis and provide data for the fiscal year ended in 2006, not the year begun in 2006. As for public education, *Giving USA* uses publicly reported large gifts to supplement the survey results.

- **Some donors make arrangements for significant deferred charitable gifts without telling the nonprofit.**

For instance, a donor can create a trust through a financial institution and take the allowed deduction subject to IRS rules for valuing such gifts. Unless the donor informs the nonprofit organization that will ultimately receive some of the trust's proceeds, the nonprofit is unaware of the gift and does not report it as revenue.

- **A donor might claim a different amount for a deduction than a charity records as a receipt.** This discrepancy can occur for an in-kind gift, in which the donor claims market value of an item, and the charity reports as charitable revenue the amount received from the sale of the item or some other value based on a different scale than the one the donor used.

Why *Giving USA* makes revisions

Because *Giving USA*'s results are a series of estimates, they are revised as additional information becomes available. A discussion of the revisions made to prior years' estimates is available at www.givingusa.org, with the user name and password appearing on the first page.

---

1 Deb, P., M. Wilhelm, M. Rooney, and M. Brown, Estimating charitable giving, *Nonprofit and Voluntary Sector Quarterly*, December 2003.

2 L. Renz, S. Lawrence, and J. Atienza, *Foundation Growth and Giving Estimates: 2007 Preview*, The Foundation Center, 2007, www.foundationcenter.org.

3 An examination of *Giving USA*'s estimate of giving to religion, compared with estimates developed using two other methods,

appears in the paper "Reconciling estimates of religious giving," written in 2005 by J. C. Harris, M. Brown, and P. Rooney. The three methods yield estimates within 5 percent of one another, offering some reassurance that using 1986 findings as a baseline is at least as good as some other approaches.

4 Joseph Claude Harris estimated Catholic giving for *Giving USA* using data from a survey of Catholic parishes. The religion chapter reports estimated contributions per household, where the number of parish is based on work done by the Center for Applied Research in the Apostolate at Georgetown University. In prior editions of *Giving USA*, Mr. Harris used an estimated number of parish households from a different source. This change does not affect the estimated total giving by Catholic households, only the estimated average amount per parish household.

5 This is a change in methodology from the past five years, when the rolling average covered the previous 10 years instead of three. The change was recommended by the Advisory Council on the grounds that the past three years are better predictors of current behavior.

6 Top 60 donors, February 22, 2007, www. philanthropy.com.

7 A. Kaplan, former editor of *Giving USA*, in personal communication with research team for *Giving USA 2007*.

8 Other types of nonprofit organizations include advocacy groups (classified under section 501(c)(4)), membership associations (classified under section 501(c)(6)), and others. Contributions made to other nonprofits are not treated as tax-deductible gifts in most cases.

9 C. Ehemann and B. Moulton, Balancing the GDP account, working paper, Bureau of Economic Analysis, May 2001, www.bea. gov, under "papers and presentations."

Some of the definitions are from the National Center for Charitable Statistics http://nccs.urban.org/glossary.htm.

Average: In statistics, the *mean*. This figure is calculated by summing the values from each respondent or reporting organization and then dividing by the number of respondents. An average can be a good representation of a trend if the organizations in the group report amounts that are relatively close together. It can misrepresent a trend if the difference between the highest amount reported and the lowest amount reported is very large. In that instance, a median might be a better point of comparison. *See also* **Median**.

Charitable revenue: Philanthropic gifts received by a charity organization. *Giving USA* asks organizations that participate in its survey to report cash received or the cash value of in-kind gifts. Where possible, we ask that unpaid pledges be excluded from the total reported charitable revenue.

Charity or charitable organization: In this book, charitable organization denotes an entity recognized as tax-exempt under section 501(c)(3) of the Internal Revenue Code. Charitable organizations are exempt from federal income taxes because of their religious, educational, scientific, and public purposes. They are eligible to receive tax-deductible gifts. *See also* **Public charity**, **Private foundation**.

Direct public support: As used on IRS Form 990, direct public support appears on line 1a and represents charitable revenue (gifts and grants).

Gift: Transfer of cash or other asset by an individual, corporation, estate or foundation. Gifts do not include government grants or contracts, allocations from nonprofit organizations, such as United Ways or communal funds, or distributions from donor-advised funds.

Indirect public support: As used on IRS Form 990, indirect public support appears on line 1b and includes transfers from one nonprofit organization to another. This includes allocations from federated campaigns, distributions from donor-advised funds, and contributions from a religious organization to another nonprofit, among other transfers.

IRS Form 990: An annual return filed with the Internal Revenue Service by nonprofit, tax-exempt organizations (even those that are not charities) with gross receipts for the year of $25,000 or more. May be submitted on a 990-EZ (when receipts are from $25,000 to $100,000 and assets are less than $250,000). Private foundations use a variation of the form, the Form 990-PF, with additional information required.

Large organization: *Giving USA* defines large organizations as those that had charitable revenue of $20 million or more.

Mean: *See* **Average**.

Median: In a summary of data, the median is the middle response. When the responses are organized sequentially, one-half of the responses given are lower than the median, and one-half are higher. Typically, when the amounts reported in a survey are close together, the median and the mean (average) will be close together. If the answers are very different from one another, the average and the median can be very different. Median values are less sensitive to the effects of outliers than are mean values. *See also* **Average**.

Medium-sized organization: *Giving USA* defines medium-sized organizations as those with total charitable revenue between $1 million and $4.99 million.

Moderately sized organization: *Giving USA* presents information about moderately sized organizations, those with charitable revenue between $5 million and $19.99 million.

National Taxonomy of Exempt Entities: A definitive classification system for nonprofit organizations that are recognized as tax-exempt under section 501(c)(3) of the Internal Revenue Code. See the online resources available at the site listed at the front of this book for a listing of the 26 major groups (named by letters of the alphabet) and examples of organizations within each group. Major groups have been clustered into 10 subsectors as follows. *See also* **Subsector**.

Subsector	Major groups included
Arts, culture, and humanities	A
Education	B
Environment/animals	C, D
Health	E, F, G, H
Human services	I, J, K, L, M, N, O, P
International affairs	Q
Public-society benefit	R, S, T, U, V, W
Religion	X
Mutual/membership benefit*	Y
Unknown, unclassified	Z

*This subsector is not tracked by *Giving USA*

Nonprofit organization: An organization whose net revenue is not distributed to individuals or other stakeholders, but is used to further the organization's mission. The organization is not owned by but is governed by a board of trustees. Not all nonprofit organizations are charities.

Nonprofit sector: A sector of the economy, apart from the government, for which profit is not a motive. Organizations may be exempt from federal, state, and local taxes. Includes houses of worship; charitable organizations formed under section 501(c) (3) of the Internal Revenue Code; and organizations formed under other sections of the Code, such as advocacy organizations, membership organizations, and others.

NTEE: *See* **National Taxonomy of Exempt Entities**.

Planned gift: The Association of Fundraising Professionals says a planned gift is structured and integrates personal, financial, and estate-planning goals with the donor's lifetime or testamentary (will) giving. Many planned gift vehicles are used, including bequests, charitable trusts, and charitable annuities.

Private foundation: Private foundation status is granted to an organization formed for a charitable purpose under section 501(c)(3) of the Internal Revenue Code that does not receive one-third or more of its support from public donations. Most, but not all, private foundations give grants to public charities. *See also* **Charity or charitable organization**, **Public charity**.

Public charity: An organization that qualifies for status as a public charity under Section 509 (a) of the Internal Revenue Code. A public charity includes tax-exempt organizations formed for certain purposes (a church; an educational organization, including public schools; a hospital or medical research facility; or an endowment operated for the benefit of a higher education institution). An organization formed for other purposes can also be a public charity if it receives a substantial part of its support from the general public. Support from a governmental unit is considered public support by proxy via taxes. Complete information about public charities can be found in IRS Publication 557. Note that some, but not all, charitable organizations formed under section 501(c)(3) are public charities. *See also* **Charity or charitable organization**, **Private foundation**.

Public support: As used by the Internal Revenue Service on IRS Form 990, line 1d, public support is the sum of line 1a or "direct public support," generally charitable gifts or grants; line 1b or "indirect public support," generally transfers from other nonprofits; and line 1c or government grants.

Reporting organization: A charitable organization that files an IRS Form 990.

Sector: The portion of the national economy that fits certain criteria for ownership and distribution of surplus. Examples include the business sector, the government sector, and the nonprofit sector. *See also* **Subsector**.

Small organization: *Giving USA* identifies small organizations as those with less than $1 million in charitable revenue.

Subsector: There are several nonprofit subsectors based on organizational purposes. *See also* **National Taxonomy of Exempt Entities**, **Sector**.

Tax-deductible: A contribution to an organization is deductible for income tax purposes if the organization is a church or is registered with and recognized by the IRS as a tax-exempt, nonprofit charity.

Tax-exempt: An organization may be exempt because it is a church or because of registration within a state or with the Internal Revenue Service. State exemptions may cover sales tax, property tax, and/or state income tax. Approved registration with the IRS will exempt an organization from federal income tax. Organizations that have more than $5,000 in gross revenues annually are legally responsible for registering with the IRS.

A-Arts, culture, humanities activities
- arts & culture (multipurpose activities)
- media & communications
- visual arts
- museums
- performing arts
- humanities
- historical societies & related historical activities

B-Educational institutions & related activities
- elementary & secondary education (preschool-grade 12)
- vocational/technical schools
- higher education
- graduate/professional schools
- adult/continuing education
- libraries
- student services & organizations

C-Environment quality, protection
- pollution abatement & control
- natural resources conservation & protection
- botanic/horticulture activities
- environmental beautification & open spaces
- environmental education & outdoor survival

D-Animal-related activities
- animal protection & welfare
- humane society
- wildlife preservation & protection
- veterinary services
- zoos & aquariums
- specialty animals & other services

E-Health-general & rehabilitative
- hospitals, nursing homes & primary medical care
- health treatment, primarily outpatient
- reproductive health care
- rehabilitative medical services
- health support services
- emergency medical services
- public health & wellness education
- health care financing/insurance programs

F-Mental health, crisis intervention
- addiction prevention & treatment
- mental health treatment & services
- crisis intervention
- psychiatric/mental health-primary care
- half-way houses (mental health)/transitional care

G-Disease/disorder/medical disciplines (multipurpose)
- birth defects & genetic diseases
- cancer
- diseases of specific organs
- nerve, muscle & bone diseases
- allergy-related diseases
- specific named diseases
- medical disciplines/specialties

H-Medical research
- identical hierarchy to diseases/disorders/ medical disciplines in major field "G"
- example: G30 represents American Cancer Society; H30 represents cancer research

I-Public protection: crime/courts/legal services
- police & law enforcement agencies
- correctional facilities & prisoner services
- crime prevention
- rehabilitation of offenders
- administration of justice/courts
- protection against/prevention of neglect, abuse, exploitation
- legal services

J-Employment/jobs
- vocational guidance & training (such as on-the-job programs)
- employment procurement assistance
- vocational rehabilitation
- employment assistance for the handicapped
- labor union/organizations
- labor-management relations

K-Food, nutrition, agriculture
- agricultural services aimed at food procurement
- food service/free food distribution
- nutrition promotion
- farmland preservation

L-Housing/shelter
- housing development/construction
- housing search assistance
- low-cost temporary shelters such as youth hostels
- homeless, temporary shelter
- housing owners/renters organizations
- housing support services

M-Public safety/disaster preparedness & relief
- disaster prevention, such as flood control
- disaster relief (US domestic)
- safety education
- civil defense & preparedness programs

N-Recreation, leisure, sports, athletics
- camps
- physical fitness & community recreation
- sports training
- recreation/pleasure or social clubs
- amateur sports
- Olympics & Special Olympics

O-Youth Development
- youth centers (such as boys/girls clubs)
- scouting
- big brothers/sisters
- agricultural development (such as 4-H)
- business development, Junior Achievement
- citizenship programs
- religious leadership development

P-Human service-other/multipurpose
- multipurpose service organizations
- children & youth services
- family services
- personal social services
- emergency assistance (food, clothing)
- residential/custodial care
- centers promoting independence of specific groups, such as senior or women's centers

Q-International
- exchange programs
- international development
- international relief services (foreign disaster relief)
- peace & security
- foreign policy research & analyses (U.S. domestic)
- international human rights

R-Civil rights/civil liberties
- equal opportunity & access
- voter education/registration
- civil liberties

S-Community improvement/development
- community/neighborhood development
- community coalitions
- economic development, urban and rural
- business services
- community service clubs (such as Junior League)

T-Philanthropy & voluntarism
- philanthropy association/society
- private foundations, funds (e.g., women's funds), and community foundations
- community funds and federated giving
- voluntarism promotion

U-Science
- scientific research & promotion
- physical/earth sciences
- engineering/technology
- biological sciences

V-Social sciences
- social science research/studies
- interdisciplinary studies, such as black studies, women's studies, urban studies, etc.

W-Public affairs/society benefit
- public policy research, general
- government & public administration
- transportation systems
- public utilities
- consumer rights/education

X-Religion/spiritual development
- Christian churches, missionary societies and related religious bodies
- Jewish synagogues
- other specific religions

Y-Mutual membership benefit organizations
- insurance providers & services (other than health)
- pension/retirement funds
- fraternal beneficiary funds
- cemeteries & burial services

Z99-unknown, unclassifiable

Source: *The Foundation Grants Index,* The Foundation Center
Note: In 1994, community funds and federated giving programs were moved from letter **S** to letter **T**. They are still in the same broad category, called "public-society benefit."

Member firms

A.L. Brourman Associates, Inc.
Advantage Consulting
Alexander Haas Martin & Partners, Inc.
The Alford Group Inc.
American City Bureau, Inc.
Arnoult & Associates, Inc.
Benevon, formerly Raising More Money
Blackburn Associates, Inc.
Campbell & Company
Carlton & Company
The Clements Group, LC
The Collins Group, Inc.
Compton Fundraising Consultants
The Covenant Group
DataFund Services, Inc.
Durkin Associates
The EHL Consulting Group, Inc.
eTapestry
Fund Inc®
Global Advancement® LLC
Grenzebach Glier & Associates, Inc.
Hodge, Cramer & Associates, Inc.
IDC
Jeffrey Byrne & Associates, Inc.
The Kellogg Organization, Inc.
Marts & Lundy, Inc.
Miller Group Worldwide, LLC
National Community Development Services, Inc.
The Oram Group, Inc.
Raybin Associates, Inc.
Ruotolo Associates Inc.
Semple Bixel Associates, Inc.
The Sharpe Group
Smith Beers Yunker & Company, Inc.
StaleyRobeson®
Viscern/Ketchum/RSI
Whitney Jones, Inc.
Woodburn, Kyle & Company

Committees

The Advisory Council on Methodology

Richard S. Belous, Ph.D.
Vice President, Research,
United Way—National Headquarters

Freddie Cross
Director of Research and Information,
Council for Advancement and Support
of Education

Kirsten Grønbjerg, Ph.D.
Efroymson Chair in Philanthropy and
Professor of Public and Environmental
Affairs, Indiana University, The Center
on Philanthropy at Indiana University

Theodore R. Hart, CFRE
President and CEO,
ePhilanthropyFoundation.Org

John J. Havens, Ph.D.
Senior Research Associate, Center on
Wealth and Philanthropy, Boston College

Nadine T. Jalandoni
Director, Research Services,
INDEPENDENT SECTOR

Amy Kao
Consultant for corporate contributions,
The Conference Board

Ann E. Kaplan
Director, Voluntary Support of Education,
Council for Aid to Education

John M. Kennedy, Ph.D.
Director, Indiana University Center for
Survey Research, Indiana University

Judith Kroll
Director of Research,
Council on Foundations

Steven A. Lawrence
Senior Director of Research
The Foundation Center

Eileen W. Lindner, Ph.D.
Editor, *Yearbook of American and
Canadian Churches*, National Council
Churches of Christ, USA

Robert B. McClelland, Ph.D.
Senior Research Economist,
U.S. Bureau of Labor Statistics

Lawrence T. McGill, Ph.D.
Senior Vice President for Research
The Foundation Center

Charles H. Moore, Executive Director,
Committee to Encourage Corporate
Philanthropy

Thomas A. Pollak
Program Director, National Center for
Charitable Statistics, The Urban Institute

Kathy L. Renzetti
Director, Communications and
Membership, Association for
Healthcare Philanthropy

Lester M. Salamon, Ph.D.
Center for Civil Society Studies
The Johns Hopkins University

Robert F. Sharpe, Jr.
President, The Sharpe Group

Frank P. Stafford, Ph.D., Director,
Institute for Social Research,
University of Michigan

Richard S. Steinberg, Ph.D.
Professor of Economics, Indiana
University-Purdue University
Indianapolis

Chapter authors

Unless otherwise listed, chapters are by Melissa S. Brown. Other authors are research department staff or doctoral students at the Center on Philanthropy at Indiana University.

The Numbers	Emily D. Krauser
Special section about hurricane response	Bridgett J. Milner
Giving by Corporations	Tamaki Onishi
Giving to Religion	Emily D. Krauser and Christine L. Weisenbach
Giving to Education	Tyrone M. Freeman
Giving to Health	Janice S. O'Rourke
Giving to Human Services	Rebecca A. Scheer
Giving to Arts, Culture, and Humanities	Diana Agidi and Christine L. Weisenbach
Giving to Environment	Austin M. Mitchell
Giving to International Affairs	Austin M. Mitchell
Legal-Legislative Overview	Suzann Weber Lupton
$5 Million and Over List	David A. Fleischhacker
Brief Summary of Methods	Heidi K. Frederick

Order Your Copy of *Giving USA 2007* Today!

First Name_____ Last Name_____

Organization_____ Address1_____

Address2_____ Address3_____

City_____ State_____ Zip_____ Country_____

Phone_____ Fax _____ Email (required for e-newsletters) _____

Prepayment is required in U.S. Dollars payable to Giving USA Foundation
Payment Type ❏ Check ❏ Visa ❏ MasterCard ❏ American Express ❏ Discover

Credit Card No._____ Exp _____

Credit Card Billing Address (if different than above) _____

Signature _____

Code	Publication	Price	Qty	Total
5005-246	**Giving USA 2007 Platinum Subscription – $370 value for $270!** *Giving USA 2007*–The Annual Report on Philanthropy for the Year 2006 *(Delivered in hard copy and in NEW searchable electronic format)* *Giving USA e-Newsletter on Topics Related to Philanthropy* – 4 issues *Giving USA 2007 Presentation on CD*	$270.00		
5006-246	**Giving USA 2007 Gold Subscription – $300 value for $210!** *Giving USA 2007*–The Annual Report on Philanthropy for the Year 2006 *(Delivered in hard copy format)* *Giving USA e-Newsletter on Topics Related to Philanthropy* – 4 issues *Giving USA 2007 Presentation on CD*	$210.00		
5007-246	**Giving USA 2007 Silver Subscription – $295 value for $200!** *Giving USA 2007*–The Annual Report on Philanthropy for the Year 2006 *(Delivered in NEW searchable electronic format)* *Giving USA e-Newsletter on Topics Related to Philanthropy* – 4 issues *Giving USA 2007 Presentation on CD*	$200.00		
5008-246	**Giving USA 2007 Bronze Subscription** *Giving USA 2007*–The Annual Report on Philanthropy for the Year 2006 *(Delivered in hard-copy format)* *Giving USA e-Newsletter on Topics Related to Philanthropy* – 4 issues	$165.00		
8001-243	***Giving USA Spotlight***, Issue 1 – Annual Survey of State Laws Regulating Charitable Solicitations as of January 1, 2008	$45.00		
1006-245	***Giving USA 2006 Presentation on CD*** Full-color, ready-made computer presentation charts with talking points	$135.00		
5004-243	***Giving USA 2007 e-Newsletter on Topics Related to Philanthropy*** – 4 issues, including Annual Survey of State Laws	$90.00		
2003-241	**BOOK ONLY:** *Giving USA 2007* – The Annual Report on Philanthropy for the Year 2006 (hard copy)	$75.00		
8005-248	**E-BOOK:** *Giving USA 2007* – The Annual Report on Philanthropy for the Year 2006 (delivered in NEW searchable electronic format)	$70.00		
2021-243	***Giving USA Spotlight***, Issue 1 – Annual Survey of State Laws Regulating Charitable Solicitations as of January 1, 2007	$40.00		

Subtotal	$
Shipping*	$
If delivered in IL, 8.25% tax	$
Total	$

*In the U.S. add $9.95 for orders up to #100
$13.95 for orders up to $149
$18.95 for orders of $150+
Outside of U.S. add $25.00 for airmail delivery

Order By Mail:
Giving USA Foundation
4700 W. Lake Ave
Glenview, IL 60025

Order By Phone:
Have your credit card ready
800/462-2372
847/375-4709

Order By Fax:
866/607-0913
Intl. – 732/578-6594

Order Online:
Visit our web store at
www.givingusa.org

In the event of a miscalculation, I authorize Giving USA Foundation to charge to the above-named credit card an amount reasonably deemed by Giving USA Foundation to be accurate and appropriate. NOTICE: It is the policy of Giving USA Foundation™ to charge credit cards when orders are received. Our 2007 products will be shipped beginning July 1, 2007.

07BOOK